Paul Simpson is th  ozen non-fiction books inclu conspiracy theories. He has e rous inter-national entertainm oversees news and reviews website SciFiBulletin.com

A BRIEF HISTORY OF

THE SPY

PAUL
SIMPSON

RUNNING PRESS
PHILADELPHIA · LONDON

ROBINSON

Constable & Robinson Ltd
55–56 Russell Square
London WC1B 4HP
www.constablerobinson.com

First published in the UK by Robinson,
An imprint of Constable & Robinson Ltd, 2013

Copyright © Paul Simpson 2013

The right of Paul Simpson to be identified as the author of this work has been asserted by him
in accordance with the Copyright, Designs and Patents Act 1988

All rights reserved. This book is sold subject to the condition
that it shall not be reproduced in whole or in part, in any form or by any means, electronic or
mechanical, including photocopying, recording, or by any information storage and retrieval system
now known or hereafter invented, without written permission from the publisher and
without a similar condition, including this condition, being imposed on the subsequent purchaser.

A copy of the British Library Cataloguing in
Publication data is available from the British Library

ISBN 978-1-78033-890-3 (paperback)
ISBN 978-1-78033-891-0 (ebook)

1 3 5 7 9 10 8 6 4 2

First published in the United States in 2013 by Running Press Book Publishers,
A Member of the Perseus Books Group

All rights reserved under the Pan-American and International Copyright Conventions

Books published by Running Press are available at special discounts for bulk purchases in the United
States by corporations, institutions, and other organizations. For more information, please contact the
Special Markets Department at the Perseus Books Group, 2300 Chestnut Street, Suite 200,
Philadelphia, PA 19103, or call (800) 810-4145, ext. 5000, or email
special.markets@perseusbooks.com.

US ISBN 978-0-7624-4803-6
US Library of Congress Control Number: 2012944547

9 8 7 6 5 4 3 2 1
Digit on the right indicates the number of this printing

Running Press Book Publishers
2300 Chestnut Street
Philadelphia, PA 19103-4371

Visit us on the web!
www.runningpress.com

Typeset by TW Typesetting, Plymouth, Devon

Printed and bound by CPI Group (UK) Ltd, Croydon, CR0 4YY

In memory of my mother, Mary Howden-Simpson, who introduced me to Simon Templar, James Bond and so many other fictional heroes.

'The one thing you can bet is that spying is never over. Spying is like the wiring in this building – it's just a question of who takes it over and switches on the lights.'

John le Carré, 1996

CONTENTS

AUTHOR'S NOTE

The invading army is coming up on the defenders' stronghold.
It's heavily fortified – a high wall surrounds the city, which
appears, at first glance, to be impregnable. The army commanders know that there is no option: they must take the city,
and quickly, or their campaign will lose momentum.

Two spies are ordered to find out the lie of the land. They
infiltrate the city, but are nearly captured. One of the locals, a
prostitute who has been harbouring them, sends the army off
in the wrong direction, while the spies manage to escape back
to their own lines. With the information they have retrieved, the
commanders make a successful plan of battle – and take the city.

A scene from the Iraq War, or perhaps one of the Balkan
conflicts of the late twentieth century? No, this is a recon-
struction of events surrounding the capture of the town of
Jericho, as described in the Book of Joshua, one of the early
books of the Bible, which can be dated to somewhere around
the fourteenth century BC. Modern spies might be able to

transmit information to their superiors using hi-tech equipment, but the core demands of the espionage world have hardly changed in thousands of years. Men and women (from ancient times, spying has always been an equal opportunity profession) have to put themselves at risk in order to obtain information that other people simply do not want them to have.

There can be few people who haven't seen a spy film, especially one of the score of movies made featuring Ian Fleming's fictional secret agent, James Bond. The suave, debonair, tuxedoed Roger Moore incarnation of that character belongs firmly in the realms of fiction, but the more gritty, determined agent, as embodied by Daniel Craig's twenty-first century version or the screen interpretation of Robert Ludlum's Jason Bourne, is a far more accurate account of life in a world of treachery and deceit. Many of the spies whose deeds are examined in this volume carried out feats that would be dismissed as pure fiction, were they not fully documented.

This *Brief History of the Spy* focuses on the period from the Second World War up to the present day, the time of the Cold War and the War on Terror. Even within that comparatively short time, the world in which spies operate has changed almost beyond recognition. The threat from terrorism is today perceived as much stronger than the fear of the Russians or the Chinese – but with events unfolding in the Middle East, will that continue to be the case?

Some of the changes have occurred for pragmatic reasons. 'The enemy of my enemy is my friend' is a precept that applies in espionage as much as it does in diplomacy. One jaded CIA officer sarcastically observes in the 007 film *Quantum of Solace*, 'You're right, we should only deal with nice people', but who are the 'nice people'? That line resonates when considering the debate over the use of 'extended interrogation techniques' (what most would regard as torture) by the CIA in the War on Terror.

One of the most fascinating things about researching and writing this overview has been the discovery of so many cases that never really entered the public consciousness. I've been intrigued by spies since reading my first Bond novel and being given *The Master Book of Spies* with its pictures of secret cameras and other cool equipment as a youngster. My first book was a history of James Bond, so I feel in a way I've come full circle, chronicling the exploits of those who labour on the real battlefields, facing imprisonment, torture or worse. To those unsung heroes this book is also gratefully dedicated.

A note on spellings: names translated from Cyrillic or Arabic languages into English can appear in many different forms. The most common (particularly Osama bin Laden, and al-Qaeda) are adopted here, but where original documents are quoted, the spellings and abbreviations within are retained (notably UBL for Usama Bin Ladin). Original newspaper and magazine articles have been referenced where possible, along with declassified documents released by the FBI and the CIA. A select bibliography is provided at the end of the book.

Paul Simpson
January 2013

PREFACE

Surprising as it may be to those of us brought up on a diet of spy books and films, at the end of the Second World War most of the government agencies whose acronyms and names have become so familiar did not exist as we know them today. There was no CIA. The letters KGB didn't instil the terror that they would from the fifties onwards. There was no state of Israel, so its intelligence organizations Mossad and Shin Bet didn't exist either. The South African espionage group nicknamed BOSS wasn't around. Pre-Communist Germany had no Stasi.

The geopolitical shifts at the end of the war, set down in agreements between the leaders of America, Great Britain and the Soviet Union at Yalta and Potsdam in 1945, meant that the intelligence communities were dealing with a very different landscape to the one between the World Wars and during the conflict itself.

Displaying the paranoia for which he is justly remembered, Soviet leader Josef Stalin was already spying on his allies – his muted reaction to US President Harry S. Truman's hints about the atomic bomb indicated to many that he was already well aware of the American progress, and, indeed, may even have known more than his counterpart. Soviet agents were already part of the British intelligence service hierarchy, and in place in strategic locations around the globe.

Truman came to realize that the Soviets were not to be trusted, and under his presidency the American intelligence community was reorganized to deal with the threat as the Cold War grew ever chillier. The British Secret Intelligence Service (popularly known as MI6, a designation used in this book for avoidance of ambiguity) also focused its attention on Russia and its satellites. The Cold War heated up and cooled down through successive regimes, with proxy wars fought around the world.

Of course, the threat from the Soviet Union wasn't the only danger that the various spy agencies in the Western world had to deal with – nor were the capitalists of America and Britain Russia's only enemies. Many countries faced domestic foes: the British in Ireland; the South Africans against those who opposed apartheid. The creation of the state of Israel added to the volatility of the Middle East, with the Israelis, unsurprisingly, expecting attack from those who vehemently objected to the Jews returning to their ancestral home: Mossad gained a reputation for ferocity and determination that continue to make it feared.

But when glasnost came, the Berlin Wall fell, and the Communist experiment proved to be a failure, those in the intelligence world slowly began to realize that there were new global threats. The World Trade Center bombings in 1993, and then, most dramatically, the events of 11 September 2001 (forever after simply known as 9/11) meant that the enemy wasn't as easy to identify, although, as the expulsion of Russian agent Anna Chapman and the other spies working for the KGB's successor, the SVR, in 2010 proves, some old enemies may not be dead, simply dormant . . .

1

EVERYTHING CHANGES

The end of the Second World War marked a sea change for the world's intelligence agencies. In some countries, such as the United States, it would lead to a major reorganization of the way in which they worked; in others, including the Soviet Union, it would mean that some operations, which had perhaps been of lesser significance during the war against Hitler, took higher priority, as former wartime allies became enemies.

In the United Kingdom, those in charge of MI6, the Secret Intelligence Service (SIS), saw the close of hostilities as a chance to put the service on a better footing, in much the same way that their colleagues at the Security Service, MI5, had needed to do at the start of the war.

Organized intelligence gathering has taken place on behalf of the English state ever since Tudor times: Thomas Cromwell, chief minister of Henry VIII, was in charge of agents reporting back from across Europe, while during the period Henry's daughter, Elizabeth I, was on the throne, her private secretary, Sir Frances Walsingham, ran a network of fifty agents, and developed a highly effective system of interception – the precursor of both MI5 and MI6 today.

The perceived threat from Germany in the early years of the twentieth century led to the creation of a Secret Service Bureau by the Committee for Imperial Defence in 1909. There were multiple reports of German agents working in Britain, often covered in a very sensationalist way by the newspapers of the time. As the MI5 website recounts, the *Weekly News* offered £10 to readers to provide information on German agents to its 'Spy Editor'; it was quickly overwhelmed with letters! Nor was it any secret that Kaiser Wilhelm was expanding the German military machine. The Bureau was therefore instructed to counter foreign espionage in the UK (the Home Section) and to collect secret intelligence abroad on Britain's potential enemies (the Foreign Section). The Home Section was led by Army Captain Vernon G.W. Kell, while the Foreign Section was headed initially by Commander Mansfield Smith-Cumming RN – his habit of initialling his correspondence 'C' led to the use of that single letter for the head of the service, a fact which author Ian Fleming adapted when creating his fictional head of service, M, for the James Bond novels.

When they were requested by the Government to investigate the growth of the German Imperial Navy, Kell and Cumming agreed to split the Bureau into two different organizations: the Home Section became the Security Service (known as MI5 from 1916 onwards) and the Foreign Section became the Secret Intelligence Service (MI6). While MI5 operated against German spies in Britain – arresting over twenty agents before the outbreak of the First World War in August 1914 – MI6 set up networks in France and Belgium that would prove highly important during the four-year conflict.

With the German menace seemingly removed following the Treaty of Versailles, which ended the war, MI6 turned its attention to a troubling development: the rise of a new political creed following the 1917 Russian Revolution – Communism. Cumming saw the rise of international communism as a major threat to the security of Great Britain, and a lot of MI6's attention during the twenties and thirties was devoted to the Comintern, the Soviet-dominated Communist International organization. The Comintern was established in 1919 to work by all available means, including armed force, for the overthrow of the international bourgeoisie and for the creation of an international Soviet republic as a transition stage to the complete abolition of the State. (The Soviets would also target MI6 in return, embedding one of their most important agents, Kim Philby, into the service: he would prove to be one of their best assets in the period immediately after the Second World War.)

MI5 was renamed the Defence Security Service in 1929, dropping the word 'Defence' from its title in 1931. Around the same time it was given responsibility for assessing all threats to the security of the UK – with the exception of Irish terrorists and anarchists, which stayed part of the police remit. (The service itself continued, and still continues, to refer to itself in shorthand as MI5, a convention adopted here.) During the period leading up to the Second World War, despite limited personnel, they dealt with the spy ring created by left-wing journalist William Norman Ewer (which led to the dismissal of various sympathizers at Scotland Yard), and leading member of the Communist Party of Great Britain and official of the League Against Imperialism, Percy Glading's spy ring based at the Woolwich Arsenal in south-east London, which was sending blueprints to the Soviets.

The rise of Nazism unsurprisingly became an important part of both services' remit during the thirties, with MI5 keeping a weather eye on British fascists, including Sir Oswald

Mosley and his blackshirt organization, the British Union of Fascists. MI5 underwent a massive reorganization in April 1941 under the aegis of Sir David Petrie. Although it was discovered post-war that only 115 agents were targeted by the Nazi regime against Britain (all bar one of whom were captured by MI5, the exception committing suicide), there were thousands of vetting requests flowing through the service's hands, as well as all the reports of potential 'Fifth Column' sympathizers who might assist the expected German invasion.

MI6 also had to carry out some drastic rethinking. Many networks of its agents were lost during the Nazi domination of Western Europe after the start of the Second World War, but subsequently many more civilians volunteered to co-operate with the service, providing invaluable information for the Allied forces. During this period, the service was formally known as MI6 (it had briefly been MI1(c) during the First World War, but had rid itself of this title post-war), partly as a flag of convenience and partly to emphasize the links with MI5.

The secret service was also responsible for the vitally important code-breaking work carried out at the Government Code and Cypher School at Bletchley Park, 40 miles north of London. The Germans believed that their vaunted Enigma code machine produced signals unreadable by anyone not in possession of a copy of the device, but in fact the experts at Bletchley Park were able to do so, and provided information, code-named ULTRA, which proved invaluable to the pros-ecution of the war.

A third organization was involved in covert (and not-so-covert tasks) during the war: the Special Operations Executive (SOE) carried out sabotage, bombing and subversive actions behind the enemy lines. Where MI6 provided the raw intelligence about troop movements, the SOE were actively haranguing the enemy. MI6 head Sir Stewart Menzies regarded them as 'amateur, dangerous, and bogus' but because they were the brainchild of Prime Minister Winston Churchill their operations continued. Some of their actions led to terrible revenge being wreaked by the Nazis: the assassination of SS deputy Reinhard Heydrich led to the extermination of 5,000 people as a reprisal. The life expectancy of an operative may have been judged in weeks, but they became feared by the forces in Occupied Europe. General Eisenhower would even comment that 'The disruption of enemy rail communications, the harassing of German road moves and the continual and increasing strain placed on German security services throughout occupied Europe by the organised forces of Resistance, played a very considerable part in our complete and final victory.'

As the tide of the war began to turn in the Allies' favour, the Foreign Office began to consider post-war plans. One suggestion in 1943 was that a unified Secret Service could be set up that combined MI5, MI6 and SOE into one organization, with branches covering Information, Security and Operations. Churchill didn't approve of this, and after many discussions between the various interested parties, the Bland Report, formally titled 'Future Organisation of the SIS', suggested that the secret service 'must start to build up a really secret organisation behind its existing, much too widely known, façade'.

The Bland Report covered all aspects of the service, including recruitment ('If ... the SIS does not succeed in attracting the right men, first-class results cannot possibly be forthcoming'), and stated bluntly that the main task was 'to obtain by covert means intelligence which it is impossible or undesirable for His Majesty's Government to seek by overt means'. The report also emphasized the need for clarity in the division of responsibility between MI5 and MI6, and suggested that SOE be wound up and operations handled by MI6.

(The SOE weren't made aware of this, since it was already clear they envisaged a role for themselves in peacetime Europe.)

The draft of the Bland Report did suggest that MI6 'should not direct its energy to investigating the activities of political organisations, e.g. Communists, Anarchists, &c' but Sir Stewart Menzies pointed out that they were dealing with this sort of work already – and indeed had set up a department, Section IX, specifically to do so. The Foreign Office 'desiderata' in regard to Europe (the guidelines by which the service operated) made it clear that while keeping an eye on any attempts by Germany to revive activities was the first priority, observing 'Russian activities . . . and the activities of national parties or groups in different countries who look to Moscow for leadership or support' came a close second. After further discussion, the non-political nature of MI6 was emphasized in the final version: the service didn't investigate people 'because of their political ideology' but only when there was 'prima facie evidence that [the] organisation in question may be used as instruments of espionage, or otherwise when specifically requested to do so . . . C would always be well advised to seek guidance from the Foreign Office as to what political parties in foreign countries need special watching, and for how long.'

And it became abundantly clear that the countries that would need watching would indeed be those from the Soviet Bloc.

During the years leading up to the start of the Cold War, the intelligence agencies of the Union of Soviet Socialist Republics were as concerned with spying on their own people as they were with counter-intelligence against foreign agents. This would continue to be the case throughout the twentieth century until the break-up of the Soviet Union, and in fact was nothing new in Russia.

The first political police force in the country, the Oprichnina, was founded by Ivan the Terrible in 1565 and was responsible for the massacre of whole cities before it was abolished seven years later. Then Peter the Great created the Preobrazhensky Prikaz so secretively that even the KGB's own histories are unsure of the exact date of its institution in the late seventeenth century. It too did not last long, but the Third Section of Tsar Nicholas I's Imperial Chancellery, founded in 1826, was to survive for over fifty years, serving as the Imperial regime's secret police. Although eventually discredited following the assassination of Tsar Alexander II, the Third Section's work against revolutionaries was carried on from 1880 by the Okhrana, the nickname for the Department of State Police and its regional security sections.

The Okhrana did operate outside the confines of Russia. Its Foreign Agency set up a centre to keep an eye on Russian emigrés in Paris – and was welcomed by the French police, the Sûreté, who went so far as to note in a report shortly before the First World War that 'It is impossible, on any objective assessment, to deny the usefulness of having a Russian police operating in Paris, whether officially or not.' When the centre was forced to close (at least publicly), the Sûreté were quick to complain that 'The French government will no longer be able to know as precisely as in the past what dangerous foreign refugees in France are doing.'

The leaders of the eventual Russian Revolution were understandably concerned about the Okhrana and its reach. The Russian Social Democratic Labour Party, which would split into the Bolsheviks and Mensheviks in 1903, was riddled with Okhrana agents. Four of the five members of the Bolshevik Party's St Petersburg Committee in 1908–9 worked for the security service. Roman Malinovsky, one of the Central Committee, was an Okhrana agent – and was shot as such when he foolhardily returned to Russia in 1918, a year after the Revolution.

The Soviet State Security organization would go through

many name changes in the period leading up to the Cold War. The Cheka (The All-Russian Extraordinary Commission for Combating Counter-Revolution and Sabotage) operated from December 1917 to February 1922, when it was incorporated into the NKVD (the People's Commissariat of State Security) as the GPU (the State Political Directorate). From July 1923 to July 1934 it was known as the OGPU (the Unified State Political Directorate) before reincorporating into the NKVD, this time as the GUGB (Main Administration of Soviet Security). For five months in 1941 it was referred to as the NKGB (the People's Commissariat of State Security) before returning to the NKVD. However, unlike in MI6, where agents who served in the First World War might still be around at the start of the Second, it was highly unlikely that anyone would survive through all of these name changes. Various errors by Soviet agents during this period – not warning of the armed uprisings in China, MI5's discovery of the Soviet spy ring in the UK – led to regular reorganizations of the State Security Service. Purges of those whom the paranoid leader Josef Stalin mistrusted meant that many NKVD officers fell victim to their own organization – particularly once it was under the control of its most feared chief, Lavrenti Beria, who rose to power as the head of the NKVD Nicolai Yezkov's deputy from 1936 before taking over on 25 November 1938, getting rid of his former boss on charges of espionage, treason and homosexuality.

Under Beria, the NKVD operated abroad extensively, with one of its agents, Ramón Mercader killing Stalin's great rival Leon Trotsky in Mexico in August 1940. The scale of their operations against their wartime allies would only become apparent in the aftermath of the Second World War. Various agents were uncovered or betrayed, and they had numerous agents in place reporting the movements of the Axis powers. One of their greatest agents, Richard Sorge, eventually became press attaché to the German embassy in Japan, and sent details of Hitler's Operation Barbarossa – the invasion of Russia – to Moscow, complete with its starting date of 22 June 1941. To Sorge's amazement, Stalin ignored the reports, until the invasion actually began, at which point the leader started to place more credence in Sorge's information. When Sorge learned that the Japanese did not intend to attack Siberia, Stalin moved his troops under Marshal Zukhov from there to the front line, which by this stage was almost within sight of the Kremlin. They were in time to rout the invading Germans. (Sorge was arrested shortly after this, and was hanged in 1944.)

Sorge wasn't the only Russian agent to warn about Barbarossa: according to KGB records, there were eighty-four separate attempts to persuade Stalin to take action. German journalist Rudolf Rössler, code-named Lucy, had a source apparently deep within the German supreme command. Werther, as this source was known, gave the start date for Barbarossa, and then, once the operation was under way, supplied details of where the German army was at its weakest – leading to the siege of Stalingrad. He also forewarned Stalin about the German invasion code-named Operation Citadel in 1943, allowing the Russian army to prepare the territory at Kursk and launch a pre-emptive attack on the Germans. Although Rössler never revealed who Werther was, some believe it might have been Hitler's deputy, Martin Bormann, who was last officially sighted in Berlin in May 1945, or possibly Admiral Canaris, who was shot following the abortive assassination attempt on Hitler by Colonel von Stauffenberg on 20 July 1944.

The Second World War also saw the creation of the NKVD's counter-intelligence section, known as SMERSH, an abbreviation of the Russian title Smert' Shpionam – Death to Spies. SMERSH, of course, became famous in the post-war years thanks to its prominent role in Ian Fleming's early James Bond novels, even though it had in fact been disbanded long before 007 was given his licence to kill. (When the stories were transferred to the screen in 1962, SMERSH was replaced as the villains by SPECTRE, a terrorist organization created for the first proposed film, *James Bond of the Secret Service*, and subsequently used in the novels.) Officially founded in April 1943, SMERSH operated for three years, both infiltrating the German secret services, and maintaining order within the Red Army: troops retreating in the face of enemy advances would be shot by their own side, and it was treason to be captured. They used any means necessary – informants, radio games, disinformation – to ensure the loyalty of both military and civilian personnel, and were highly regarded by Stalin, to whom they reported directly. They were tasked with finding Hitler's body at the end of the war, and, some sources claim, even removing it to Russia (leading to the inevitable claims that SMERSH agents recovered Hitler alive, and took him back to Moscow for interrogation and execution).

There was another Moscow Centre operation that began running before the Second World War, would continue through the war, and still be effective during the critical first few years of the Cold War. Hailed by the KGB as the ablest group of foreign agents it ever recruited, the quintet of spies became nicknamed 'The Magnificent Five'. The spy ring comprising Kim Philby, Guy Burgess, Donald Maclean, Anthony Blunt and John Cairncross, provided invaluable information during the war and in its immediate aftermath.

Some agents are motivated by greed, others by ideology. The Magnificent Five were all recruited during the thirties when, as Anthony Blunt explained after his treachery was made public in 1979, 'It seemed to me and many of my contemporaries that the Communist Party and Russia constituted the only firm bulwark against fascism, since the Western democracies were taking an uncertain and compromising attitude towards Germany.' British Labour Party leader Ramsay MacDonald's agreement to head a National

Government in 1931 was seen as a sell-out by the Magnificent Five and the Russian model seemed the only way forward.

The prime mover initially was Guy Burgess, a flamboyant Old Etonian whose Communist leanings were inflamed further by the book *Hitler over Europe?* by Ernst Henri, which proselytized the use of cells containing five members (*Fünfergruppen*, as they were named in Germany) to help foment anti-fascism. Henri was in fact OGPU agent Semyon Nikolayevich Rostovsky, who was a major recruiter for Moscow Centre, talent-spotting in Cambridge during the thirties. Burgess set out to create his own 'light-blue ring of five'.

Around the same time, one of his friends, former Cambridge man Harold 'Kim' Philby was signing up for Soviet Intelligence. Philby graduated in 1933 with 'the conviction that my life must be devoted to Communism'. He travelled in Europe, and in Vienna met and married Litzi Friedmann, who was a Comintern agent, and attracted the attention of the OGPU for his work on behalf of the party. He was recruited by Teodor Maly, and according to Philby, at that stage 'given the job of penetrating British intelligence . . . it did not matter how long it took to do the job'. He was sent back to England in May 1934 with a new controller, Arnold Deutsch, code name Otto.

Deutsch was instructed to work with both Philby and Burgess, but when Philby unsuccessfully tried to join the civil service (he was passed over because his referees had doubts about his 'sense of political injustice'), Deutsch ordered him to be patient. Philby therefore publicly claimed to have changed his political orientation, and started to become a member of the establishment, working for the liberal monthly *Review of Reviews*.

Burgess had been busy, gathering his ring of five. They included mathematician Anthony Blunt, and language scholar Donald Maclean, both of whom were Burgess' lovers at different times. He also recruited another modern languages student, John Cairncross, into his Comintern cell.

When Burgess was formally recruited by Deutsch, the controller suggested that the idea of a group was perhaps not the best way forward. Burgess, though, maintained the links of friendship between the five men throughout the next few years – which would almost prove catastrophic for Kim Philby when he was tarred by association with Maclean and Burgess when they were forced to defect to Russia in 1951.

On Deutsch's instructions, Maclean and Cairncross both broke off their contact with the Communist party, and applied to join the civil service. Burgess became personal assistant to MP Jack Macnamara; Maclean was accepted into the Foreign Office in October 1935, with Cairncross joining him there a year later. While the personable Maclean made friends and started to gain access to useful material, Cairncross was less successful, and eventually Deutsch suggested that he apply to work at the Treasury. Burgess became a popular producer for the British Broadcasting Corporation, making contacts across the spectrum – including MI6 deputy department head David Footman, who would recommend Burgess for a job in the secret service in 1938, working for MI6's new Section D, broadcasting propaganda to Nazi Germany. Blunt remained in Cambridge, sourcing new recruits for the NKVD, including Leo Long, who would be an important asset during the Second World War.

Philby, meanwhile, was becoming involved in the sort of assignment more usually to be found in the contemporary thrillers of Helen MacInnes or Leslie Charteris than the more mundane copying of secrets and passing of information carried out by the other Cambridge Spies. The Spanish Civil War broke out in 1936, and early the next year, Philby was sent under journalistic cover to penetrate General Franco's entourage and help organize his assassination. That particular mission was abandoned that summer in favour of gaining information about the other intelligence services operating in Spain. The following spring, Philby became a local hero when the car he was travelling in was hit by a shell and he was the sole survivor; the medal he received was pinned on by Franco himself!

The Magnificent Five, though, were shortly to find themselves without a controller. Following the great purges of the NKVD in 1937, both Maly, who had been working with Philby, and Deutsch were recalled to Moscow. Maly faced execution, while Deutsch survived into the war years before being executed by the SS as part of the anti-Nazi resistance in Vienna.

When war broke out, the Magnificent Five ensured that they were in prime positions to assist their Soviet paymasters. Cairncross became private secretary to Lord Hankey, the Chancellor of the Duchy of Lancaster, who chaired many secret committees and was even overseeing the intelligence services. This meant that Cairncross could pass across 'literally tons of documents', according to the NKVD, including warnings about Operation Barbarossa, and the findings of the Scientific Advisory and Maud Committees regarding the prospect of creating a weapon using Uranium-235 – making him one of the Soviet Union's first atomic spies. When Hankey was sacked from the Government in 1942, Cairncross turned his attentions to Bletchley Park, home of the Engima codebreakers.

Burgess was already ensconced in MI6 at the outbreak of war, and he assisted Kim Philby's smooth entry to the organization. Philby and Burgess would work together as instructors at a training school for the sabotage division Section IX (known as Section D, for 'Destruction') before that was folded into the new SOE. Burgess was let go while Philby remained with SOE until he moved across to Section V, the Counter-Intelligence section of MI6. (Moscow had other agents in SOE, including Donald Maclean's schoolfriend James Klugmann.)

While at Section V, Philby was able to pass on information on pre-war MI6 agents operating against the Soviets from the Registry, and, by volunteering for night duty at service headquarters at 54 Broadway, near St James' Park in central London, he could keep Moscow informed of all current developments. He liaised with MI5 when Section V moved into central London in 1943, and when a new Section IX was established in 1944, specifically to deal with the Soviet threat past and present, Moscow Centre insisted that he 'must do everything, but everything, to ensure that [he] became head of Section IX'. Philby manoeuvred the main contender – a staunch anti-Communist – out of the running, and as his colleague Robert Cecil wrote, thereby 'had ensured that the whole post-war effort to counter Communist espionage would become known in the Kremlin. The history of espionage records few, if any, comparable masterstrokes.'

Although Philby undoubtedly made the greatest contribution overall to Soviet intelligence, during the war it was Cairncross and Blunt who attracted the most plaudits from Moscow Centre. Blunt would eventually work himself into a nervous breakdown, and effectively become little more than a courier after the war. He was recruited into MI5 in the summer of 1940, and was soon in charge of surveillance of neutral embassies, as well as gaining surreptitious access to the various diplomatic bags of their couriers – which he would photograph and pass over to the Five's new London contact, Anatoly Gorsky. He also ran Leo Long as a sub-agent, gaining material courtesy of Long's access to ULTRA material from Bletchley Park as a member of MI14.

Cairncross was also at Bletchley at this point early in the Second World War, passing on information about German troop movements, and contributing to the Soviet victory at the Battle of Kursk. In 1944, he then moved across to MI6, working on the German desk at Section V, before moving to the Political Intelligence section, where he didn't prosper so well, lacking Burgess' or Maclean's innate talents for getting along with people easily.

Guy Burgess' contributions to the Soviet war effort were in a different field, following his dismissal from SOE. He ended up working once more as a talks producer for the BBC, and even managed to get the author of his own inspiration, Ernst Henri, on the air, proclaiming how great the Soviet Union's intelligence network was!

Maclean was the only one of the Five not to have a distinguished war career – at least at first. He didn't handle the strain of his double life well, and although he was part of the General Department of the Foreign Office, he seemed to lack energy, not helped by problems with his domestic life. However in Spring 1944, he was posted to Washington DC, and seemed to regain his previous enthusiasm. He had access to information about the Allies' plans after the war ended, and also became involved with liaison with the atomic-bomb project. His wife was in New York, and he travelled there from Washington regularly to see her – and pass on information to Gorsky, who had crossed to the United States to handle Centre agents there. Of course, this meant that there was signals traffic between the various Soviet missions on the East Coast regarding his movements – something that would come back to haunt Maclean a few years later, and eventually cause the downfall of the entire Cambridge Magnificent Five.

Compared with their British or Russian allies, the Americans were latecomers to the espionage field – partly, of course, because as of the start of the Second World War, the United States as an entity had only existed for just over 150 years.

During the First World War, which America only entered in 1917, the Army's G-2 section along with the Office of Naval Intelligence (ONI) had operated against pro-German groups, and American cryptologist Herbert O. Yardley helped to organize the US Army's Cipher Bureau, known as

MI-8. This had some notable successes against German agents operating in the US, but its peacetime operations were brought to a close in 1928 when incoming president Herbert Hoover's new secretary of state Henry L. Stimson shut it down, stating that 'Gentlemen do not read each other's mail'.

G-2 and the ONI continued to function between the wars, working in tandem with the newly created Federal Bureau of Intelligence (formerly the Department of Justice Bureau of Investigation) to keep an eye on actual and potential subversive elements, including the Communist Party of the United States of America (CPUSA). It seems they didn't realize the scale of Soviet infiltration: the daughter of the American ambassador to Germany was an early recruit, while Congressman Samuel Dickstein, a key member of the Special Committee on Un-American Activities, which was seeking to eradicate Nazism in the States, was on the NKVD books during the late thirties, and earned the nickname Crook for his financial demands.

Inevitably there were overlapping operations between the various groups, but it was only after the outbreak of war in Europe in September 1939 that President Roosevelt decided to regularize the situation. In June 1940, internal security was divided between the various parties: the FBI remained in charge of civilian investigations, while G-2 and the ONI dealt with those involving the military (including defence plants that had major Army or Navy contracts). They would also be responsible for the Panama Canal Zone, the Philippines and major Army reservations.

Despite the shutdown of the Cipher Bureau, code-breaking had continued to form a major part of the intelligence work of the US forces, and a debate continues to this day about how much was known by President Roosevelt about the impending attack on Pearl Harbor in December 1941. It seems probable that the president was not aware of the danger, but what is absolutely certain is that the men in charge in Hawaii were not up to speed with everything that Washington knew and didn't take the appropriate action. The code-breakers would redeem the reputation of their profession by breaking the Japanese code known as JN25, which prevented the invasion of Northern Australia and gave US Fleet Admiral Nimitz a vital edge before the Battle of Midway.

Five months before Pearl Harbor, President Roosevelt appointed William 'Wild Bill' Donovan, a successful Wall Street lawyer and Medal of Honor winner, as Coordinator of Intelligence (COI). Donovan had spent the previous year liaising with William Stephenson, the Scottish-Canadian millionaire who became an unofficial channel for British influence in the States following the outbreak of war in Europe. Donovan became convinced that a central coordinated American intelligence agency was required, and his appointment as COI, consulting with the heads of the existing agencies and reporting directly to the president, was a major stepping-stone towards that.

The declaration of war with Japan and Germany in December 1941 led to a division of the COI's responsibilities, with its propaganda work transferred to the Office of War Information, and the rest incorporated into the new Office of Strategic Services (the OSS). Donovan remained in charge of this new organization, but instead of reporting to the president as formerly, he now answered to the military Joint Chiefs of Staff.

The OSS was split into three divisions: the Special Intelligence division gathered intelligence from open sources, and from agents in the field. Allen Dulles was in charge of a crucial station in Bern, Switzerland, which supplied a lot of vital information regarding the Nazi rocket programme, and the German atomic bomb project. The Special Operations group was an equivalent to the British Special Operations Executive, and carried out many of the same functions, sometimes in tandem with the British, but on other occasions, as in

Yugoslavia, working with different groups opposing the Nazis. The Morale Operations division used the radio station *Soldat Ensender* as a propaganda weapon against the German army. Many senior figures in American intelligence circles after the Second World War were OSS agents, including future CIA chiefs Allen Dulles and William Colby.

Although the FBI were involved with what might be termed traditional activities during the war years – dealing with potential saboteurs and other threats to national security – they did operate their own Special Intelligence Service (confusingly referred to as the SIS by the Bureau) in Latin America. According to the FBI's own history its role 'was to provide information on Axis activities in South America and to destroy its intelligence and propaganda networks. Several hundred thousand Germans or German descendants and numerous Japanese lived in South America. They provided pro-Axis pressure and cover for Axis communications facilities. Nevertheless, in every South American country, the SIS was instrumental in bringing about a situation in which, by 1944, continued support for the Nazis became intolerable or impractical.'

At much the same time as the heads of British Intelligence were contemplating what would happen once the Axis was defeated, William Donovan was considering the future for American Intelligence. In a memorandum to President Roosevelt on 18 November 1944 he wrote:

Once our enemies are defeated, the demand will be equally pressing for information that will aid us in solving the problems of peace. This will require two things:
1. That intelligence control be returned to the supervision of the President.
2. The establishment of a central authority reporting directly to you, with responsibility to frame intelligence objectives and to collect and coordinate the intelligence material

required by the Executive Branch in planning and carrying out national policy and strategy.

This central authority would be led by a director reporting to the president, aided by an Advisory Board consisting of the Secretary of State, the Secretary of War, the Secretary of the Navy, and such other members as the President might subsequently appoint. Its primary aim would be to coordinate all intelligence efforts and the collection 'either directly or through existing Government Departments and agencies, of pertinent information, including military, economic, political and scientific, concerning the capabilities, intentions and activities of foreign nations, with particular reference to the effect such matters may have upon the national security, policies and interests of the United States'.

The memo was leaked to the press, and caused an uproar. Columnist Walter Trohan said that it would be 'an all-powerful intelligence service to spy on the post-war world and to pry into the lives of citizens at home' which 'would operate under an independent budget and presumably have secret funds for spy works along the lines of bribing and luxury living described in the novels of [British spy novelist] E. Phillips Oppenhem'.

Roosevelt took no action on Donovan's suggestion, and, following the president's death, his successor Harry S. Truman decided not to allow the OSS to continue post-war, fearing that it would become an 'American Gestapo'. The order to disband was given on 20 September 1945, and the OSS ceased functioning a mere ten days later, with some of its key capabilities handed over to the War Department as the Strategic Services Unit.

Yet only four months after he had seen fit to shut down America's key central intelligence-gathering organization, President Truman signed an executive order establishing the Central Intelligence Group to operate under the direction of the National Intelligence Authority. What had changed?

2

A NEW REALPOLITIK

'I can say even today that I do not think any insoluble differences will arise among Russia, Great Britain, and the United States,' President Roosevelt informed the American people in his 'fireside chat' broadcast around the world on Christmas Eve, 1943, following meetings with his counterparts – British Prime Minister Winston Churchill, Soviet leader Josef Stalin, and the Chinese Generalissimo, Chiang Kai-shek – in Cairo and Tehran. He went on to say:

> In these conferences we were concerned with basic principles – principles which involve the security and the welfare and the standard of living of human beings in countries large and small.
>
> To use an American and somewhat ungrammatical colloquialism, I may say that I 'got along fine' with Marshal Stalin. He is a man who combines a tremendous, relentless determination with a stalwart good humour. I believe he is truly representative of the heart and soul of Russia; and I believe that we are going to get along very well with him and the Russian people – very well indeed . . .

The doctrine that the strong shall dominate the weak is the
doctrine of our enemies – and we reject it.

Roosevelt certainly seemed prepared to accept Stalin's assurances that people in the Baltic states (Lithuania, Latvia and
Estonia) would be free to choose whether they stayed under
Soviet domination. Although Stalin made it clear that he
wanted a far western border for Poland, bringing much of the
country under Soviet control, the discussion was postponed.
However Stalin's appetite for increasing Soviet hegemony was
noted by Roosevelt's adviser Charles Bohlen, who told the US
ambassador to the Soviet Union that 'the Soviet Union would
be the only important military and political force on the
continent of Europe. The rest of Europe would be reduced to
military and political impotence.' It has been suggested that
Roosevelt agreed to Stalin's plans in return for the Soviet
leader's support for the establishment of the United Nations.
(It's worth noting that the NKVD had the US delegation's
property bugged, and that the Soviets regarded another of
Roosevelt's advisers, Harry Hopkins, almost as one of their
own – Hopkins wasn't a Communist by conviction, but he
accepted that the Soviets would inevitably be the dominant
power in Europe after the end of the war, and advised the
president accordingly.)

When the leaders met at Yalta in 1945, following the
successful invasion on D-Day, the war was all but over.
Russian and Allied troops were virtually in Berlin, and great
swathes of Eastern Europe were now to all intents and
purposes governed by Moscow. As one of Roosevelt's advisers
Bernard Baruch pointed out, it would be futile 'to demand of
Russia what she thinks she needs and most of which she now
possesses'. Poland would be under Soviet rule, although Stalin
promised there would be elections. Germany would be
divided into four zones, with Berlin itself divided, an island
within the Soviet zone.

Charles Bohlen felt that Stalin was hoodwinking the president. 'What [Roosevelt] did not understand was that Stalin's enmity was based on profound ideological convictions,' he wrote. 'The existence of a gap between the Soviet Union and the United States, a gap that could not be bridged, was never fully perceived by Franklin Roosevelt.' Roosevelt himself said, 'I think that if I give him everything that I possibly can and ask nothing from him in return, noblesse oblige, he won't try to annex anything and will work for a world of democracy and peace.'

But Stalin had no intention of following through on his promises. Roosevelt told Congress that he hoped the Yalta agreement would 'spell the end of the system of unilateral action, the exclusive alliances, the spheres of influence, the balances of power, and all the other expedients that have been tried for centuries – and have always failed'. It was a naive view, at best. Stalin refused to allow Western observers in for the elections, and Roosevelt realized, less than three weeks before his death, that: 'We can't do business with Stalin. He has broken every one of the promises he made at Yalta.'

On 12 April 1945, Roosevelt died of a cerebral haemorrhage. His successor, Harry S. Truman, was a great deal blunter than Roosevelt had ever been: when the Soviet Foreign Minister complained that he had never been addressed in such a way, after a dressing-down by the president, Truman replied, 'Carry out your agreements and you won't get talked to like that.' It was Truman who sat down with Churchill – and then new British Prime Minister Clement Atlee, whose Labour Party took power in the post-war election that occurred mid-conference – and Stalin at Potsdam, a suburb in the south-west of Berlin, and discovered that most of the important decisions had already been taken and Stalin had no intention of accepting any decisions that didn't directly benefit the Soviet Union's plans. Truman's priority, initially, was the still-continuing war in the Far East, and gaining Soviet support for that. In the end, though, the use of the atom bomb, first at Hiroshima and then Nagasaki, prompted the Japanese surrender – and Truman could focus on the Soviet duplicity that he saw. Duplicity that would be revealed in detail when a cypher clerk at the Soviet embassy in Ottawa, Canada, defected to the West that September.

Just as the record executive who turned down the Beatles has gone down in history as missing one of the great opportunities of the twentieth century, in espionage terms so did the night editor at the *Ottawa Journal* in failing to take adequate notice of the nervous Russian standing in the offices on the evening of 5 September 1945.

Igor Gouzenko had decided to defect from his post at the Soviet embassy in Ottawa. Although he was officially employed as a cypher clerk, he was in fact a lieutenant in Soviet Army intelligence, the GRU, and became determined to claim asylum when he learned that he and his family were due to return to the Soviet Union. He was well aware that anyone who served overseas was regarded with suspicion by the Soviet secret police, and he knew that life in Canada, even with the inevitable austerity post-war, would be better than in his homeland. In order to ensure that the Canadians would allow him to stay, rather than simply returning him to the embassy, he appropriated a packet containing more than a hundred decrypted messages that provided details of recent Soviet espionage against both Canada and the US.

Gouzenko tried to interest both the *Ottawa Journal* and the Canadian Ministry of Justice in his story, but no one listened. Eventually his neighbour, a Canadian Air Force officer, took pity on him, and allowed Gouzenko to hide on his property. He then contacted the Royal Canadian Mounted Police (RCMP), who watched from Dundonald Park as NKVD agents searched Gouzenko's apartment, desperately looking for the defector.

The papers that Gouzenko brought with him were

dynamite. Although they referred to agents by code-names, there was enough in plain language to reveal a string of Soviet informants in all manner of places. 'The amazing thing,' Canadian Prime Minister Mackenzie King wrote in his diary after he had been briefed on the information Gouzenko provided, 'is how many contacts have been successfully made with people in key positions in government and industrial circles.'

In their official history, the Canadian Security Intelligence Service (CSIS) credits Gouzenko's revelations with:

> ... usher[ing] in the modern era of Canadian security intelligence. Previously, the 'communist menace' had been viewed by authorities in terms of its threat to the labour movement. Gouzenko's information showed that the Soviets of the day were interested in more than cultivating disaffected workers: they were intent on acquiring military, scientific, and technological information by whatever means available to them. Such knowledge had become the key to advancement, and the Soviets intended to progress.

The information he provided led to a sweeping investigation and arrests under the Canadian War Measures Act. Eleven of the twenty-one Canadians arrested were convicted, including member of parliament Fred Rose, the only Communist ever elected to the Canadian governing body.

The British and Americans, understandably, wanted to know more about Gouzenko's revelations, particularly since it was 'supported by convincing documentary [evidence of] political and scientific espionage', according to the official report. MI5 agent Roger Hollis was sent to assist with debriefing, and passed information back to London – although since one of the contacts there was Soviet agent Kim Philby, Moscow Centre was kept up to speed on the revelations, and able to attempt to minimise the damage.

There was little they could do, though. Gouzenko's material revealed one of the key Soviet agents involved with Moscow Centre's attempts to obtain information about the American atomic program – something that the Soviets had been interested in for some considerable period.

The Gouzenko papers specifically identified the scientist Alan Nunn May as one of the agents in place within the Manhattan Project, the code-name for the development of the atomic bomb. A member of the Communist Party of Great Britain since the thirties, Nunn May had offered information to the Soviets about the possibility of a 'dirty' nuclear bomb in 1941. When he was sent to Canada in January 1943 to work on the Manhattan Project, he became part of the GRU network run out of the Ottawa embassy by Colonel Nikolai Zabotin, and passed both information and samples of Uranium-235 to the Soviets, apparently in exchange for two bottles of whiskey and $700, which Nunn May said he burned. When he returned to Britain he was eventually arrested by MI5, and confessed. He would later be sentenced to ten years in prison, despite his barrister's argument that at the time he passed the materials, the Soviets were British allies. The Soviets' other key mole within the Manhattan Project would remain safe for a while longer.

While the RCMP and MI5 were probing Gouzenko's secrets, the FBI were dealing with revelations of their own when one of the longest-standing Soviet agents on American soil came in of her own free will and began blowing open various Soviet intelligence operations.

Elizabeth Bentley, later known as the Red Spy Queen, had joined the CPUSA in 1935, and when she got a job working for the Italian Library of Information – a propaganda bureau for the fascist Italian regime – based in New York City three years later, she offered her services as a spy. NKVD agent Jacob Golos became her controller, although Bentley maintained that she was unaware that she was in the employ of

Moscow Centre for at least two years. In 1940, when Golos was forced to register under the Foreign Aliens Registration Act, Bentley became the intermediary with his rings of agents, and took charge of Golos' cover operation, the United States Service and Shipping Corporation. During the war, she ran the Silvermaster group, a network based around Nathan Gregory Silvermaster, an economist with the War Production Board, which passed information on German military strength and American munitions production, as well as other useful material, back to Moscow.

When Golos died of a heart attack in 1943, Bentley, code-named *Umnitsa* (Miss Wise) by Moscow, continued with his spying activities, now reporting to Iskhak Akhmerov, the leading NKVD agent in the USA. The CPUSA General Secretary Earl Browder supported her desire to keep agents reporting via her, rather than directly to Akhmerov, but in June 1944 Browder changed his mind. 'I discovered then that Earl Browder was just a puppet, that somebody pulled the strings in Moscow,' Bentley would later say, suggesting that this was what led her to defect.

Soviet intelligence began to become mistrustful of Bentley when she began dating Peter Heller, who they suspected worked for the FBI. They suggested that she emigrate to the Soviet Union, but Bentley refused. Instead, she visited an FBI field office in August 1945, but didn't defect at that stage. After a row with her new controller, Anatoly Gorsky (who had come over to deal with the American networks following his successes with Philby and the other members of the Magnificent Five in London from 1940 onwards), she realized that she was in serious danger from Moscow Centre – and Gorsky indeed recommended that they get rid of her. When she learned that Louis Budenz, one of her sources, had defected, her mind was made up.

Elizabeth Bentley began to tell her story to the FBI on 7 November 1945, and from that date onwards provided reams of information that would reveal the extent of Soviet infiltration of all levels of American society. She named around 150 agents working for the Soviet Union, including thirty-seven federal employees, and informed the Bureau that 'the Russians are most interested in placing someone in the employment of the FBI, especially as a special agent . . . The Russians have been trying for two years to place someone in the employment of the FBI, with negative results . . . The FBI was the only government agency that they could not crack and money was no object to accomplish this.'

Perhaps buoyed by the news that the Russians considered them impregnable, the FBI thought that they were on the verge of rounding up multiple spy rings, particularly when the information Bentley provided tallied with the material from Igor Gouzenko – but once again, Moscow Centre seemed to know everything ahead of time, and the various agents were no longer contacted by their Russian controllers. The reason? Once again, in his role with MI6, Kim Philby was kept in the loop – and passed on the bad news to Moscow, who cabled out to their American agents to 'cease immediately their connection with all persons known to Bentley in our work [and] to warn the agents about Bentley's betrayal'.

While they may not have led to the great coup for which the FBI had been hoping, Elizabeth Bentley's revelations were a bad blow for Moscow Centre. As well as blowing the cover of numerous useful sources, her 107-page testimony listed all aspects of Soviet tradecraft and operations in the United States. Coupled with Igor Gouzenko's material, and the sudden loss of all of their agents inside the OSS when that organization was suddenly shut down at the start of October 1945, things did not look good for the Soviets. However, they still had their ace in the hole – Kim Philby, and the other members of the Magnificent Five. But even their time was running out.

Igor Gouzenko and Elizabeth Bentley's testimony and

information may have given American and British counter-intelligence organizations much to ponder, but one of the greatest sources of information about the Soviet activity in the West – and the one that led directly to the uncovering of Kim Philby's spy ring – came from the Russians themselves. Even though much of the intelligence gleaned from it was dis-covered in the first few years of the Cold War, its existence, and the insight it gave into Soviet activities against the West, were factors in the emergence of the decades-long conflict, and the decision by President Truman to go pro-active in his dealings with the Soviets.

On 1 February 1943, Soviet diplomatic communications came under greater scrutiny than before, when the US Army's Signal Intelligence Service began the project that would later be code-named Venona. Based at Arlington Hall in Virginia, this code-breaking programme would eventually be as im-portant to those fighting Soviet infiltration as the work done at Bletchley Park on the Enigma material was to the Allies during the Second World War.

Put simply, the code-breakers on Venona were looking at literally thousands of messages that had been sent back and forth between Moscow and its diplomatic missions around the world. They realized that in addition to orders and reports for the various trade delegations and diplomats at the missions, there were instructions going to the representatives of the different Soviet intelligence groups: the NKVD, the GRU and the GRU-Naval (the Soviet Naval Intelligence staff).

The process of breaking the code was painstaking, and progress was slow. A weakness in the Soviet cryptographic system was discovered within a year of Venona's inception, and further breakthroughs followed in 1944, but it wasn't until 1946 that cryptographer Meredith Gardner was able to read portions of NKVD messages. As William P. Crowell explained when the Venona project was declassified in 1995:

The Venona cryptosystems . . . should have been impossible to read. They consisted of a code book in which letters, words, and phrases were equated to numbers. So a code clerk would take a plain text message and encode the message using numbers from the code book. This would have presented a significant challenge itself depending on how long the code book was used. However, the messages were further modified, in other words double-encrypted, by use of a one-time pad. The use of a one-time pad effectively randomizes the code and renders it unreadable. The key to the Venona success was that mistakes were made in the construction and use of the one-time pads – a fact that was discovered only through brute force and analysis of the message traffic.

According to Oleg Gordievsky's history of the KGB, the sheer number of messages travelling between the USSR and the various missions worldwide was so great towards the end of the Second World War that Moscow Centre sometimes sent out the same 'one-time' pad again. (The cypher officer responsible was apparently shot.)

As the work continued, more and more code names of Soviet agents were revealed – backing up information given by Gouzenko and Bentley – and the team at Arlington Hall were supplemented by British analysts as well as representatives from the FBI.

By no means all the messages were decoded, but enough was revealed to allow investigators to pursue leads. A burned codebook, found on the battlefield at the end of the war, proved eventually to be useful when some of its contents correlated to Venona, but this only came to light nearly a decade after its discovery.

The Soviets were, unsurprisingly, concerned about this work. Elizabeth Bentley mentioned in one of her debriefings that Moscow had been aware to a certain extent of the work going on there as early as 1944. In 1945, they managed to infiltrate an agent, Bill Weisband, into Arlington Hall, whose identity was ironically uncovered when the relevant instructions formed one of the Venona documents. However, even after his treachery was discovered in 1950, Weisband was never prosecuted for espionage since both the British and Americans agreed that the Venona project was too valuable to be mentioned even at an 'in camera' hearing.

The Soviets could do little about Venona: they didn't know which messages the Arlington Hall cryptographers would be able to read, so, as Gordievsky said, 'It was immediately clear ... that Venona represented a series of time-bombs of potentially enormous destructive force for its agent networks.'

The biggest secret that Moscow wanted kept quiet was its access to American and British research into the atomic bomb. One of the first intelligence messages from 1944 that was decoded, in December 1946, related to code name ENOR-MOZ – the Manhattan Project – providing the Soviets with a list of the names of the leading scientists working on the atomic bomb. Other messages gave specific details about progress on the development of the device, which the Soviet agents planted at the top secret Los Alamos base in New Mexico hoped would enable their scientific counterparts to maintain parity with the American project.

The main Soviet agent was Dr Klaus Fuchs, a German Communist Party member who had moved to England in 1933. He was brought on board the British atomic bomb project under Professor Rudolf Peierls in 1941. MI5 had been reluctant to give Fuchs security clearance, but eventually he was passed – at which point he immediately travelled to London to offer his services to the Russians! He would later claim that he didn't know whether he was working for the GRU or the NKGB, protesting that he didn't realize there was more than one branch of Soviet intelligence.

Fuchs was sent across to America in December 1943, and transferred to the control of another key Russian spy, Harry Gold, to whom he passed numerous details on the bomb, supplementing the material that another Russian spy, David Greenglass, was providing. This would continue throughout the rest of the Second World War, with Greenglass leaving the Los Alamos headquarters in February 1946, and Fuchs heading over to the British Atomic Energy Research Establishment at Harwell, Oxfordshire, four months later.

However, at almost exactly the same time as the Russians were benefitting from Fuchs' treachery and exploding their own atomic bomb, the Venona transcripts were providing clues to both Fuchs' and Greenglass' identities. Fuchs was arrested and confessed in January 1950, while Greenglass admitted his role in June that year. Information that Greenglass provided would prove critical in winding up the Soviet network run by Julius and Ethel Rosenberg (see chapter 4).

In addition to cutting off the Soviets' inroads into the atomic establishment, Venona also crippled one of their major operations in Australia. Since 1943, the NKVD residency in Canberra had great success penetrating the Australian Ministry of External Affairs, which gave them access to a lot of British secrets. Jim Hill and Ian Milner, the two best Soviet agents there, were compromised by the Venona material. Early in 1948, MI5 sent their Director-General, Sir Percy Sillitoe, accompanied by Roger Hollis, to conduct an investigation, maintaining the cover story that a British mole in Soviet intelligence had passed on the agents' details, rather than risk compromising Venona. The loss of these agents was such a serious blow to Moscow Centre that by the time the KGB Resident Vladimiri Petrov defected in 1954, they had still not been able to achieve more than minor breaches of Australian security.

However, perhaps the most damaging discovery of the Venona material as far as the Soviets were concerned was the seemingly trivial item that a Russian agent, code-named Gomer (Homer in English), had been travelling from Washington to New York in 1944 to visit his pregnant wife. When this final piece was put into place, it meant that Homer could only be one person: Donald Maclean. And with Maclean would go the whole of the Magnificent Five.

Kim Philby had stayed in MI6 after the end of the war, becoming head of the Secret Service station in Turkey from 1947 to 1949 (using that position to betray any British agents who attempted to use the Turkish border crossing to gain access to the Soviet Union), and then was sent as MI6 representative in Washington from 1949, during which time he had access to both American and British case files. Not long before his recall in 1951, he passed over information about three groups of six agents who were parachuting into the Ukraine – sending them to their deaths, noting in his diary that 'I can make an informed guess' as to their fate.

During the same period, Guy Burgess and Donald Maclean were able to pass over reams of information from the Foreign Office, with Anthony Blunt occasionally assisting Burgess with the material. Although Burgess was gradually becoming more dissolute, often under the influence of drink or drugs, he could still charm information out of unsuspecting colleagues, as he did in the Far Eastern Department of the Foreign Office before he was posted to Washington in 1950. Maclean was posted to Cairo in 1948, but his drinking also slipped out of control, as did other aspects of his behaviour. According to Gordievsky, Moscow Centre blamed both his and Burgess' excesses on their concerns that the Venona information might compromise them. After a drunken rampage in Cairo in 1950, Maclean was sent back to Britain, where he seemed to pull himself together – and was able to provide the Russians with useful intelligence regarding the onset of the Korean War.

As MI6 liaison with American intelligence and counter-intelligence services, Kim Philby very quickly realized who code name Homer really was, but it was eighteen months before further decrypts would give enough clues for the FBI to gain sufficient evidence against Maclean. The field of suspects narrowed to thirty-five by the end of 1950, and just nine by April 1951. Philby tried to divert attention away from Maclean, but a crucial piece of evidence both cleared Philby's suggested suspect and became the fatal one for Maclean. However, because neither the FBI nor MI5 wanted to reveal the existence of Venona in court (Fuchs and Greenglass had confessed, so it wasn't necessary in their cases), there was a period during which MI5 tried to gain new evidence of Maclean's treachery.

Guy Burgess had been posted to Washington, and was staying with Philby (something that would compromise the latter tremendously after Burgess' defection). However, he was spiralling out of control, and Philby used Burgess' recall to Britain to get a message to Maclean, who had realized that his access to top-secret papers was being restricted, and that therefore he was probably under surveillance. When Burgess reached London he received a letter from Philby stating, 'It's getting *very* hot here.' Burgess was finding it hard to deal with the situation, and Yuro Modin, his KGB controller, put pressure on him to defect alongside Maclean. Before MI5 could bring Maclean in for interrogation, Burgess and Maclean disappeared, travelling across the English Channel and then the continent before arriving in Moscow a few weeks later.

News of both men's departure sent the intelligence community into uproar. Anthony Blunt was under no suspicion and was able to gain access to Burgess' flat, where he disposed of a large number of incriminating documents (although he would inadvertently leave some handwritten notes which would lead directly to the unmasking of John Cairncross). Modin had tried to persuade Blunt to join Burgess and Maclean but he refused. (He would eventually confess in 1964, but gained immunity from prosecution.) Kim Philby, on the other hand, decided to brazen things out – but the CIA would have other ideas.

3

THE COLD WAR BEGINS

By the end of 1945, President Truman had come to the conclusion that the Soviets could not be trusted, but he still hoped that in some way peace could be maintained. Despite the clear evidence of Soviet networks operating in America, thanks to the testimony of Oleg Gouzenko and Elizabeth Bentley, and the emerging material from Venona, he was reluctant to expose them publicly. However, events in the first few weeks of 1946 would start to educate the American people that the wartime alliance with the Soviets was not going to extend beyond the end of the conflict.

In the USSR, Stalin was making it clear that he saw the way forward very differently from his erstwhile allies. In February 1946, he gave a speech to the voters of Moscow, in which he blamed the outbreak of the Second World War on 'monopolistic capitalism' and went on to say, 'Perhaps catastrophic wars could be avoided if it were possible periodically to redistribute raw materials and markets among the respective countries in conformity with their economic weight by means of concerted and peaceful decisions. But this is impossible under the present capitalist conditions of world economic development.'

A week later, the news of the arrests in Canada based on the Gouzenko information was released in America and a few days after that, political adviser George F. Kennan sent a briefing telegram from the US Embassy in Moscow, which would shape American foreign policy for much of the next forty-five years. It set out his belief that the 'USSR still lives in antagonistic "capitalist encirclement" with which in the long run there can be no permanent peaceful coexistence'; that 'Russians will participate officially in international organizations where they see opportunity of extending Soviet power or of inhibiting or diluting power of others'; and that 'we have here a political force committed fanatically to the belief that with [the] US there can be no permanent *modus vivendi*, that it is desirable and necessary that the internal harmony of our society be disrupted, our traditional way of life be destroyed, the international authority of our state be broken, if Soviet power is to be secure.'

On 5 March, respected statesman Winston Churchill gave a speech at Westminster College, in Fulton, Missouri. Accompanied on the platform by President Truman, Churchill expressed his belief that the world had changed irrevocably, and coined a phrase that would epitomize the Soviet-dominated fiefdom. He told the audience of students:

From Stettin in the Baltic to Trieste in the Adriatic, an iron curtain has descended across the Continent. Behind that line lie all the capitals of the ancient states of Central and Eastern Europe. Warsaw, Berlin, Prague, Vienna, Budapest, Belgrade, Bucharest and Sofia; all these famous cities and the populations around them lie in what I must call the Soviet sphere, and all are subject, in one form or another, not only to Soviet influence but to a very high and in some cases increasing measure of control from Moscow.

In a great number of countries, far from the Russian frontiers and throughout the world, Communist fifth columns are established and work in complete unity and absolute obedience to the directions they receive from the Communist centre. Except in the British Commonwealth and in the United States where Communism is in its infancy, the Communist parties or fifth columns constitute a growing challenge and peril to Christian civilization ... I do not believe that Soviet Russia desires war. What they desire is the fruits of war and the indefinite expansion of their power and doctrines.

The Central Intelligence Agency was created by a National Security Act passed by Congress on 26 July 1947 and began operating in September, replacing the Central Intelligence Group which had been brought into existence in January 1946, once Truman appreciated that coordination of the various sources of intelligence data was vital. Admiral Sidney Souers, General Hoyt Vandenburg and then Admiral Roscoe Hillenkoetter were successive Directors of Central Intelligence during the CIG years, with Hillenkoetter transferring over to the CIA on its formation.

It's fair to say that the CIA was not an immediate success. According to some reports, they simply weren't up to the job. There's a story that is still told in Berlin about the early days of the Agency's involvement there: networks of agents would be set up secretly operating within the Soviet sector, in accordance with normal espionage principles, but then all those involved were invited to a cocktail party at the American base. This was great in terms of boosting morale for the agents – but it meant that all the Stasi, or the NKVD, had to do was arrest one person, and they could ascertain the identities of not just their one or two contacts, but potentially a whole host of them.

A similar error of judgement caused the loss of multiple teams during the Korean War: ethnic agents who were going to be parachuted into mainland China were trained and lived together, and inevitably shared information about their missions. Betrayal of one team would lead to betrayal of others.

There certainly appeared to be a sorry litany of key world events that the fledgling agency failed to predict, which were highlighted by an article in the *New York Herald Tribune* in August 1950. Much of this work was carried out by the Office of Reports and Estimates (ORE), which would pay the price for the various failures when the Agency was reorganized in late 1950.

This began with the Soviet takeover of Czechoslovakia in the spring of 1948. The Communists had become the single largest political party in Czechoslovakia in the elections held in 1946, with Klement Gottwald taking office as prime minster under President Edvard Beneš. Even though Beneš hoped to maintain diplomatic links with the West, the Communists took control of key ministries and started a drive towards total power. In September 1947, the newly formed Cominform (a group comprising members from the Communist parties around the world which aimed to spread the communist creed worldwide) noted that Czechoslovakia was the sole East European country in which 'the complete victory of the working class over the bourgeoisie' had not been achieved.

Action against non-communist ministers was stepped up, leading to the mass resignation by twenty-one of them in February 1948. Beneš was pushed into a corner, unable to back the non-communists for fear of the Red Army using a communist-backed insurrection as a pretext to invade. Gottwald threatened a general strike unless Beneš created a communist-led government – still technically a coalition, since it included the Communist Party, and the (pro-Moscow) Social Democrats. It meant that Czechoslovakia was now in the Soviets' hands, and the elections held that May were purely for show.

The CIA weren't expecting things to develop so quickly – a refrain that would be heard frequently under Hillenkoetter's leadership – and they sorely misread the intentions behind the actions. 'The timing of the coup in Czechoslovakia was forced upon the Kremlin when the non-Communists took action endangering Communist control of the police. A Communist victory in the May elections would have been impossible without such control,' Hillenkoetter told Truman in a letter on 2 March, while on 10 March, a report suggested that 'the Czech coup and the [Soviet's] demands on Finland [for a 'treaty of mutual assistance' – a prelude to a takeover] ... do not preclude the possibility of Soviet efforts to effect a rapprochement with the West'.

Three months later, the American government was shocked by a communiqué issued by the Cominform on 28 June, expelling Yugoslavia from its ranks. 'The leadership of the Communist Party of Yugoslavia has pursued an incorrect line on the main questions of home and foreign policy, a line which represents a departure from Marxism-Leninism,' it stated. The Communist Party had placed itself 'outside the family of the fraternal Communist Parties, outside the united Communist front and consequently outside the ranks of the Information Bureau'. The CIA had not put the various pieces of intel together to foresee Stalin splitting with someone regarded as one of his staunchest allies, Yugoslav prime minister Marshal Josip Tito.

In fact, the relationship between the two men had been rocky for some time, despite some surface signs of trust, such as the Cominform placing its headquarters in Belgrade. Tito had his own very clear ideas about how much he wanted his country to be under Soviet domination – he was happy to cooperate with Russia, and to emulate such concepts as the Five-Year Plan (Stalin's grandiose centralized economic plans), but they would be implemented in a way that suited Yugoslavia, not the USSR. There were tensions over Tito's use of troops in Albania, and his plans for a joint Yugoslav-Bulgarian Balkan Federation, which Stalin at first denounced, and then suddenly demanded be speeded up (possibly so he could plant pro-Moscow Bulgarians in strong positions in the joint organization).

Letters were flying between Moscow and Belgrade, with Tito eventually pointing out that 'No matter how much each of us loves the land of Socialism, the Soviet Union, he can in no case love less his country, which is also building Socialism.' Moscow announced on 12 June that Belgrade would no longer be hosting the Danube navigation conference, claiming the city would have 'difficulty in providing the necessary facilities', a charge the Yugoslavs denied. The split followed two weeks later – and would lead to Yugoslavia ploughing a different course from other Communist countries for many years to come.

Although the CIA had noted developments, they were criticized for not predicting the cataclysmic nature of the split, and the potential for change within the Soviet-dominated countries. In his written response to President Truman following the *Herald Tribune* article, DCI Hillenkoetter would point out:

CIA noted that Tito was taking energetic steps to purge the Yugoslav Communist Party of diversionists, and on 10 June reported that the Yugoslav government was groping for a policy that would make it 'the Balkan spearhead of evangelical and expansionist Communism'. When Yugoslavia defied the USSR on June 20 by insisting that the Danube Conference be held at Belgrade, the CIA estimated that the Kremlin faced a serious problem in reconciling within the Satellite states the conflict between national interests and international Communism.

In other words, yes, they did spot what was going on, but no one could have guessed it would be that serious.

The split between Yugoslavia and the Soviet Union was thrown into shadow by the start of another major rift between Russia and its former wartime allies, with the blockade of the non-Soviet sectors of Berlin that began in earnest on 24 June 1948. However, on this occasion, the accusation that the CIA failed to give adequate warning of this was not just unfair – it was manifestly wrong.

As part of the Potsdam Treaty which divided Germany into four sectors – run by Britain, France, the US and the USSR – Berlin itself was similarly divided. This was a constant thorn in Stalin's side: it provided a staging-post for American and British intelligence deep in the heart of Soviet East Germany; disaffected and reluctant citizens could find a haven from Communism by claiming asylum there and it was a reminder that Stalin had failed to achieve everything he wanted from the end of the war. The Western sectors were heavily reliant on cooperation from the Soviets, and when Stalin took exception to the way in which Britain, France and America were advancing with democracy and a new currency within occupied Germany, he decided that he wanted the allies out of Berlin. Pressure on what he regarded as the weak point of the coalition might also lead to a permanent split between the various states.

A policy of harassment began: trains travelling between the non-Soviet parts of Germany and Berlin were stopped and searched; a Soviet Yak-9 fighter came too close to a British airliner, killing all aboard. On 19 June 1948, the Russians stopped all rail traffic into the city; four days later, road and barge traffic was also halted. Then they cut the electricity supplies to West Berlin. It could have been a prelude for war, but all analysis indicated that if the Western powers held firm, Stalin would eventually back down. An incredible feat of logistics ensured that the blockade of Berlin, while still materially affecting everyone within the city, never brought the Western powers near to capitulation. For ten months, a constant stream of aircraft brought supplies along the internationally agreed air corridors over East Germany, keeping the Berliners alive.

Three months before the blockade began, at a time when the Soviets were carrying out military manoeuvres and beginning their harassment, DCI Hillenkoetter briefed President Truman:

> The USSR ... cannot expect the US and the other Western Powers to evacuate [Berlin] voluntarily. The USSR, therefore, will probably use every means short of armed force to compel these powers to leave the city.
>
> These devices may include additional obstruction to transport and travel to and within the city, 'failure' of services such as electric supply, reduction of that part of the food supply which comes from the Soviet Zone ... [T]he day-to-day developments in the immediate future will test the firmness, patience, and discipline of all US personnel in Berlin.

As a prediction of the nearly year-long crisis, it couldn't really be bettered. It certainly seemed as if Stalin wasn't being served with nearly as good intelligence from his people in Berlin, since he fatally underestimated the resolve of the coalition, and had little option but to back down and eventually reopen the borders.

The Cold War wasn't the only consideration for the CIA in 1948. Events in the Middle East were the focus of attention, as Jewish forces fought tooth and nail to create an independent state of Israel. On numerous occasions during that year, it seemed as if the Arab forces would deal a decisive blow to the nascent state, which had been declared on 14 May 1948, and recognized by the US and the USSR. However, the tenacity of the Jewish people – together with aid from foreign countries, sometimes in direct breach of United Nations declarations – ensured their survival. Hillenkoetter answered criticisms that the CIA hadn't predicted the outcome by pointing out that no one could have anticipated the amount of overseas aid that Israel would receive.

What proved to be one of the biggest mistakes the early CIA would make came with regard to the Soviet atomic programme. Neither the CIA nor the FBI was fully aware of the extent of the spy rings that had been set up during the Second World War to elicit the information – although Alan Nunn May had been arrested following the Gouzenko revelations, he was proud in later life that he never betrayed any of his colleagues to the security forces. The Venona transcripts showed that there were others involved, but there wasn't clear evidence as to whom – and without that information it was impossible to judge what could have been passed across.

Although the Western allies had tried to prevent German atomic scientists from being inducted to the Soviet programme at the end of the war, they knew that some key German personnel, including Dr Nicolaus Riehl of the Auer Company, Professor Gustav Hertz, and Professor Adolf Thiessen, were in Russian hands. Intelligence reports concluded that Germany's foremost cyclotron constructor, as well as an expert in the biophysics of radiation, were also working for them. Four East German scientists who defected to the West in 1947 helped to fill in some of the gaps, and evidence obtained by covert CIA operatives suggested that plutonium production was taking place at Elektrostal, a small town about sixty miles east of Moscow, using material produced at the IG Farben plant near Berlin.

Unfortunately, the CIA's own analysts didn't pay much heed to that information, and instead relied on pre-war geological analyses which stated that the Soviet Union wouldn't be able to threaten America's near-monopoly on suitable ore. In October 1946, the CIA's Office of Reports and Estimates suggested that 'It is probable that the capability of the USSR to develop weapons based on atomic energy will be limited to the possible development of an atomic bomb to the stage of production at some time between 1950 and 1953. On this assumption, a quantity of such bombs could be produced and stockpiled by 1956.' The ORE admitted its projections were 'educated guesswork' but based it on 'the current estimate of existing Soviet scientific and industrial capabilities, taking into account the past performance of Soviet and of Soviet-controlled German scientists and technicians, our own past experience, and estimates of our own capabilities for future development and production.' Although the information received regarding the Soviets progress brought the projected date forward to a certain extent, the earliest possible date was still being given as 'mid-1950' with mid-1953 being the most probable. That report was dated a mere five days before the Soviets exploded their first atomic device, nicknamed Joe-1 at Semipalatinsk, a site in north-eastern Kazakhstan, on 29 August.

Internally at the CIA, the failure to predict the timing of the test firing was described as an 'almost total failure of conventional intelligence' by assistant director Willard Machie. Summoned before the Joint Committee on Atomic Energy on 17 October, Hillenkoetter maintained that 'I don't think we were taken by surprise' – an assertion that didn't go down too well with the members of the committee.

'Our estimates were not too far off,' Hillenkoetter said, explaining that the CIA assumed that the Russians didn't begin work on an atomic programme until after the explosion at Hiroshima in August 1945, but it was now clear that they had started in 1943 – so the ORE's estimate of five years from start to finish was still accurate. He also noted that now the Russians had exploded a bomb, it meant that they could better correlate the various pieces of information that they had. (One Senator pointed out that even 'the Russians themselves didn't know that they had the bomb until it went off', unconsciously

echoing the concerns of Soviet ministers at the time, who
sought reassurance that there had been the distinctive mush-
room cloud before reporting to Stalin.)

At least one of the Senators present caught the mood: 'We
have not had an organisation adequate to know what is going
on in the past and [the DCI] gives me no assurance that we are
going to have one in the future.'

Failing to predict the rise of the Communist party and the
declaration of the People's Republic of China was another
charge levelled against Hillenkoetter by the *Herald Tribune*.
Once again this wasn't accurate: the Agency had been
repeatedly pointing out that the nationalist forces in China
were disintegrating, and the rise of the Communist party
under Mao Tse Tung was a corollary of that.

In the words of a later deputy DDI at the CIA, John
Gannon:

> [There was] a widely held but incorrect perception that the job
> of intelligence officers is to predict the future. That is not the
> case. Only God is omniscient, and only the Pope is infallible;
> intelligence officers are too savvy to compete in that league.
> Rather, the function of intelligence is to help US decision
> makers better understand the forces at work in any situation,
> the other fellow's perspective, and the opportunities and
> consequences of any course of action so that US policymakers
> can make informed decisions.

Hillenkoetter's job at the CIA was made much harder by the
lack of cooperation that he received from other intelligence
agencies. As he told President Truman, 'The [military] services
withhold planning and operational information from the CIA
and this hampers the CIA in fulfilling its mission.' The FBI
could be obstructive, and the military sections overestimated
Soviet capabilities in their own fields to ensure their own
departments received the necessary support.

It wasn't all bad news: the CIA were able to prevent a Communist party victory in the 1948 Italian elections. This wasn't the spy work of the Second World War, sneaking behind enemy lines. However, for an American government seriously worried about the spread of Communism, it was equally important, and for the agents actively involved in passing money to contacts and other clandestine activities, it wasn't that different in reality.

Former CIA operative F. Mark Wyatt was one of those involved in this new form of spying. As he told CNN in 1995:

> The run-of-the-mill operative in the [CIA] was hopeful that we could get into a [covert] operation ... My colleagues in the CIA, in 1946–47, when I was involved, were gung-ho. We had been in the war; we didn't question authority – 'Should we do it this way, should we not?' We definitely knew that the Soviet empire was, as Reagan said, the Evil Empire, and that was it. And when we were stationed abroad ... whether we were in Sri Lanka or we were in Iceland, we knew what our target was: it was the Soviet target. We were interested in what was going on in that country, and the connections of that country with the pervasive expansionist Soviet power.

DCI Hillenkoetter wasn't convinced that the CIA had the authority to take an active role in the Italian election and was advised by the agency's general counsel, Lawrence Houston, that he needed a specific mandate. This he received from the National Security Council in NSC directive 4a, which ordered the CIA '[to] initiate steps looking toward the conduct of covert psychological operations designed to counteract Soviet and Soviet-inspired activities'. The Special Procedures Group (SPG) was tasked with finding a way to do this.

In reality, this meant working with the Christian Democrats to defeat the Popular Democratic Front, a coalition formed by the Italian Communist and Socialist Parties. In addition to letter-writing campaigns by Italian-Americans, propaganda broadcasts by the Voice of America warning of the dangers of a rerun of the Czechoslovakian fall into Communism, and food and grain assistance, the SPG undertook more covert operations. As Wyatt recalled:

> We had bags of money that we delivered to selected politicians, to defray their political expenses, their campaign expenses, for posters, for pamphlets, what have you ... And we did many things to assist those selected Christian Democrats, Republicans, and the other parties that were completely reliable – that could keep the secret of where their funds came from. They were talked to by CIA experts: 'What do you say if all of a sudden you have in Turin the greatest extravaganza of propaganda? Who pays for it? Does the Fiat Corporation pay for it, or what? You've got to have some reason for your munificence at this time, and we don't want an indication that it's young Americans that are passing the money to you ... [in] black bags.

It meant training the Italian politicians in tradecraft so that the money could be passed surreptitiously, but, perhaps to the surprise of some of the agents involved, it worked. The Christian Democrats won by a landslide – 48 per cent to 31 per cent for the Popular Democratic Front. How much of this can be ascribed to the CIA's activities has been questioned over the years, but it was a rare victory for the early agents of the CIA to celebrate.

4

FIGHTING THE COLD WAR ON NEW FRONTS

With the Soviet Union proving that they had the atomic bomb in August 1949, it was evident that the escalation between the two opposing forces could result in a third world war, and the fifties would see many proxy conflicts between West and East. Eastern Europe and China were held by the Communists – even if everyone in power in the countries didn't necessarily bow down before Josef Stalin, they were of similar mindset, and to the Western intelligence agencies, they were a common foe.

All three of the main agencies involved in that conflict – Britain's MI6, the American CIA and the Russian KGB – would undergo major reorganization in the early years of the decade. The British had to reassess their entire set-up in the light of Donald Maclean and Guy Burgess' defection to Russia – and MI5's strong conviction that Kim Philby was the 'Third Man' who had persuaded them to leave. (Philby would continue to be a problem for MI6 until his eventual departure to Russia in 1963.) The death of Stalin in 1953 directly led to the restructuring of the Soviet State Security Service into the form in which it is best known. And the CIA had to deal with yet another failure of intelligence-gathering.

A lack of confidence in the reports coming from the CIA's Office of Reports and Estimates had been expressed as early as Spring 1949, and it was criticized heavily for not putting together the pieces regarding the Soviet atomic test. However, it was its failure to predict the invasion of South Korea by the North Koreans of the Democratic People's Republic of Korea (DPRK) in June 1950, and the involvement of the Chinese People's Army in October that year that led to the departure of Hillenkoetter.

In January 1950, the CIA reported their analysis of the troop movements in North Korea:

> The continuing southward movement of the expanding Korean People's Army toward the [border at the] thirty-eighth parallel probably constitutes a defensive measure to offset the growing strength of the offensively minded South Korean Army ... Despite this increase in North Korean military strength, the possibility of an invasion of South Korea is unlikely unless North Korean forces can develop a clear-cut superiority over the increasingly efficient South Korean Army.

They believed that the invasion would have to be ordered by Russia: 'The DPRK is a firmly controlled Soviet satellite that exercises no independent initiative and depends entirely on the support of the USSR for existence,' the CIA stated on 19 June, six days before the North Koreans did indeed act independently.

Once the war was under way, the CIA believed that the Chinese would not intervene in the situation, despite numerous coded and open warnings from the Chinese authorities. The authorities in Beijing made it clear that they would take action as they saw fit to protect their country as General

MacArthur and his troops pushed the DPRK Army back towards the 38th Parallel and then across it, entering North Korean territory on 1 October. 'While full-scale Chinese Communist intervention in Korea must be regarded as a continuing possibility, a consideration of all known factors leads to the conclusion that barring a Soviet decision for global war, such action is not probable in 1950,' stated the CIA report on 12 October. The next day, the Communist Chinese army entered North Korea. By mid-November, they were in full operation.

In light of these errors – and even before the Chinese intervention in the Korean War was confirmed – in October 1950, President Truman appointed General Walter Bedell Smith to the post of DCI with instructions to shake up the three-year-old agency and make it fit for purpose.

Smith created three directorates – intelligence (CDI); plans (DP); and administration (DA) – and the Korean War became a baptism of fire for the newly reorganized CIA. Turf wars between them and the Army's intelligence units continued, reaching as high as the President, who backed the CIA, although he required them to liaise with the Joint Chiefs of Staff. The Agency carried out a number of successful operations. Both they and the Army created units for special ops, and the CIA trained thousands of Koreans for infiltration into the DPRK for intelligence gathering and sabotage, as well as setting up escape and evasion networks. Missions, such as Operation Bluebell, were run by an operational arm known by the acronym JACK (Joint Advisory Commission, Korea), and, while the Agency acknowledged that some of the North Koreans and Chinese who volunteered for service were simply using them as a way of getting transport back home, many provided intelligence which helped the war effort.

In addition, the CIA also tried to continue its mission of subverting Communism by carrying out missions in China. The Agency created a cover airline, Civil Air Transport Co.

Ltd (CAT), which was used to drop agents and supplies into China, not always successfully. America still officially backed the nationalist government of China, which had been replaced by the Communists in 1949 and had moved to Formosa, and the CIA's Operation Paper supported invasion attempts from Burma by the Kuomintang, which it was hoped might draw some troops away from the Korean conflict.

Not every mission was a success, and misjudgements could have catastrophic consequences. Details of one such, in which agents John T. Downey and Richard G. Fecteau were shot down on their first mission over northern China in 1952, were only released under the Freedom of Information Act in 2011. Believing that they were extracting an undercover agent, they were actually walking into a trap. Their plane was shot down, and both men were captured alive, tortured and put on trial by the Chinese, and then held prisoner for the next twenty years. Although the CIA initially told their families that they had been lost in a CAT plane crash, back channel diplomacy would eventually lead to their release. Jack Downey refused to return to the Agency, pointing out, 'I don't think I'm cut out for this line of work!' Both men were able to retire with full pensions from the CIA and were awarded the Director's Medal for Extraordinary Fidelity at a special ceremony at CIA Headquarters in 1998.

While the CIA was concentrating on the conflict in south-east Asia, the FBI was having more success winding up Russian networks. The arrest in Britain of atomic scientist Klaus Fuchs as a result of the Venona project would lead to many more agents coming to light. Interrogated by MI5's James Skardon, Fuchs tried to conceal his contacts' identities, but Skardon did learn about a courier named 'Raymond', to whom Fuchs had passed top secret information about the atom bomb in June 1945, on the Castillo Street bridge over the river in the small town of Santa Fe near the Las Alamos base. 'Raymond' had made contact with Fuchs through the scientist's sister and the descriptions given by her and Fuchs tallied with someone the FBI had already interrogated as a result of Elizabeth Bentley's testimony: Harry Gold. Faced with evidence found at his own apartment that placed him in Santa Fe (which he had denied visiting), Gold confessed.

However, parts of Gold's story didn't add up, in particular why he had stopped in Albuquerque on one of his trips to Santa Fe. Eventually he admitted that he had visited a soldier who gave him technical drawings from Los Alamos – and this turned out to be Fuchs' colleague, David Greenglass. In turn, Greenglass broke under interrogation, and confessed that his wife Ruth and brother-in-law Julius Rosenberg were spies. This tallied with further Venona transcripts, which identified Rosenberg as a key agent known as 'Antenna' or 'Liberal', David Greenglass as 'Kalibr', and his wife as 'Osa'. Another agent, radar engineer Morton Sobell, was also taken into custody in Mexico when he tried to flee.

Julius Rosenberg and his wife Ethel were arrested and charged with espionage, but unlike the other members of their spy ring, they refused to admit their guilt. Accordingly they, along with Sobell, were brought to trial, where the FBI had to rely on the testimony of David Greenglass, which included details of the way the side piece of a box of Jell-O was used as a means of identification between agents Harry Gold and Elizabeth Bentley. Sobell was sentenced to thirty years' imprisonment. The Rosenbergs were sentenced to death. They were executed at Sing Sing Prison in June 1953, after multiple legal appeals and pleas for clemency.

President Dwight D. Eisenhower, who succeeded Harry S. Truman in January 1953, summed up the general public's revulsion at the Rosenbergs' activities:

These two individuals have been tried and convicted of a most serious crime against the people of the United States. They have been found guilty of conspiring with intent and reason to believe that it would be to the advantage of a foreign power, to deliver to the agents of that foreign power certain highly secret atomic information relating to the national defence of the United States. The nature of the crime for which they have been found guilty and sentenced far exceeds that of the taking of the life of another citizen; it involves the deliberate betrayal of the entire nation and could very well result in the death of many, many thousands of innocent citizens. By their act these two individuals have, in fact, betrayed the cause of freedom for which free men are fighting and dying at this very hour.

The Rosenbergs' trial concluded in April 1951; a month later, Guy Burgess and Donald Maclean defected to the USSR. Questions were asked about the strength of the British security vetting that had been taking place: Fuchs had gained clearance from MI5; Maclean and Burgess had similarly passed muster. There was much talk of a 'Third Man' in the British set-up who had warned Burgess and Maclean, and many in MI5 were convinced it was Kim Philby. The mistrust didn't prevent the two countries working together, though.

Two of the most important joint operations took place in continental Europe – the Vienna-based Operation Silver, and its Berlin equivalent, Operation Gold. The Russians were increasingly using landlines for phone calls and teletype traffic. This presented a problem for intelligence-gathering, as it was no longer a case of monitoring radio frequencies.

Like Berlin, Vienna was partitioned into different sectors in the immediate post-war period, and Operation Silver was the brainchild of the MI6 head of station in 1949, Peter Lunn, who realized that they were in a position to tap into the Soviet landlines. A tunnel was dug from a house seventy feet away from the lines, and to provide cover for the project, MI6 opened a store selling Harris Tweed – which proved to be almost too successful!

The CIA were also interested in gaining access to the Soviet's landlines, particularly after they realized that Mos-

cow's encoding machines had a flaw which sent a faint echo
of the uncoded message along with the encrypted version.
When the CIA's Carl Nelson visited Vienna, he came across
the MI6 operation, and the two sides joined forces – although
it seems that Nelson didn't share the information about the
clear versions with his allies.

The Vienna project was the inspiration for a similar
operation in Berlin, which would in the end produce over
forty thousand hours of telephone conversations and six
million hours of teletype traffic. Ironically Operation Gold is
best known because of the nature of its discovery by the
Soviets.

The Berlin Tunnel would be deemed 'one of the most
valuable and daring projects ever undertaken' by then-DCI
Allen Dulles who gave the go-ahead for the digging in
conjunction with the British in December 1953. The tunnel
was a major engineering feat, travelling nearly 1,500 feet
beneath the ground to reach a cable that was only 27 inches
from the surface. The cable's location had been provided by an
agent inside the East Berlin post office, and the construction of
an Air Force radar site and warehouse was used as a cover for
the work which began in February 1954. The tunnel itself was
completed in February 1955, and taps were in operation until
April the following year when it was discovered, with the
Soviets trying to make a great propaganda coup from it. (This
backfired: *Time* magazine commented that 'It's the best
publicity the US has had in Berlin for a long time.')

As far as the CIA were concerned at the time, 'Analysis of
all available evidence . . . indicates that the Soviet discovery of
the Tunnel was particularly fortuitous and was not the result
of a penetration of the agencies involved, a security violation,
or testing of the lines by Soviets or East Germans.' It seemed
as if the Soviets had got lucky – but in fact, they were aware
of the tunnel all the time, thanks to yet another KGB spy
within MI6's ranks, this time George Blake (see chapter 5),

who had been present at the initial briefing in October 1953, two months before Dulles had approved the project. It seemed, though, that the KGB was more concerned with protecting Blake than keeping the secrets that would be revealed via the wiretaps, so didn't act sooner.

The CIA's successful involvement in the Italian election of 1948 was just the start of their intervention in the affairs of other countries. Sometimes this was by invitation of some of the parties involved – such as in China, where the nationalist government of Chiang Kai-shek welcomed the CIA assistance – but by no means was this always the case.

Operation Ajax was a case in point. The CIA's actions in Iran helped keep the Shah in power until the coup of 1979, but as its instigator, Kermit Roosevelt, would later note: 'If we, the CIA, are ever going to try something like this again, we must be absolutely sure that the people and the army want what we want. If not, you had better call in the marines.' The problem was: the CIA was acting against what a democratically elected government had decided.

The problem arose when the concession that granted oil rights in Iran to the British-run Anglo-Iranian Oil Company (AIOC) came up for review in 1950. The Iranian parliament, the Majlis, called for the terms to be renegotiated so they weren't so favourable to the AIOC. One member of the Majlis, Mohammed Mossadegh, a Europe-educated lawyer in his early seventies, became the focal point for the opposition, and in March 1951, the AIOC's holdings were nationalized. Mossadegh was then elected prime minister on 29 April. The British didn't take kindly to this: describing it as 'a series of insensate actions', they claimed that 'Unless this is promptly checked, the whole of the free world will be much poorer and weaker, including the deluded Iranian people themselves.' The Iranian people themselves, however, considered Mossadegh to be a hero for standing up to the British.

Although the Americans wouldn't initially assist the British with removing Mossadegh, the Iranian's unwillingness to deal with the increasing influence of the Communist party meant that he came into focus for the CIA as a potential enemy, and so Project Ajax was born. In March 1953, an Iranian army general approached the Americans about backing an Army-led coup, and there was concern that the Communists would step in during the chaos. DCI Allen Dulles approved the operation to 'bring about the fall of Mossadegh' on 4 April. General Zahedi was seen as the ideal figurehead for the new regime, and CIA and MI6 agents discussed how best to run the operation (with the CIA not trusting the British with details of their own assets inside the country).

The operation came close to collapse because of the weakness of the Shah of Iran, whose role was to dismiss Mossadegh and appoint Zahedi. After much vacillating, he eventually did so on 13 August, but the coup was very nearly a disaster. On more than one occasion, Roosevelt was advised to leave Tehran, the operation a failure, but, more by luck than judgement, it was eventually successful.

The CIA's own official history of the project – leaked to the *New York Times* – describes the final day of the coup as 'a day that should never have ended for it carried with it such a sense of excitement, of satisfaction and of jubilation that it is doubtful whether any other can come up to it'. It would lead to a similarly aimed operation in Guatemala the following year; it can also be seen as a forerunner of the disastrous CIA operation which came apart at the Bay of Pigs in Cuba in 1961.

According to the CIA's own in-house historians, their operation in Guatemala, confidently code-named Success, was 'an intensive paramilitary and psychological campaign to replace a popular elected government with political non-entity. In method, scale, and conception it had no antecedent and its triumph confirmed the belief of many in the Eisenhower administration that covert operations offered a safe, inexpensive substitute for armed force in resisting Communist inroads in the Third World.' Assassination plots, paramilitary and economic warfare, provocation techniques, psychological operations, rumour campaigns and sabotage all played their part in toppling Jacobo Árbenz Guzmán, the second legally elected president in Guatemalan history and replacing him with Colonel Carlos Castillo Armas.

Árbenz was tolerant of locally known Communists, making him what the Americans regarded as a 'fellow traveller' and possibly a Communist himself, and when he brought in an Agrarian Reform Law that redistributed land belonging to the United Fruit Company this made some in the US administration believe that the Communists had now established a beachhead in Latin America via Árbenz.

The CIA felt that the military were 'the only organized element in Guatemala capable of rapidly and decisively altering the political situation', but the agency was aware that they would need considerable encouragement to make the right decision. Graffiti, political pamphlets, character assassinations and the daily delivery of fake death-notices to Árbenz and members of his cabinet all helped to prepare the way for the eventual invasion.

In the end, the army did turn on Árbenz, and he was forced to resign – but their actions perhaps were dictated more by the concern that the Americans would invade if Guzman remained in power, than because they feared the frankly feeble Colonel Armas and his very small *Ejército de liberación*. Dulles presented the results of Operation Success to President Eisenhower as a virtually bloodless coup, although he was aware that more than four dozen people had actually been killed.

After losing so many key agents in the West thanks to the various defections and revelations from the Venona transcripts, the KGB needed to rebuild its networks. In addition to infiltrating George Blake into MI6, they also targeted

French intelligence and the new West German organization. Many of these were never discovered, unlike one of their best agents (in his own opinion) Georges Pâques, who was Chef de Cabinet and adviser to several French ministers in the post-war period before becoming a key agent during de Gaulle's administration in 1958.

Former SS captain Hans Clemens, already working for Moscow, was recruited by the West German intelligence agency and in 1951 was able to turn another former SS officer Heinze Felfe, who distinguished himself in Western eyes by allegedly setting up a network of agents in Moscow – all of whose 'information' was carefully prepared by Moscow Centre, in the full knowledge it would reach West German Chancellor Konrad Adenauer.

In Norway in 1949, the KGB was able to recruit Gunvor Galtung Haavik, an employee at the Norwegian embassy in Moscow, by threatening to send her Russian lover to Siberia. Sent back to Oslo in 1955, she became an important source for the KGB at her new posting at the Norwegian Ministry of Foreign Affairs for the next twenty-two years, until her cover was blown by British agent Oleg Gordievsky in 1977.

However, as many, if not more, of State Security's operations would be directed internally. Stalin believed that the break between Russia and Yugoslavia was simply part of a wide-ranging imperialist conspiracy to undermine the Soviet power bloc, and agents were on the hunt for conspirators. The Hungarian Minister of the Interior, László Rajk was accused of being part of a grand Titoist conspiracy against the Soviets and was subject to a show trial in Budapest in 1949. An anti-Semitic witch-hunt began after Stalin perceived links between the new state of Israel and the USA, and switched Soviet support to Israel's Arab enemies. This was to form the last great purge of Stalin's life, with all Jewish officers (bar a number of so-called 'hidden Jews' who were officially part of other ethnic groups) removed from positions of power, and from the MGB. A perceived plot against the state by doctors saw the dictator's rage vented on those who 'trampled the sacred banner of science' – agents of British and American intelligence working through 'a corrupt Jewish bourgeois nationalist organisation'.

Josef Stalin died in March 1953, and during the inevitable power struggle in the Kremlin, Beria expanded the power of the state security organs under his control, bringing the MGB into the Ministry of the Interior (the MVD). Perhaps unwisely, he ordered a reorganization of the MVD network in East Germany, and in the absence of nearly a thousand officers, an uprising took place that the newly promoted General Fadeykin failed to handle properly.

Beria had overplayed his hand, and on 26 June he was accused of being an 'imperialist agent' by the ruling Presidium. He was tried, convicted and executed for working for British intelligence, supposedly ever since he had worked in Baku in 1919 when the area was under British control.

While the MGB still formed part of the MVD, a foreign assassination mission went disastrously wrong. Operation Rhine was designed to eliminate Georgi Sergeevich Okolovich, a Ukrainian émigré living in West Germany. Instead of killing him, however, the assassin, Nikolai Kholkov, defected to the West; he was one of five agents who would transfer allegiance in the first few months of 1954, with defections from the Tokyo and Vienna residencies, as well as two in Canberra in April 1954.

By that time, the KGB had been reorganized one last time. Removed from the MVD, but downgraded to committee status, the KGB was attached to the Council of Ministers to keep it under some form of control – the post-Stalin leadership was determined that it would never have the unbridled power that its predecessors had enjoyed. That wouldn't stop it from becoming one of the most ruthless intelligence agencies in the world.

5

CAT AND MOUSE

In the press, in Parliament, in the United Nations, from the pulpit, there is a ceaseless talk about the rule of law, civilized relations between nations, the spread of democratic processes, self-determination and national sovereignty, respect for the rights of man and human dignity.

The reality, we all know perfectly well is quite the opposite and consists of an ever-increasing spread of lawlessness, disregard of human contract, cruelty and corruption. The nuclear stalemate is matched by the moral stalemate.

It is the spy who has been called on to remedy the situation created by the deficiencies of ministers, diplomats, generals and priests.

Men's minds are shaped of course by their environments and we spies, although we have our professional mystique, do perhaps live closer to the realities and hard facts of international relations than other practitioners of government. We are relatively free of the problems of status, of precedence, departmental attitudes and evasions of personal responsibility, which create the official cast of mind. We do not have to

develop, like Parliamentarians conditioned by a lifetime, the
ability to produce the ready phrase, the smart reply and the
flashing smile. And so it is not surprising these days that the spy
finds himself the main guardian of intellectual integrity.

That's the way that MI6 regarded the work of the spy in the
late fifties, in this circular by George Young, who was part of
the joint MI6/CIA operation to remove Mossadegh from Iran,
as well as the abortive coup against Egyptian President
Nasser, and would later become Vice Chief of the service. It's
the background against which Ian Fleming created master spy
James Bond. It wasn't a world of glamour or mystique, just
people doing their jobs to gain the information necessary to
keep the world on an even keel.

It wasn't just those in the West who saw it that way.
Interviewed by CNN in 1998, after the collapse of Communism, East German spy chief Markus Wolf pointed out:

> At that stage of the twentieth-century European history,
> developments at times bordered on a hot war, and that's why
> I think that if something positive can be said about the work
> of the intelligence services, it's that through their work
> they may have avoided this going over the threshold to a hot
> war . . .
>   I'm pretty sure that the intelligence services on the whole,
> and the spies both in the East and the West, tended towards a
> more realistic assessment of the balance of power than that of
> politicians and military leaders; so that actions, or even
> adventurous actions which could easily have led to an escalation
> [of tension] or even to a war, would have been desisted from.

The CIA were still intent on blocking Communism wherever
they thought that it might gain a foothold. Building on their
perceived successes in Italy, Iran and Guatemala, they sought
to take a lead role in Vietnam, following the 1954 United
Nations resolution that divided that country in preparation

for national elections in 1956. The difference between their previous operations and working in Vietnam derived primarily from the nature of the country. As the CIA's own history points out: 'In the territory south of the 17th parallel, which Americans at first called Free Vietnam, there existed neither a sense of nationhood nor an indigenous administration . . . The 17th parallel designated a truce line, not an international boundary, and the entirely provisional entity lying south of it was supposed to disappear after national elections in 1956.' Effectively, rather than backing one side against another, they were trying to create a country.

The CIA had been active in Vietnam since 1950, trying to boost French efforts against the Communist insurgent organization, the Viet Minh, and now they put Colonel Edward Lansdale in as a 'kingmaker', much the same role as he had played in the Philippines where his actions had helped stave off the Communist political movement, the Hukbalahap, from taking power. Lansdale told CIA Director Allan Dulles that his goal was to build a 'political base' in Indochina which, if successful, would 'give CIA control [of the] government and change [the] whole atmosphere'. This would be focused around Ngo Dinh Diem, a certified anti-Communist and Catholic who had lived in New York from 1951–53.

The CIA put a lot of effort into backing Ngo Dinh Diem, who became prime minister in 1954. Lansdale helped to train the Vietnamese National Army, and ran a propaganda campaign to encourage the country's Roman Catholic population to move into Diem's part of Vietnam, using the slogan 'God has gone south'.

Diem called a referendum in October 1955, the campaign for which was characterized by dirty tricks. Even though his advisers were convinced that Diem would win comfortably and oust the sitting head of state, former Emperor Bao Dai, there was still massive electoral fraud, with Diem winning 133 per cent of the vote in Saigon. (The US State Department congratulated him on running the referendum 'in such an orderly and efficient manner'!) Diem went on to proclaim himself president of the Republic of Vietnam – and, at least initially, it did seem as if this was another job well done by the CIA.

Things weren't doing so well in the heart of Communism itself. There wasn't a CIA officer stationed at the Moscow embassy for the first six years of the Agency's life, and when the State Department finally reluctantly agreed for one to be put in place in 1953, the first head of station, Edward Ellis Smith, was seduced by his MGB maid. (He wasn't well regarded by his peers, 'his work was not only worthless, but much had been fabricated', the CIA's chief of operations in the Soviet bloc division would later comment.) According to the KGB, a dozen embassy personnel admitted succumbing to the temptations of State Security's 'swallows' before being sent home in disgrace over the next few years. The KGB didn't need to worry that much about the Americans' activities anyway: during the building of the new US embassy in 1953, key rooms were bugged during the night when no American guards were keeping watch on the building site.

The CIA did score one notable success within the Soviet bloc during this time, after a GRU officer, Pyotr Semyonovich Popov, slipped a note into an American diplomat's car in Vienna in January 1953, stating: 'I am a Soviet officer. I wish to meet with an American officer with the object of offering certain services.' With the experienced George Kisevalter as his case officer firstly in Austria and then later in Berlin, Popov proved to be a highly effective asset for the fledgling Agency, providing the CIA with details of the organization of the Soviet military command, the structure of the GRU, and the names and operations of Soviet intelligence agents in Europe. He was also able to alert the CIA to spies entering the US, and it was after the FBI frightened one of these off that

Popov came under suspicion, since he was one of the few on the Soviet side who knew the illegal agent's travel plans. Popov was recalled to Moscow in November 1958 – although the CIA tried to persuade him not to go – where he was able to pass a coded message back to the Agency to say that although he was safe, he had been transferred out of the GRU and was unable to leave the USSR.

It became clear from the standard of material that Popov was passing once he was back in Moscow that he had been turned by the KGB. Although for a time it was believed that Popov was betrayed by KGB agent George Blake, it has also been claimed that a Russian mole within the CIA passed on the information, and that poor tradecraft by the CIA in Moscow meant that a letter designed for Popov reached the KGB. In September 1959, Popov was able to pass a message surreptitiously to his Moscow CIA handler, Russell Langelle, confirming he was now a double agent, and saying that he hoped to be posted to Berlin once more, from where he could escape to the West. His note concluded: 'Could you not ask your kind President Eisenhower to see if he might cause restitution to be made for my family and my life?'

Unfortunately for him, the KGB decided to wrap up the operation before Popov could be transferred, arresting and expelling Langelle. Popov was tried and executed the following year.

One aspect of the CIA's activities that began during the fifties about which much has been written, a lot of it sensationalist, was Project MKULTRA, the agency's top secret behavioural research programme. Everything from the assassination of President John F. Kennedy to the death of singer John Lennon has been blamed on test subjects either being controlled by the CIA, or struggling to deal with the after-effects. Many of the ideas behind the *Bourne Identity* trilogy of films were inspired by MKULTRA: original director Doug Liman's father was one of those responsible for revealing other CIA dirty tricks during the Iran-Contra scandal of 1986.

MKULTRA was set up in response to the belief that the Communist nations were making great steps in the fields of brainwashing and mind control, as evidenced by the 'voluntary' testimony being given by captured American soldiers during the Korean War. The thinking was that Western agents and soldiers should therefore be prepared to deal with the effects of such techniques.

The Technical Services staff at the CIA were authorized to begin MKULTRA in April 1953; it became the responsibility of the Chemistry Division, headed by Dr Sidney Gottlieb. As an internal CIA report from 1963 explained, MKULTRA was 'concerned with the research and development of chemical, biological and radiological materials capable of employment in clandestine operations to control human behaviour'. It had wide-reaching aims – everything from finding ways to make alcohol more or less effective, as required, to creating instantly acting knock-out drops, to locating substances that would help people's ability to resist brainwashing.

The project tried many different methods to achieve its goals. Initially, hypnotism was tried. In February 1954, Gottlieb was able to implant a post-hypnotic suggestion into a woman who was normally loath to handle a weapon. Under the command, she was told to try to wake another woman up by any means possible, and 'failing in this, she would pick up a pistol nearby and fire it'. According to the declassified report, she 'carried out all these suggestions to the letter including firing the (unloaded pneumatic pistol) gun . . . and then proceeding to fall into a deep sleep . . . [On waking] she expressed absolute denial that the foregoing sequence had happened.'

The substance with which MKULTRA is most associated is lysergic acid diethylamide, better known as LSD. To begin with, the subjects of the experiments gave their consent, but

Gottlieb needed to know how people who were not aware that they were being drugged would react. This would lead to many people's rights being violated, and in some extreme cases, to death – the most notable case being army scientist Dr Frank Olson, who was given LSD in November 1953 without his knowledge or consent and jumped from a hotel room to his death a few days later. Eventually, as they had with hypnosis, the MKULTRA scientists dismissed LSD as being too unpredictable in its results – although not before many Americans were tested, including the author Ken Kesey, who would become of the great proselytizers of the drugs culture.

Less well known are some of the side-products of the MKULTRA research – including the CIA's investigations into magic. It was all very well coming up with secret drugs that would have the desired effect, but pointless if there was no way of administering them to the chosen target. John Mulholland, one of the most highly respected American magicians of the time, was brought on board, and applied the secrets of sleight of hand to the problem. His 1954 paper entitled 'Some Operational Applications of the Art of Deception' formed the basis of a training manual for agents, and the agency picked his brains further to investigate possible methods of covert signalling.

MKULTRA's days were numbered when the CIA's own internal monitor, the Inspector General, reported in 1963 that the controls over its operations were inadequate, and that the moral and ethical implications were too great. Much as many of those who would like to believe that the CIA's quest to create the perfect unwitting assassin – usually referred to as a Manchurian Candidate, after the Richard Condon 1959 novel, which featured a serviceman programmed by the Communists to commit murder – continued (and perhaps continues to this day), MKULTRA was disbanded by the end of the sixties. However, the revelation of its existence would have a critical effect on the CIA in the seventies; perhaps the best epitaph on it came from Senator Edward Kennedy in 1977: 'The Agency itself acknowledged that these tests made little scientific sense.'

Downgrading the organs of State Security in the Soviet Union from a Ministry to a Committee when the KGB was set up in 1954 did not mean that the organization's power would be any the less effective. This was amply shown by the extremely pro-active stance taken by its leader during the Hungarian Revolution of 1956, its first major test – with the Chairman of the KGB, Ivan Aleksandrovich Serov, going undercover himself.

Just as the Americans were concerned about protecting any area into which Communism might spread, so the Kremlin wanted to make sure that all parts of the Soviet bloc were toeing the party line. After the split with Yugoslavia (which didn't heal after the death of Stalin) and the rising in East Berlin in 1953, the Presidium wanted to nip any potential activity in the bud. Trouble began to foment in Hungary, following a speech by Soviet leader Nikita Khruschev that denounced Stalin's cult of personality, and those – like the Hungarian First Secretary Mátyás Rákosi – who followed in its footsteps. Rákosi was pressured into resigning but was replaced by a hardliner, rather than by the popular Imre Nagy. A revolution began on 23 October when a crowd demonstrating outside the Radio Building were shot by AVH (Hungarian State Security) troops.

Serov flew to Budapest, but was simply introduced to the Hungarians as a new Soviet adviser, rather than as head of the KGB. He was present as the situation worsened – Nagy was brought in as Prime Minister, but this didn't stop the popular uprising, as workers united with students against the Soviet-backed government. It reached the stage on 30 October, a day after the AVH had been abolished, where Kremlin representatives agreed to the removal of Soviet troops, and Nagy announced he was forming a multi-party government.

Soviet Ambassador Yuri Andropov, later to become chief of the KGB and Soviet leader himself, was responsible for countering this counter-revolution. He ordered fresh Red Army units to enter Hungary, while reassuring Nagy that they were only there to safeguard the security of the units that were supposed to be leaving. On 3 November, the Hungarian minister of defence was invited to Soviet military headquarters – and at midnight he, along with the rest of the national delegation, was arrested by Serov and a group of KGB officers. When the Red Army launched its assault the next day, Nagy made a desperate plea for help before seeking asylum in the Yugoslav embassy. At this point, Serov identified himself to the Budapest police chief, Sándor Kopácsi, who had stood up to him initially, and took open charge of the operation. Unsurprisingly, when Nagy and his colleagues left the Yugoslav embassy believing the guarantees of safe conduct they had been given by the new Soviet-backed government, they were arrested by the KGB, taken for trial. Two of them died, or were killed, during the interrogation process; Nagy's other colleagues were shot. Nagy himself was taken to Romania, then returned to Hungary and tried in secret. He was hanged in June 1958.

Not long before the Hungarian Revolution, the KGB also claimed another success in Europe, although this time with considerably less bloodshed, and much less negative publicity in the outside world. According to the KGB themselves, one of their greatest foreign coups was the rise to power of the Finnish politician Urho Kaleva Kekkonen, who became President of Finland in 1956, a post he held until 1981. While there is no doubt that Kekkonen had good relations with the KGB, and often acted in a way that benefited the Soviets, it seems far more likely that rather than being an active Soviet agent, he was a very pragmatic man who saw the relationship with Moscow as a good way to maintain an independent Finland. The Soviets certainly assisted him by pressurising other candidates to withdraw from elections against Kekkonen, but the number of KGB and GRU agents who were caught by the Finnish Security Police without Kekkonen's intervention would suggest that, for once, it was the KGB who were being manipulated.

Manoeuvres against the Soviets had major repercussions for the British Secret Intelligence Service in 1956, when a mission to investigate the Soviet cruiser *Ordzhonikidze* while moored in Portsmouth Harbour went badly wrong. It would lead to questions in the Houses of Parliament, and, some claim, the relocation of the U-2 spy flights from Lakenheath in Norfolk, in the east of England, to Weisbaden in West Germany. It has often been blamed for the resignation of the head of MI6 later that year, although the official history of MI5 notes that the decision for Sir John Sinclair to step down at this point had been taken two years earlier. And it was the inspiration for one of James Bond's more seemingly outrageous missions as recorded in the book and movie *Thunderball*.

The Navy wanted more information about the propeller design of the Soviet cruiser, which had brought Khruschev on an official visit to the UK. MI6 officer Nicholas Elliott hired a freelance frogman, Commander Lionel 'Buster' Crabb, to carry out the mission. The Prime Minister, Sir Anthony Eden, was keen to promote friendly relations with the USSR, and had ordered MI5 and MI6 not to carry out operations against the Soviets during the visit, so he was highly embarrassed when the Soviet sailors reported seeing a frogman wearing a diving suit around the ship on 19 April 1956. That it was Crabb, there is no doubt – but he was never seen again.

The Soviets made political capital out of the incident, with Khruschev making reference to 'underwater problems' in a press conference. Despite attempts by the security services to throw reporters off the scent by claiming Crabb was diving three miles away, eventually Eden had to come clean: 'As has already been publicly announced, Commander Crabb was engaged in diving tests and is presumed to have met his death whilst so engaged,' went the official note from the Foreign Office. 'The diver, who, as stated in the Soviet note, was observed from the Soviet warships to be swimming between the Soviet destroyers, was presumably Commander Crabb. His approach to the destroyers was completely unauthorised and Her Majesty's Government desire to express their regret at the incident.' Added Eden in the House of Commons, 'It would not be in the public interest to disclose the circumstances in which Commander Crabb is presumed to have met his death.'

It may not have been in the public interest to reveal what happened, but in fact no one knew for sure exactly what did occur. A headless, handless body was identified as Crabb in June 1957 and buried in his place, but the man who made the identification admitted later he had been coerced by the security services. Crabb may have been brought aboard the *Ordzhonikidze* and died in their sickbay. There were claims that he was taken to Russia and worked in the Soviet Navy. Even when papers released under the Freedom of Information Act suggested that there was a second diver with Crabb, they shed no further light on the mystery.

The CIA weren't the only intelligence agency in favour of pro-active regime change during this time. The Suez crisis, which brought about the fall of Sir Anthony Eden, and caused major difficulties for the Anglo-American relationship for years, proved that such plans don't always work out.

The usual accounts of the crisis note that it was precipitated by Egyptian President Gamal Abdel Nasser nationalizing the Suez Canal in July 1956. Eden saw this as the act of a fascist dictator and as he proclaimed at the time, 'we all remember only too well what the cost can be in giving in to fascism'.

Three months later, Israel invaded Egypt via the Sinai peninsula; this led to French and British forces landing, apparently to separate the combatants – but coincidentally with the aim of forming a peacekeeping force around the Suez Canal, taking it out of Nasser's hands. However, after pressure from both the US and the USSR at the United Nations, a ceasefire was declared and the foreign troops had to leave. Nasser survived.

However, as a CIA memorandum from April – three months before the nationalization of the canal – shows, MI6 wanted to take far more drastic action against Nasser much earlier, since he had 'accepted full scale collaboration with the Soviets. Nasser has now taken the initiative for the extension of Soviet influence in Syria, Libya, and French North Africa. Nasser must therefore be regarded as an out-and-out Soviet instrument. MI6 asserted that it is now British government view that western interests in the Middle East, particularly oil, must be preserved from Egyptian-Soviet threat at all costs.'

Their plan to achieve this was threefold:

Phase one – complete change in government of Syria. MI6 believes it can mount this operation alone, but if necessary will involve joint action with Iraq, Turkey, and possibly Israel. Phase two – Saudi Arabia. Believe MI6 prepared to undertake efforts to exploit splits in Royal Family and possibly hasten fall of King Saud. Phase three – to be undertaken in anticipation of violent Egyptian reaction to phases one and two. This ranges from sanctions, calculated to isolate Nasser, to use of force, both British and Israeli, to tumble Egyptian government. Extreme possibilities would involve special operations by Israelis against Egyptian supply dumps and newly acquired aircraft and tanks, as well as outright Israeli attack on Gaza or other border areas.

The Foreign Office didn't share MI6's view that there would be a group of Egyptians who would rise up against Nasser, and indeed when the invasion happened – at the same time as the Russians were dealing with the Hungarian uprising – the expected internal revolt failed to materialize. MI6's plan to assassinate Nasser with nerve gas was never put into effect. And when President Eisenhower, perhaps hypocritically given the CIA's penchant for regime change elsewhere in the world, made it clear that 'We believe these actions to have been taken in error, for we do not accept the use of force as a wise or proper instrument for the settlement of international disputes,' it was evident that the attempt to retake the canal, let alone remove Nasser, was over.

1957 would see the end of another of the KGB's assets in the United States, Colonel Rudolf Invanovich Abel – although he would be known by many names, including his birth name William Fisher, Emil Goldfus, and Martin Collins. His arrest by the FBI in June that year, and their discovery of 'virtual museums of modern espionage equipment' in his workplace and hotel room, which 'contained shortwave radios, cipher pads, cameras and film for producing microdots, a hollow shaving brush, cufflinks, and numerous other "trick" containers' would lead to his conviction for conspiracy to obtain and transmit defence information to the Soviet Union.

Giving the FBI the name Abel during his interrogation was probably a move designed to let his KGB controllers know his situation, a typical act by this veteran operative, who had spent years in Soviet intelligence before the Second World War prior to entering the US in 1948, as code name Mark. He was involved with the Volunteer network of atomic spies that operated out of New York, but had to rein back his activities following the arrest of Julius and Ethel Rosenberg. The arrival of a new assistant, Reino Häyhänen, in October 1952, was supposed to mark a new phase in his career, but in fact would lead to disaster for Abel. Häyhänen was not a good agent, misusing KGB funds, losing important reports, and even mislaying one of the hollowed-out coins in which information was transmitted. This coin found its way into the hands of the FBI, who spent years trying to decode the message within.

At the start of 1957, Abel demanded that the KGB recall Häyhänen to Moscow, but his assistant decided instead to defect, fearing for his life if he returned to the USSR. He claimed asylum at the Paris embassy, stating, 'I'm an officer in the Soviet intelligence service. For the past five years, I have been operating in the United States. Now I need your help.' The CIA station officers thought he was drunk or delusional, but eventually passed him back for interrogation by the FBI. Searches of Häyhänen's home found another hollowed-out coin, and the KGB officer gave his interrogators enough information to allow the original message from 1953 to be decoded.

Häyhänen was also able to give the FBI sufficient information to identify a number of Soviet agents, including Army Sergeant Roy Rhodes, code-named Quebec; UN delegate Mikhail Nikolaevich Svirin, who had already returned to the USSR; and Rudolf Abel, code-named Mark. Abel was arrested on 21 June, but initially refused to give any information to his captors, in the end only providing his 'real' name and demanding to be deported.

Abel would only serve five years of his thirty-year sentence; in 1962 he was exchanged for Francis Gary Powers, the pilot of an American U-2 spy plane shot down over Russia in 1960. Although he lectured on intelligence work to Russian school children and did some work in the Illegals Directorate, Abel became disillusioned in the years before his death in 1971 – perhaps because he realized that for all that he had propaganda value to the KGB for not breaking under interrogation, he had done little to advance the cause. KGB records indicate that his nine-year stint in New York had little practical effect, since he had failed to set up a new network.

* * *

Some KGB agents were successes, almost despite themselves. One such was Robert Lee Johnson, an army sergeant and part-time pimp, who had tried to cross into East Berlin in 1953 to ask for asylum for himself and his prostitute fiancée. The KGB persuaded him to remain in the US Army, and for three years, he provided them with low-grade information. In 1956, he left the army, cut his connections with Moscow, and tried to make his fortune in Las Vegas. This failed, and in January 1957, the KGB reactivated him, giving him $500 and telling him to enlist in the US Air Force. Johnson was turned down, but was able to sign up again with the US Army. Over the next few years, he passed over photographs, plans and documents, and when he was transferred to the Armed Forces Courier Centre at Orly Airport in France, he was able to access a triple-locked vault. His methods seem like something from a Bond film: Johnson used a key for the first lock taken from a wax impression; he found a copy of the combination for the second in a wastepaper basket; and the KGB provided him with a portable X-ray device which allowed him to crack the combination for the third. This allowed him to pass over cypher systems, the locations of the nuclear warheads in Europe and defence plans for both the US and NATO. He was eventually caught following testimony provided by the defector Yuri Nosenko.

The late fifties saw other Soviet agents move into stronger positions around Europe: in France from 1958 onwards, Georges Pâques had access to defence documents including the entire NATO defence plan for Western Europe; he would continue to provide information until 1963. Canadian economist Hugh Hambleton was also working for the Russians inside NATO between 1957 and 1961, and provided so much material that the KGB had to provide a black van equipped with a photographic laboratory so that it could be speedily copied. Hambleton, who was recruited in 1951, would eventually work for Moscow for thirty years before he was arrested.

In West Germany, Soviet agent Heinz Felfe became head of the Soviet counter-intelligence section of the BND – a similar role to that held by Kim Philby in the UK a decade earlier. Enquiries from the CIA and other agencies for information held by the BND gave Felfe, and thus Moscow, an insight into their operations. The damage that he achieved was considerable (although perhaps not as great as he claimed in his self-serving autobiography, released in the mid-eighties): 'Ten years of secret agent reports had to be re-evaluated: those fabricated by the other side, those subtly slanted, those from purely mythical sources,' pointed out one CIA officer.

British naval clerk John Vassall penetrated the British Admiralty, and was blackmailed into working for the KGB after attending a homosexual party set up by Moscow Centre. On his return to the UK, he was able to provide his handler with thousands of highly classified documents covering naval policy and weapons development. He continued working for the Soviets for five years until his lifestyle attracted suspicion, and he was arrested for espionage.

Not everything went according to plan for the KGB. After the fiasco caused by Nikolai Kholkov's failure to kill Okolovich and the assassin's subsequent defection in 1954, an attempt on the Ukrainian Vladimir Poremsky failed the following year when his prospective killer told the West German police of his mission. The KGB couldn't even kill Kholkov; an attempt on his life using radioactive thallium failed.

One assassin working for the KGB's 'wetworks' section, Department 13, did chalk up some successes. Bogdan Stashinsky used a cyanide gas-spraying gun to assassinate two Ukrainian emigrés, Lev Rebet in October 1957 and Stepan Bandera, two years later. However, Stashinsky's German-born wife persuaded him into a change of heart and they defected to the West in Berlin, a day before the Berlin Wall went up in August 1961. He stood trial for the murders, but, as BND chief Reinhard Gehlen explained in his autobiography: 'The court identified Stashinsky's unscrupulous employer [KGB Chairman Alexasandr] Shelyepin as the person primarily responsible for the hideous murders, and the defendant – who had given a highly credible account of the extreme pressure applied to him by the KGB to act as he did – received a comparatively mild sentence.' As a result of Stashinsky's defection and the very public trial, the Kremlin reconsidered the use of assassination as a weapon. Contrary to the belief of spy thriller writers, 'wet affairs' became a last resort for the Kremlin in the early sixties, rather than standard operating procedure.

While agents in place continued to make a valuable contribution to the espionage activities of the American intelligence community during the late fifties, their work was supplemented by two other sources – the advent of the spy-plane program, and the increased use of cryptographics, courtesy of the newly established National Security Agency.

The early fifties saw the 'Reds under the Bed' scares, fomented by Senator Joseph McCarthy, and despite his downfall, there were many who believed that the Soviet Union was considerably stronger than it actually was. All the various agencies had to make estimates, and inevitably used worse case scenarios as the basis for these. The launch of the Sputnik satellite in 1957 did nothing to quell those fears – not only could the Russians launch missiles at the US from their various territories around the world, but they could now do so from space as well.

The CIA's Project Aquatone went a long way to dealing with the queries raised by the various other agencies. As a CIA report written a few days after the initial operation pointed out, 'Five operational missions have already proven that many of our guesses on important subjects can be seriously wrong, that the estimates which form the basis for national policy can be projections from wrong guesses, and that, as a consequence, our policy can indeed be bankrupt.'

Project Aquatone involved a pilot flying at 70,000 feet above the Soviet Union, photographing everything that he could see. After President Eishenhower gave the go-ahead in November 1954, a special plane, the U-2, was devised by Lockheed engineer Clarence Kelly Johnson, and in July 1955 became the first to be tested at the Groom Lake facility in Nevada – now better known as the conspiracy-inspiring Area 51. A new camera was developed by James Baker and Edwin Land, the creator of the Polaroid camera, with the resolution necessary to gain detailed information from the air.

The first flight took off from Wiesbaden in West Germany on 4 July 1956, and despite Khruschev ordering it to be shot down, it carried out five of its seven allotted missions, providing information on the Soviet Navy's Leningrad ship-yards as well as causing a drastic revision of the armed forces' estimates of Soviet bomber strength and the military's state of readiness. For the rest of the decade, the CIA would maintain the cover story that the missions were purely of a scientific nature, all the while improving the U-2's capabilities, and working on a new plane, Project Oxcart, which could supersede it.

Although the U-2 would continue in active operational service for a further fifty years – and is still in use today by the US armed services – the program of overflights across the Soviet Union came to a sudden halt on 1 May 1960, when the twenty-fourth mission, flown by Captain Francis Gary Powers, was shot down. The wreckage of the plane was put on display by the Russians, and Powers was the subject of a show trial. He would only serve two years of his sentence, before being swapped for KGB Colonel Rudolf Abel.

As far as CIA DCI Allen Dulles was concerned, the U-2 project 'was one of the most valuable intelligence-collection operations that any country has ever mounted at any time, and

. . . it was vital to our national security'. It also had the added benefit that 'It has made the Soviets less cocky about their ability to deal with what we might bring against them.'

The U-2 program may have become public as a result of Powers' crash, but another aspect of the intelligence community that was becoming increasingly valuable would remain secret for considerably longer – the National Security Agency (NSA), based from 1956 onwards out of Fort Meade, near Washington DC. Whereas now the NSA's address and phone number come up in a Google search, in the fifties this well-funded signal intelligence service was so secret that those insiders aware of it would joke that its acronym stood for 'No Such Agency'.

Although the combined British and American SIGINT (signal intelligence) codebreakers had achieved some success in the years immediately after the Second World War in reading then-current Soviet codes, the Kremlin's decision on Friday 20 October 1948 to change all of their codes and cypher machines created what has been described as 'perhaps the most significant intelligence loss in US history'. Black Friday, as it quickly came to be known, marked the start of an eight-year period when there was little knowledge about what was going on inside the Soviet Union, only alleviated by the U-2 missions. The codebreakers had been able to decipher the North Korean signals during the war there, providing invaluable information that saved many lives during the early part of that conflict, but it became clear that there were too many different agencies all carrying out their own code-breaking activities. President Truman created the NSA in 1952 to coordinate the collection and processing of communications intelligence, with the secretary of defence as the government's executive agent for all SIGINT activities, taking the new agency outside the jurisdiction of the CIA.

Black Friday's effect continued to be felt through the early years of the NSA, with the agency not picking up on Stalin's death or the subsequent uprising in East Berlin in spring 1953. By 1955, the lack of ability to crack the highest-grade Russian codes was causing serious concern. However, when the Hungarian Revolution and the Suez Crisis sprang up simultaneously, the NSA was able to provide sufficient information for President Eisenhower to take action to help defuse the situations and not overreact – they knew about Soviet tank movements on the Hungarian borders, and the Israeli/British/French plans regarding Egypt.

The NSA cooperated with the CIA over the U-2 missions, monitoring Soviet air-defence transmissions, and even intercepting communications from their radar operators who were tracking the planes – giving the CIA real-time information on the missions' progress. They could also deduce the size of the Soviet air force from the nature of the force sent up to intercept the spy plane. The relationship grew a little cooler following the downing of Captain Powers' plane: the NSA insisted that Powers was much lower than he claimed, although the official report would back Powers' story, much to the annoyance of the NSA.

Unsurprisingly, the NSA became a prime target for the KGB. Although all the Soviet operations would take advantage of 'walk-ins' (Western volunteers prepared to betray their country, rather than agents infiltrated into position), the NSA became the target of a major plan by KGB chief Alexsandr Shelyepin, who set up better coordination between the relevant directorates with the Security service and established a Special Section whose primary objective was to collect intelligence on cypher systems of particular interest to the Soviet cryptanalysts.

By 1960, three NSA agents were also working for Moscow but then two cryptologists, William Hamilton Martin and Bernon F. Mitchell, who had been based at the NSA for four years, defected during their annual leave in June. Arriving in

Moscow that September, they gave a press conference that revealed great swathes about the NSA's activities, including the embarrassing revelation that the agency wasn't just focusing their attentions on their enemies. Italy, Turkey, France, Yugoslavia, the United Arab Republic, Indonesia and Uruguay were all specifically mentioned by Martin. It became commonly accepted that the two men were in a homosexual relationship, which had left them open to blackmail. This led to a witch-hunt within the NSA and the enforced resignations of over two-dozen officers who were believed to be 'sexual deviates'. Oddly, the NSA's own internal investigations, while noting that 'Beyond any doubt, no other event has had, or is likely to have in the future, a greater impact on the Agency's security program,' believed that their defections were impulsive, and not caused by blackmail over their sexuality.

The KGB still had another agent in place: Staff Sergeant Jack Dunlap, the chauffeur to the chief of staff at Fort Meade, who offered his services to the Soviet embassy in Washington in 1960. He became a source of instruction books, manuals, and conceptual and engineering designs for the cypher machines, but he found it hard to deal with his double life, and committed suicide in July 1963. His treachery was only discovered a month after his death.

By then, though, the KGB had other problems to deal with, as the early years of the sixties brought some of their longest-serving agents' careers to an end.

6

DEFECTIVE INFORMATION

There are many ways in which spies' careers come to a sudden halt: sometimes they're caught red-handed, carrying out the missions set by their bosses; other times tradecraft errors, either their own or mistakes made by other people, lead to their capture. But probably the worst way to be taken out of action is through betrayal, particularly if it's by one of your own.

The KGB suffered a number of such setbacks at the end of the fifties and early sixties following assorted defections to the West. Once the FBI, MI5 or the other Western counter-intelligence agencies got hold of the information, they would pursue every lead until as many possible Soviet agents were identified. Sometimes this would take time. Unless defectors were particularly well placed, they were unlikely to possess exact details of particular agents, but usually they provided sufficient clues to enable the authorities to put a group under surveillance and then eliminate them from the investigation.

Polish Lieutenant Colonel Mikhail Goleniewski juggled being a triple agent between 1959 and his defection in January

1961, working as head of the Technical and Scientific Department of the Polish Secret Service, reporting to Moscow, and also providing information jointly to MI6 and the CIA, which the CIA described as 'Grade 1 from the inside'. The Americans called him 'Sniper'; the British knew him as 'Lavinia'. Even before his defection, he informed his controllers that 'The Russians have got two very important spies in Britain: one in British Intelligence, the other somewhere in the Navy.' Working from the documents Goleniewski had seen, there were ten potential suspects within MI6 (including 'rising star' George Blake), but when investigated all appeared to be in the clear – the most likely source of the papers, so the British believed, was a burglary at the MI6 station in Brussels, and that's what they told the Americans.

When Goleniewski passed along some more information about the naval spy in March 1960, it was the clue that blew open a complete Soviet spy network, known as the Portland Ring, after the naval base from which the secrets were being extracted. 'Sniper' said that the spy's name was something like 'Huiton': this correlated with one Harry Houghton, who was at the time working in the Underwater Weapons Establishment at Portland, Dorset, and fitted the other information provided. What followed was a classic example of counter-intelligence at work.

Houghton was followed by MI5 operatives (known as Watchers) on his monthly visit to London with his girlfriend, Ethel Gee. There they watched him hand over a carrier bag in exchange for an envelope. MI5 followed the man Houghton had met, whom they believed was a Polish intelligence officer, but hit a snag when they learned that the car he drove was registered to a Canadian importer of jukeboxes named Gordon Arnold Lonsdale. At Lonsdale and Houghton's next meeting, the Watchers overheard Lonsdale say he was heading to America on business; before he left, he deposited a parcel at the Midland Bank. MI5 opened the parcel, and discovered a treasure trove: 'The complete toolkit of the professional spy,' according to case officer Peter Wright. The materials identified Lonsdale as a KGB agent.

Lonsdale was followed on his return to the UK in October, and MI5 discovered he was staying with a New Zealand couple, Peter and Helen Kroger, in the London suburb of Ruislip. The Krogers and Lonsdale were monitored until their arrest in January, shortly before Goleniewski was going to defect.

Far from being innocent booksellers, the Krogers were in fact long-term Russian agents, who, then going by the names of Lona and Morris Cohen, had been part of the Soviet penetration of the Manhattan Project. They had fled to Mexico when the Rosenbergs were arrested and then established a new cover in the UK a few years later. When MI5 raided their home, they found everything from multiple passports to a high-speed radio transmitter and short-wave receiver.

Lonsdale, alias Konon Trofimovich Molody, had joined the NKVD during the Second World War, and had adopted the identity of the deceased Gordon Lonsdale in 1954 when he entered Canada. As well as sending copious material to Moscow from his agents, Lonsdale's natural business acumen meant that he was actually making a profit for the KGB!

In addition to Houghton, Lonsdale was running a spy inside the Germ Warfare Research Centre at Porton Down (87 miles south-west of London), as well as Melita Norwood, a seemingly innocent secretary who worked at the British Non-Ferrous Metals Research Association. Norwood had provided atomic secrets to the Russians during the Second World War, and would continue to work for the KGB until her retirement in 1972. Nicknamed 'The Spy Who Came In From the Co-op', she was acclaimed as one of the KGB's most important female assets, and remained undetected until Vasili Mitrokhin defected to the West in 1992.

Lonsdale was sentenced to twenty-five years in jail, but was exchanged in 1964 for Greville Wynne; the Krogers were exchanged in July 1969 for a British anti-subversive held by the KGB. Houghton and Gee received fifteen-year sentences, although they were released in 1970, and married the following year.

The other KGB spy exposed by Goleniewski's testimony was indeed George Blake, who had evaded suspicion when 'Sniper' first mentioned the existence of the mole. Blake, whose real name was George Behar, had joined MI6 in 1948, after studying Russian at Cambridge. He was posted to Seoul in South Korea the following year but was captured by the invading North Koreans. Blake was interrogated by MGB officers, who were allowed access to prisoners of war by Chinese intelligence, and by the time he was repatriated to Britain at the end of the Korean War, he was a Soviet agent. Whether he changed sides because of natural antipathy to the British system or because he was a true Manchurian Candidate and was brainwashed by the Chinese is open to debate: in 2007, he said he wasn't a traitor: 'To betray, you first have to belong. I never belonged.'

Blake's importance to the KGB can be judged by the fact that even though he warned Moscow about the tapping of the phone lines in Berlin in Operation Gold, they allowed that operation to proceed rather than risk blowing his cover. He was posted to Berlin, where he was in a position to betray numerous British and American operatives, as well as helping to identify the CIA's man in the GRU, Pyotr Popov. Blake would later admit that he didn't know exactly what he handed over to the KGB 'because it was so much'.

As a result of Goleniewski's debriefing by the CIA after his defection, it was clear that Blake was the mole, and he was arrested in April 1961 when he was summoned back to London from a training course in the Lebanon. J. Edgar Hoover's reaction to the news was atypically understanding:

'After all, Christ Himself found a traitor in His small team of twelve.' Sentenced to forty-two years, Blake escaped from Wormwood Scrubs prison in 1966 and fled to the Soviet Union, where he was awarded an Order of Friendship by former KGB head Vladimir Putin in 2007. At that point Blake was still taking an active role in the affairs of the secret service, according to the head of the Russian SVR, the successor to the KGB.

Goleniewski's testimony would also be responsible for the downfall of Heinz Felfe within the BND; he was arrested in October 1961 and eventually sentenced to fifteen years' hard labour. Felfe's legacy, though, was that much of the West German counter-intelligence work over the previous decade had to be deemed suspect, injuring Reinhard Gehlen's hard-won reputation for backing his own judgement.

The defector himself started to lose some credibility when he began to maintain that he was the Tsarevich Alexei Nikolaevich, who most believe had been killed with the rest of the Russian royal family in 1917 at Ekaterinburg. Goleniewski claimed that he gave his date of birth as 1922 to explain why he looked so young (the Tsarevich was born in 1904) since he suffered from haemophilia. Unsurprisingly, the CIA released him from its payroll in 1964, a year after he started making these claims publicly.

While the KGB were losing agents, the CIA was apparently going from strength to strength. The death of Congolese leader Patrice Lumumba in January 1961 certainly came at a convenient time for the Agency, even if they were not finally responsible for his demise. Lumumba was the first prime minister of the independent Republic of Congo after it gained independence from Belgium, but the tumultuous nature of his administration, and the civil war that quickly broke out there, gave rise to panic in Washington. CIA director Allen Dulles noted that 'We are faced with a person who is a Castro or worse. Lumumba has been bought by the Communists,' and in a memo wrote, 'In high quarters here, it is the clear-cut conclusion that if [Lumumba] continues to hold high office, the inevitable result will [have] disastrous consequences ... for the interests of the free world generally. Consequently, we conclude that his removal must be an urgent and prime objective.'

While the CIA were supporting Joseph Mobutu's faction in the civil war, enter MKULTRA's chief scientist, Dr Sidney Gottlieb, who was sent to Leopoldville with a plan to arrange for Lumumba's assassination with poisoned toothpaste. The CIA station chief, Lawrence Devlin, claimed that he refused to carry out the instructions and that after Lumumba was arrested by opposing forces in December, he threw the poison into the Congo River. Some declassified documents suggest that CIA agents assisted with the disposal of Lumumba's body after his execution on 17 January 1961 – his corpse was certainly never found – but Devlin would later deny any CIA involvement, even after the Belgians admitted their role.

The early part of the sixties would be dominated by the relationship between incoming US President John F. Kennedy and his Soviet counterpart, Nikita Khruschev, with the world coming closer to war during that period than at any time since 1945. Although Russian and American tanks would come face-to-face at Checkpoint Charlie in Berlin for a perilous sixteen hours on 22 October 1961, shortly after the construction of the wall dividing East and West Berlin, the real flashpoint was Cuba.

The problem there had begun when Fidel Castro took power in the Caribbean island country in 1959. Castro seemed to be an improvement on the previous leader, dictator Fulgencio Batista. He tried to reassure Americans of his good intentions: 'I know what the world thinks of us, we are Communists, and of course I have said very clearly that we are not Communists; very clearly.' However, it quickly became clear that he would very easily become a thorn in America's side, particularly given how close the country was to US shores.

The KGB began dealings with Castro's chief of intelligence as early as July 1959, sending over a hundred advisers to help overhaul the security and intelligence services, and later that year, Castro began to nationalize American plantations as well as close down lucrative concessions run by the Mafia. In March 1960, President Eisenhower approved a programme of action against the Cuban government, its stated purpose was to 'bring about the replacement of the Castro regime with one more devoted to the true interests of the Cuban people and more acceptable to the US in such a manner to avoid any appearance of US intervention'. Anti-Castro Cubans who had fled to Florida were recruited for the cause and started to undergo training.

The Soviet leadership began to publicly support Castro: 'We shall do everything to support Cuba in her struggle,' Khrushchev proclaimed in July 1960, adding ominously, 'Now the United States is not so unreachable as she once was.' Suspecting that Americans could be thrown off the island shortly, three CIA technical officers were sent into Cuba in August to put surveillance devices into an enemy embassy, but when that proved impossible they were captured during their attempt to bug the New China News Agency. They would stay in Cuban jails throughout the dramatic events of the next three years.

John F. Kennedy succeeded Eisenhower in January 1961. The incoming president was informed of the plot against Castro, and the plan to promote regime change in Cuba. The briefing suggested 'Moscow had put in place a puppet ruler who ... promoted dissent in Nicaragua, Haiti, Panama and the Dominican Republic in order to surround the southern United States with Communist satellites.' Buoyed by their previous successful regime changes in Iran and Guatemala, the CIA intended to land their trained exiles near Trinidad in southern Cuba, close to anti-Castro groups, and set off an uprising.

The new president wasn't so keen. Kennedy did not want his term of office to begin with an American-sponsored invasion, and he insisted that the exiles land at the Bay of Pigs, a hundred miles from their original target. He also scaled back the air support that the CIA intended to provide, removing the initial air strike, and postponing the second until after it was clear the invasion had succeeded. CIA Deputy Director Richard Bissell felt this would seriously jeopardize the outcome, but his hands were tied.

Launched on 17 April 1961, the invasion was a catastrophic failure, with hundreds of the Cuban exiles killed or captured, and thousands on both sides injured. Kennedy took full responsibility publically: 'There's an old saying that victory has a hundred fathers and defeat is an orphan . . . What matters is only one fact, I am the responsible officer of the government.' Behind the scenes, he accepted Allen Dulles' resignation as DCI of the CIA, and Richard Bissell resigned after he was demoted. An internal CIA report castigated the Agency for 'exceed[ing] its capabilities in developing the project from guerrilla support to overt armed action without any plausible deniability' and its 'failure to realistically assess risks and to adequately communicate information and decisions internally and with other government principals.'

This didn't mean that the US government's desire to see Castro removed from power disappeared, and in November 1961, Kennedy approved Operation Mongoose, whose aim was to 'help Cuba overthrow the Communist regime', through 'a revolt which can take place in Cuba by October 1962'. This was masterminded by the administration's Attorney-General, Kennedy's brother Robert.

Over the next few years, assorted plans to assassinate Fidel

Castro were drawn up by the CIA, many of these focusing on the dictator's trademark cigars. At different times, they considered lacing them with hallucinogenic drugs, poisons, depilatory chemicals and even explosives! To cover their tracks, the agency contemplated an alliance with the Mafia: documents declassified in 2007 recount meetings between a CIA go-between, Robert Maheu, and mob bosses Momo Salvatore Giancana and Santos Trafficante, with Giancana suggesting that 'some type of potent pill that could be placed in Castro's food or drink would be much more effective'.

The NSA increased its surveillance of Cuba greatly, generating nearly six thousand reports during the six months from April 1962. However, as the NSA's own history points out, the events of that autumn 'marked the most significant failure of SIGINT to warn national leaders since World War II'. Equally, they would prove that one man in the right place can dramatically alter the course of world history.

That man was Colonel Oleg Vladimirovich Penkovsky, a GRU officer who actively spied jointly for the CIA and MI6 from spring 1961 until his arrest at the height of the Cuban Missile Crisis in October 1962. Penkovsky had approached American authorities in Moscow after the Powers trial, but his overtures were rebuffed. Penkovsky was eventually brought on board by a British businessman with links to MI6, Greville Wynne. The material Penkovsky was able to provide gave both British and American intelligence an insight into the workings of the KGB and the GRU, and the sometimes tetchy relationship between the two. He also passed over technical information on the Soviet war machine, especially with regard to their missile and rocket-launching capabilities, and suggested that Premier Khruschev may not be as willing to push the world to nuclear war as his rhetoric might suggest.

Penkovsky visited London with a trade delegation in summer 1961 and returned to the Soviet Union that autumn. The KGB began to suspect there was a leak in spring 1962 after observing Janet Chisholm, the wife of the British station head, receiving a package from an unidentified man. Surveillance on Western embassies showed Penkovsky making an unauthorized, and un-cleared visit to a British embassy reception – which one of Penkovsky's drinking friends, head of the GRU and former KGB chief General Serov would later try to excuse – and then in July he was seen visiting Wynne in his hotel room, and taking standard precautions to avoid being overheard (turning on the taps and the radio). Penkovsky's apartment was searched and bugged.

By this time, the situation in Cuba had escalated. Khruschev had taken Kennedy's inaction during the Bay of Pigs crisis – in particular, not sending troops in to back up the Cuban exiles when it was clear that things were going wrong – to indicate that he lacked a strong backbone. He therefore decided that the Soviet Union would install missiles in Cuba, and Kennedy would have to accept it as a fait accompli. Soviet scientists travelled to Cuba under cover of an agricultural delegation, and began constructing the sites.

New CIA Director John A. McCone was suspicious of the Soviet activity that was revealed by the NSA signal tapping as well as by agents on the ground. This included a report from the French intelligence's Washington chief of station, Thyraud de Vosjoli, who had visited the Cuban capital, Havana, and noted that four to six thousand Soviet military personnel had arrived there since the start of July. This prompted a U-2 mission that confirmed that the Soviets had brought Surface to Air Missiles (SAMs) to the island. Unfortunately, a release of information to the *Washington Post* by the State Department resulted in the Russians adopting radio silence, severely denting the NSA's ability to gain further information about their activity – which meant that the imminent arrival of nuclear ballistic missiles aboard merchant ships steaming towards Cuba was not picked up by the NSA. Based on the information they did have, they believed that Khruschev was telling the truth: 'The Soviet Union is supplying to Cuba exclusively defensive weapons intended for protecting the interests of the Cuban revolution.'

That was all to change on 14 October when the first overflight of the island in six weeks revealed the presence of Soviet ballistic missiles, which had actually arrived over a month earlier. President Kennedy was briefed early the next morning, and for the next few days, the ultimate game of brinkmanship took place between him and Nikita Khruschev. The information that Penkovsky provided had assisted in the identification of the missile sites, and in reading Khrushchev's character.

Other spies would also play their part in the crisis. A KGB agent in Washington, journalist Georgi Bolshakov, had built a relationship with Attorney-General Robert Kennedy, and this was used by Khruschev as part of the attempt to blindside the Americans. President Kennedy regarded the communications as a private hotline to Khrushchev, and felt that he had been personally betrayed when the truth about the missiles was revealed.

As the crisis reached its climax, with Kennedy preparing for an invasion of Cuba, which was pretty certain to lead to nuclear war if the Soviets reacted militarily, the KGB Resident in Washington, Aleksandr Feklisov, rang an ABC reporter, John Scali, whom he knew had access to the White House. He passed on a message: if the Soviets removed their missiles, would the US pledge not to invade Cuba? It was the first move in the negotiations that would bring the crisis to a resolution, with Khrushchev sending a personal letter shortly after that in similar terms which officially started the endgame (albeit one that still came perilously close to going wrong, when a Soviet SAM downed a US plane, and the US Navy depth-charged a Soviet submarine that was carrying a tactical nuclear warhead).

Penkovsky and Greville Wynne did not see the resolution

of the crisis as free men. Seen handling a forged passport at his flat, Penkovsky was arrested; Wynne was apprehended in Budapest a few days later. Both were tried; Penkovsky was shot and Wynne was eventually exchanged for Gordon Lonsdale in 1964. Penkovsky's friend, General Serov was dismissed from the GRU and committed suicide shortly afterwards.

Also coming to a head during the latter part of 1962 was a scandal that would lead to the resignation of the British Secretary of State for War, John Profumo, the following June. This involved the Soviet naval attaché, Yevgeny Ivanov, who for a time was sleeping with the same call girl, Christine Keeler, as Profumo. There were concerns that Dr Stephen Ward, who acted as Keeler's pimp, had manipulated a situation whereby Profumo might pass 'pillow talk' regarding nuclear secrets to Keeler that could be of use to the Soviets. Challenged about this, Profumo initially denied there had been any impropriety in his relationship with Keeler, but later admitted he had lied to the House of Commons, and in accordance with the then-prevalent code of behaviour, he resigned his position.

The situation was complicated by Ward's behaviour. Initially it seemed as if he was acting for the Soviets, but when MI5 warned Profumo and Ivanov, and Profumo ended his affair with Keeler, Ward offered to try to persuade Ivanov to defect. Certainly Ward was used as a back channel to pass messages between the British Foreign Office and Moscow via Ivanov. But according to Keeler, Ward had been already working for MI5, spotting those foreign diplomats whose sexual behaviour might lend themselves to being blackmailed. MI5's official history denies this.

After Profumo's resignation, Ward was tried for living off immoral earnings; he was found unconscious in his flat before the guilty verdict was delivered – conspiracy theorists believe he may have been killed by one of the intelligence agencies whose secrets he could have revealed in exchange for a lighter sentence. A joint MI5-MI6 working party looked into 'the possibility that the Russian Intelligence Service had a hand in staging the Profumo Affair in order to discredit Her Majesty's government'. By the time it reported in the negative, Prime Minister Harold Macmillan had resigned through ill health.

The defection of Anatoliy Golitsyn in December 1961 originally looked as if it might be as much of a treasure trove for the counter-intelligence forces of the West as Mikhail Goleniewski's testimony had been earlier that year. Certainly he provided information that exposed the KGB's agent in France, Georges Pâques, and ended the careers of Elsie Mai, a Finn who had infiltrated the British consulate in Helsinki, and John Vassall, the spy within the British Admiralty. He also gave further evidence that proved Kim Philby's involvement as a Soviet agent – faced with this, Philby finally defected to Moscow in 1963 – but the major problem with most of his assertions were that, unlike previous defectors, he didn't bring evidence that could be checked out. Often his knowledge of operations was vague – such as in France, where he claimed that there was an agent network code-named Sapphire operating within the French intelligence agency, the SDECE – and he seemed to believe that the KGB's influence had spread everywhere, to the extent that he wouldn't trust any interrogator who could speak to him in Russian, and maintained that Moscow Centre had a key agent within the CIA.

The KGB certainly took his defection seriously: a month later, they sent orders to fifty-four stations worldwide on the actions necessary to minimize the damage, and in November 1962, an order was given for his assassination. There were some within the CIA, including James Jesus Angleton, the

counter-intelligence director who interviewed Golitsyn on his
arrival in the States, who took his accusations very seriously
and called him 'the most valuable defector ever to reach the
West'. Others were far more sceptical. Golitsyn's theories
about the KGB's activities became ever wilder: he accused
British Labour Party leader, later Prime Minister, Harold
Wilson of working for Moscow Centre, and claimed that his
predecessor Hugh Gaitskell had been poisoned by the KGB
in order to secure the position for Wilson. MI5 officer Peter
Wright was one of those who believed there was some truth
to Golitsyn's claims about Wilson.

The situation regarding Golitsyn was complicated by the
defection of another Russian, Yuri Nosenko, who had worked
for Soviet State Security since 1953. After a posting to
England, Nosenko started to consider defecting, and in 1960
tried to contact a Western intelligence officer without success.
Eventually in 1962 he was recruited by the CIA in Geneva.
His information also helped to identify John Vassall and
Robert Johnson as KGB agents, and he provided some
information on the fate of Pyotr Popov, as well as revealing
the existence of the many bugs in the US Embassy planted
there during its building in 1953.

Nosenko defected in February 1964, fearing he was under
suspicion. Unfortunately for him, his information didn't tally
with that of Golitsyn. The earlier defector had said that the
KGB would send false defectors across to try to discredit his
testimony, and that's certainly what Nosenko appeared to be
doing. Nosenko was adamant that the KGB did not have a
mole within the CIA, no matter what Golitsyn might say.

President Kennedy had been assassinated in November
1963, and some within the CIA believed that the Soviets were
involved – but Nosenko made it clear that Lee Harvey
Oswald, who most believed was the assassin, may have
travelled in Russia and been investigated during his time there,
but he was not a KGB agent. This may have led to the intense

treatment that Nosenko received – as CIA case officer Robert Baer noted, 'When Nosenko offered a version of Lee Harvey Oswald and the Kennedy assassination that didn't fit with the Agency's corporate view he was sent to solitary confinement at the farm for three years.' This treatment was so rigorous that it merited a public apology from later CIA DCI Stansfield Turner in 1978: 'The excessively harsh treatment of Mr Nosenko went beyond the bounds of propriety or good judgment.'

Nosenko was interrogated for three years, and failed two lie-detector tests during this time (although he claimed that a doctor inserted a finger into his anus to stimulate his blood pressure prior to the second one to give a false reading). However, after a change in interrogators, he was released in April 1969.

The after-effect of the two defections was that neither man was fully believed. Both had given important information about Soviet operatives in the West, but there were many questions left unanswered. One of the responses to this was the establishment of the Fluency committee. This was a group of MI5 and MI6 officers, created in November 1964 to investigate all allegations of infiltration of the British security services. The committee met for seven years, and came up with a list of two hundred instances of possible Soviet penetration. These included Dick Ellis, an MI6 employee who had already come under suspicion after Burgess and Maclean's defection, and had retired as an active agent in 1953. The evidence uncovered seemed to indicate that Ellis had been an agent for Nazi intelligence during the Second World War, and for the GRU and then the KGB. Ellis eventually admitted he had spied for both at the start of the war, but then lied about his contact with Kim Philby, leading the committee to conclude that he had been a Soviet agent for around thirty years.

Peter Wright was the chair of the Fluency committee and made it his life's work to pursue Roger Hollis, the Director-

General of MI5 from 1956 to 1965, whom he believed was a Soviet agent. Wright had originally decided that the Deputy Director-General, Graham Mitchell, was the Soviet agent, based on such circumstantial evidence as the placement of dust in his office drawer. The CIA and FBI, as well as the RCMP (who handled intelligence in Canada prior to the establishment of the CSIS) all expressed doubt, and Mitchell was eventually cleared in 1970.

However, Roger Hollis' actions lay him open to suspicion: he prevented a key interrogation during the investigation into John Vassall; his reports during the Profumo affair were not adequately compiled. In 1964, Anthony Blunt had finally admitted his role in the Philby/Burgess/Maclean spy ring in return for immunity from prosecution, and Wright was convinced there was a Fifth Man who had protected the others. (The Fifth Man's identity as John Cairncross wasn't revealed until 1990.) Wright made himself extremely unpopular with his allegations, admitting 'There was talk of the Gestapo.'

Once he had retired from MI5, Wright wrote his autobiography, *Spycatcher*, in which he made his allegations about Hollis public. Wright claimed that when Hollis was sent to interrogate Igor Gouzenko in 1945, he had stayed in disguise in case Gouzenko recognized him as a Soviet agent, and Hollis had then tried to persuade Gouzenko not to make further allegations. Based on this shaky evidence, he declared Hollis a traitor.

Now, with access to the KGB records, courtesy of defector Oleg Gordievsky, we know that George Blake was the last key agent that Moscow Centre had within either MI5 or MI6, but at the time what may well have been incompetency was seen as something much worse. The Trend Committee, headed by Lord Trend, investigated Hollis and the Soviet penetration of MI5 in the seventies, and reported that the allegations against Hollis were inconclusive. An internal MI5 report from

1988 noted that the belief in a traitor had persisted for so long because of 'a lack of intellectual rigour in some of the leading investigators ... dishonesty on the part of Wright, who did not scruple to invent evidence where none existed ... [and] the baleful influence of Golitsyn who realised in 1963 that he had told all he knew and set about developing his theory of massive and coordinated Soviet deception ("disinformation") supported by high-level penetration of all western intelligence and security services.' Couple that with an overwhelming belief that Moscow Centre was a lot more efficient than it really was, and the stage was set for the witch-hunts. As Allen Dulles wrote in 1963: 'Soviet intelligence is over-confident, over-complicated, and over-estimated.'

7

POWER CORRUPTS

The 2003 invasion of Iraq wasn't the first time that the United States has gone to war based on inaccurate information supplied to the administration by the intelligence agencies. Sometimes intelligence agencies will choose not to send the White House information that they know will anger the president. The Gulf of Tonkin incident did not play out in the way in which it was initially presented to President Johnson, upon which he based the Gulf of Tonkin Resolution of 7 August 1964.

Between 1960 and July 1962, the CIA had tried sending teams of trained South Vietnamese agents into North Vietnam; these had been unsuccessful. Thereafter, responsibility for actions against the North Vietnamese was transferred to the Defence Department, which began OPLAN34-63, a series of offensives against the North Vietnamese coastline in autumn 1963, and then refined them as OPLAN34A that December (although it seems no one thought to inform the NSA's Asian desk of the operation.)

The USS *Maddox* was equipped for SIGINT work and sent into the Gulf of Tonkin on 28 July 1964, reassured by the commander of the SIGINT group in Taiwan that their ship would be in no danger. However, an OPLAN34A raid which took place on 31 July seriously annoyed the North Vietnamese – and they responded by sending three torpedo boats after the *Maddox*. The *Maddox* was warned of the impending engagement by NSA intercepts of North Vietnamese orders; when the boats approached, the US ship fired warning shots before the Vietnamese fired. At the end of combat, one of the torpedo boats had been sunk, and the other two damaged.

President Johnson was briefed on the attack the next day, and decided to keep his cool: he ordered the *Maddox* to resume its mission, albeit guarded by a destroyer, the *Turner Joy*, and air support. Further OPLAN34A attacks took place the following day, and SIGINT suggested that the North Vietnamese would respond again.

On 4 August, everything seemed to indicate that the *Maddox* was about to be attacked again. North Vietnamese patrol boats had shadowed them for part of the time, and in the evening, they believed they were being followed by two surface and three air contacts. The *Turner Joy* and the *Maddox* opened fire on a radar contact at 9.30 that night, and it seemed as if they engaged in a pitched battle with around six patrol boats.

But while that news electrified Washington, and preparations for airstrikes were made, in the Gulf the captains on the *Turner Joy* and the *Maddox* were reviewing the action, and realized that, as Captain Herrick said, 'Certain that original ambush [on 2 August] was bonafide. Details of action following present a confusing picture.' In Washington, Robert McNamara, the Secretary of Defence, and the Joint Chiefs of Staff decided that an attack had taken place – based on two NSA intercepts, one stating that a North Vietnamese boat had shot at American aircraft; the other that two planes had been shot down, and two Vietnamese ships had been lost. As the NSA's own history explained, 'The reliance on SIGINT even went to the extent of overruling the commander on the scene. It was obvious to the president and his advisers that there really had been an attack – they had the North Vietnamese messages to prove it.' There was one serious problem though. The messages were timed during the 'battle' itself – yet referred to the reaction of the North Vietnamese to its conclusion. It was enough to start the conflict. (With the benefit of hindsight, McNamara accepted that the evidence wasn't strong enough, and that the attack didn't happen; based on a number of comments he made, President Johnson had doubts from the start.)

However, much as this may have been a misuse of the spies' work, it is clear that Johnson's administration was looking for a trigger to begin the war, and as the NSA themselves pointed out, 'Had the 4 August incident not occurred, something else would have.'

The latter half of the sixties was, to a large degree, a time when spies engaged in the Cold War got on with their business. There weren't many events that caused major changes to the way espionage was carried out – to the extent that many histories of the period touch on the Vietnam War, and the continuing hunts within the security services for KGB moles as revealed by Golitsyn, but mention little else.

This is slightly ironic, given that this is the era when spies were at the forefront of popular culture: the James Bond movies, based increasingly loosely on the novels by Ian Fleming, were released virtually annually in the sixties. They gave rise to many imitators, including the Matt Helm film thrillers featuring Dean Martin as the sort of self-promoting agent that no self-respecting agency would want near them (but whose weaknesses they would be more than happy to take advantage of to blackmail him), and the TV series *The*

Man From U.N.C.L.E., which predated glasnost with its partnership of American agent Napoleon Solo (a pre-*Hustle* Robert Vaughn) and Russian Illya Kuryakin (*NCIS'* David McCallum). (The CIA even includes memorabilia from the series in its museum at Langley, Virginia, USA.) The backlash to these over-the-top adventures gave rise to the more realistic novels of John le Carré, such as *The Spy Who Came in from the Cold*, and Adam Hall (the *Quiller* series). Le Carré had served in the British security services in the post-Second World War period, although he acknowledged that he was one of those whose covers would have been blown by Kim Philby before the defection of Burgess and Maclean removed him from office.

The KGB assisted in the removal of Nikita Khruschev from office in 1964 and the rise to power of Leonid Brehznev. Shelyepin found himself sidelined, with Yuri Andropov promoted to Chairman of the KGB in 1967. For them, the sixties were a period of re-entrenchment, to make up for the loss of the spy rings thanks to the various defectors.

Although they weren't able to infiltrate an agent into either MI5 or MI6, the KGB were active in Britain during the decade. One of their most useful men was Sirioj Husein Abdoolcader, who worked as a clerk at the Greater London Council motor licensing department. Recruited in 1967, Abdoolcader had access to the number plates of the cars of all the MI5 and Special Branch vehicles, so any surveillance carried out by the security services on the London residency personnel was immediately compromised.

Following on from their success in penetrating the Manhattan Project two decades earlier, Moscow Centre targeted scientific and technological personnel, creating a new 'Directorate T' specifically to deal with the new intelligence field. Some agents may have had lucky escapes, thanks to the difficulties that the security services faced in proving their case. Dr Guiseppe Martelli, who had worked at the Atomic

Energy Authority, was arrested in 1963 but, even though he was found with one-time pads and other spy tools, MI5 were unable to gain a conviction, since they couldn't provide evidence that he had been in contact with those who had access to classified information. Two workers at the Kodak factory accused of selling film-process material to the East German intelligence agency, the HVA, were similarly acquitted in 1965. It seems probable that a number of similar cases didn't get to court – according to Oleg Gordievsky, the Directorate T records indicate those that ended in conviction were only 'the tip of the iceberg'.

Two cases were successfully prosecuted during this decade in Britain. Frank Bossard, a project manager at the Ministry of Aviation, was recruited by the GRU around the time that he was transferred to working on guided weapons in 1960. Until he was betrayed by the testimony of GRU officer and CIA asset Dimitri Polyakov in 1965, he was regularly leaving film of classified documents in dead letter boxes in return for cash.

Douglas Britten, described as 'a good actor and an accomplished liar' by a Security Commission following his conviction, also betrayed secrets for cash. Recruited in 1962, he tried to break off contact during his posting to the listening stations on Cyprus in 1966, but was then blackmailed by his KGB controller with a photo showing him receiving payments from the Soviets. He was transferred back to RAF Digby in Lancashire, where the KGB pressured him to provide more information. Britten was photographed visiting the Soviet consulate, arrested, and although he cooperated with MI5, he was sentenced to twenty-one years' imprisonment.

Nicholas Praeger also worked assiduously for the Eastern bloc during the sixties, although he was turned and handled by the Czech intelligence agency, the Státní Bezpeènost (StB). A committed Communist, Praeger was a top radar technician with access to secret material by the time he was recruited by the StB in 1959. His value to the StB increased after he left the

RAF, and joined the English Electric Company, which was working on radar-jamming equipment aboard British nuclear strike bombers. Moscow described his information as 'the best intelligence yet provided by the StB'. When StB officer Josef Frolik defected to the West in 1969 following the Soviet invasion of Czechoslovakia the previous year (leaving from a secret holiday camp for secret agents in Bulgaria!), he gave his interrogators sufficient information to help identify Praeger, who was eventually arrested and convicted in 1971.

The StB were instrumental in turning important people in other professions too: they found that British politicians and trade unionists were more susceptible to a friendly approach from a Czechoslovak than a Russian, usually maintaining that the mistrust between London and Prague was unjustified. Once they received payment for their time writing about promoting new links, they belonged to the StB.

One key agent was Labour politician Will Owen, about whom his fellow MP Leo Abse said later, 'Owen certainly did his best to rape his motherland.' Recruited in 1954, he was known as 'Greedy bastard' by his StB controllers, interested solely in the fees and free holidays in Czechoslovakia he could get. Owen passed over highly secret material on the British Army of the Rhine and the British portion of NATO until he too was betrayed by Frolik.

John Stonehouse, the Labour MP who infamously faked his own suicide in 1974, worked for the StB for an extended period of time, although he denied that he was an agent when accused by MI5, following Frolik's defection. Frolik claimed that Stonehouse 'put [the StB] in a position to know a great deal about certain British military and counter-intelligence operations', but at the time that was the only real evidence against him. A later defector, code-named Affirm, confirmed in 1980 that Stonehouse had been working for the Czechs, but the StB had been disappointed by the amount of intelligence he was able to provide once he became a minister.

The StB had their hands full with Tom Driberg, who was a double or triple agent, also working for MI5 and the KGB. An MP since 1945, and even chairman of the Labour party for a year, Driberg was able to provide his various masters with information about the habits of MPs, which could be used to blackmail them. Known as 'Lord of the Spies' when elevated to the peerage in 1975, he claimed to MI5 that he only ever passed harmless stuff to his Communist contacts.

A fourth MP, code-named Gustav by the StB, has never been properly identified; some claim that Frolik's description matched Sir Barnett Stross, who died in 1967, but it has been pointed out that any information he was in a position to pass on could as easily have been obtained openly from the Transport & General Workers' Union headquarters at Transport House in London.

In June 2012, as this book was being written, Conservative minister Raymond Mawby's career working for the StB through the sixties was uncovered: code name Laval was first contacted in 1960 at a cocktail party at the Czechoslovakian embassy. His weakness was money: 'His leisure time he spends in bars . . . and also loves gambling,' one Czech agent noted. 'While playing roulette and other games he is willing to accept a monetary "loan" which was exploited twice.' Mawby was the only Conservative MP known to work for the Eastern bloc, passing over details of key members of the party as well as official and handwritten floor plans of offices at the House of Commons. The relationship only ended in 1971 after a number of Eastern bloc agents were thrown out of the UK: 'Considering the worsening operational conditions in Great Britain and after evaluating dangerous signals . . . we are forbidding all contacts with him,' states a note in his file.

The StB didn't confine its operations to the United Kingdom. In October 1968, a rash of apparent suicides in West Germany could be linked to the discovery of a spy ring run by the Czech security service. On 8 October, Major-General

Horst Wendland, the deputy chief of the BND, shot himself in his office; it was later confirmed that he had been working for the StB. The same day, his friend Rear-Admiral Hermann Lüdke, the deputy head of NATO's logistics division, was found dead on a private hunting estate, shortly after the discovery of photographs of top-secret documents taken by him with a Minox camera of the sort used by the Eastern bloc services. Incredibly, they had been found by a darkroom assistant alongside holiday snaps that Lüdke was having developed. Within a few days, Colonel Johannes Grimm, who worked in the German Defence Ministry, was found fatally shot; Gerald Bohm, also in the Defence Ministry, was found drowned in the Rhine river; Edeltraud Grapentin, a liaison with the Information Ministry, died from an overdose of sleeping pills; and Hans-Heinrich Schenk, a researcher at the Economics Ministry, was found hanged in an apartment in Cologne.

Nor were the StB the only agency outside the KGB to run agents in the West. Markus Johannes Wolf, the head of the East German HVA (also known as the Stasi) was an expert at spying on his own people within the German Democratic Republic, but was renowned for the penetration programme that he ran for over a generation within West Germany. According to a defector in 1958, Wolf had two to three thousand penetration agents already in place at that point. One particularly successful tactic was using agents to seduce secretaries in key positions: in the mid-fifties, Irmgard Römer, who worked at the Bonn Foreign Office, was passing copies of telegrams to embassies to her seducer, Carl Helmers. In 1967, Leonore Sütterlein, another secretary at the Foreign Office, was convicted of passing over 3,000 classified documents to her husband, who was in reality a KGB officer; Sütterlein committed suicide when she learned he had married her simply to recruit her. Other secretaries at the Science Ministry and at the embassy in Warsaw were convicted, but many of Wolf's best agents went undetected.

Wolf's greatest agent's most important coup took place following the election of Willy Brandt as chancellor of West Germany in 1969. Some years earlier, Stasi agent Günter Guillaume had apparently defected from the East, and built up a successful cover, working for the Social Democrat Party. He was elected to the Frankfurt city council in 1968, and when Brandt came to power, Guillaume went to work for his office. Within a few years, he would become Brandt's most trusted aide – and able to pass back through Wolf to Moscow key details of the Federal Republic's future plans.

The KGB played its part in dealing with 'internal' unrest within the Soviet bloc, notably during the Prague Spring of 1968, when liberalization in Czechoslovakia (so-called 'socialism with a human face') was deemed to be a threat to the Soviets. As negotiations and discussions went on between Leonid Brezhnev and Alexander Dubček, the Czech leader, Andropov's KGB were paving the way for a Soviet takeover. Although this ended up being military in nature, in June 1968 KGB reserve officer Mikhail Sagatelyan made various recommendations to the Kremlin based on a visit he had made to the country the previous month. In particular, he suggested creating a 'pro-Soviet faction' within the Czechoslovak leadership, which would oust Dubček ('a lesser evil than a military invasion,' according to Sagatelyan).

The KGB had already increased their presence within Czechoslovakia, and now carried out two operations: Progress and Khodoki. Progress saw KGB agents, including future CIA spy Oleg Gordievsky's brother, pose as Westerners making contact with opposition groups in Czechoslovakia; Khodoki involved agents fabricating proof that the opposition was planning an armed coup – thereby giving the USSR a pretext to come to the government's aid.

Andropov genuinely believed that Western agencies were trying to promote the political changes that Dubček was proposing. He even discarded a report from his trusted resident in Washington, Oleg Kalugin, which stated clearly that the CIA were not involved based on documents which he had seen. Where hard evidence didn't exist, the KGB invented it, using their agents to 'discover' arms caches and promote unrest.

The Red Army, supported by units from other Warsaw Pact countries, invaded Czechoslovakia on the night of 20 August 1968, removing Dubček from power. Unfortunately, the opposition to Dubček's policies was nowhere near as strong as the Kremlin had believed, and in the end he was returned to power, albeit on a very tight leash from Moscow, with a heavy KGB presence in the country monitoring for signs of disquiet.

The Prague Spring's conclusion had two major repercussions within the spy world: the Brezhnev Doctrine, formally stated in September 1968, noted that while each country had a right to take 'its own separate road to socialism', their policies mustn't damage either socialism in their own country, or anywhere else. If such damage did occur, the Soviet Union had 'an internationalist duty' to 'act in resolute opposition to the anti-socialist forces'. This would keep the KGB busy for the next twenty years. The other result was its personal effect on Oleg Gordievsky; the way in which the Prague Spring was dealt with by Moscow would be a motivating factor in his decision to work with the CIA.

Although the CIA's primary activities during the second half of the sixties were involved with the conflict in south-east Asia, they also continued with their intelligence-gathering missions against the Communist countries. The decade saw a number of technological advances, with improvements in the quality of listening devices and the other paraphernalia of espionage – some of these prompted by the wilder ideas seen on TV shows like *The Man From U.N.C.L.E.* or *Mission:*

Impossible. According to the CIA's Technical Services Division (TSD), they would need to bring in extra telephone assistance to cope with the calls that would come from agents following the broadcast of these shows.

One project that the TSD invested some time in was nicknamed 'Acoustic Kitty', which, although it sounds like something from an episode of spy spoof *Get Smart*, genuinely involved transmitters being implanted into cats. Feral felines were common to the region where a targeted Asian head of state was holding private meetings. The idea was to embed a power source, transmitter, microphone and antenna into an animal, with the mike going in the cat's ear, the transmitter at the base of the skull, and the antenna woven into its fur. Once the go-ahead was given, the operation took an hour to perform, and the audio quality was adequate. Chances are, though, the technician who thought of the idea wasn't a cat owner, since Acoustic Kitty refused to go where the CIA wanted it to, despite training. A CIA memo closing down the project noted: 'Our final examination of trained cats ... convinced us that the program would not lend itself in a practical sense to our highly specialized needs ... The work done on this problem over the years reflects great credit on the personnel who guided it.'

A rather more conventional spy worked for the CIA for nearly twenty-five years and was described as a jewel in the crown by more than one senior member of the agency. Dimitri Fedorovich Polyakov was a GRU agent who had worked as a member of the Soviet mission at the United Nations, and run illegal agents into West Germany during a posting in Berlin.

Initially offering his services to the FBI as a counter-intelligence source during his second stint at the UN in 1961 and working with them for a year, he was handed over to the CIA before he returned to Russia in 1962. Polyakov didn't appear to be motivated by money: he accepted no more than

$3,000 a year, and mostly took that in the form of tools, fishing gear or shotguns. According to one CIA case officer who worked with him for fifteen years, Polyakov 'articulated a sense that he had to help us out or the Soviets were going to win the cold war, and he couldn't stand that. He felt we were very naive and we were going to fail.' It's also been suggested that he felt disillusioned when he was refused permission to allow his son to enter a New York hospital for life-saving treatment and the boy died.

Polyakov was posted to Rangoon, Burma, and was able to assist the US war effort in Vietnam by passing over the GRU's details on the Chinese and Vietnamese military forces, as well as revealing the identity of the GRU spy in the British Ministry of Aviation, Frank Bossard. His material would continue to influence American policy through the following decade, notably with its insight into the relationship between Russia and China, which had deteriorated through the sixties.

Discussion of the US military's role during the Vietnam War will often turn to darker actions, such as the massacre of Vietnamese civilians by American soldiers at My Lai. The CIA's reputation was not enhanced when news reached the American public about the abuses carried out in the name of Operation Phoenix, although it wasn't all negative. Many US servicemen and their families were extremely grateful to the Agency for their work in establishing contact between prisoners of war and their homes.

The purpose of Operation Phoenix was to root out supporters of the Viet Cong, otherwise known as the National Front for the Liberation of South Vietnam. The Viet Cong wanted to 'overthrow the camouflaged colonial regime of the American imperialists', and to all intents and purposes were carrying out the wishes of the North Vietnamese government in Hanoi. They carried out acts of violence and terrorism against government employees and anyone assisting those they regarded as the enemy, which at times could include medical personnel.

The Viet Cong carried out what became known as the Tet Offensive in early 1968, attacking more than a hundred towns around South Vietnam. They even mounted a commando raid on the US embassy in Saigon. They hoped that an urban uprising would follow, but it didn't, and between forty thousand (the US estimate) and seventy-five thousand (the Viet Cong's own figure) of their own troops were killed, as compared to around six thousand American and South Vietnamese. Although this was presented as a major defeat for the Americans by the anti-war media in the States, it was equally devastating for the Viet Cong, whose infrastructure was weakened, and numbers depleted to such a level that they were unable to ever fully regroup: 'We failed to seize a number of primary objectives. We also failed to hold the occupied areas. In the political field we failed to motivate the people to stage uprisings,' the Viet Cong themselves admitted. However, as Richard Nixon pointed out: 'Though it was an overwhelming victory for South Vietnam and the United States, the almost universal theme of media coverage was that we had suffered a disastrous defeat. The steady drumbeat of inaccurate stories convinced millions of Americans that we had lost a major battle.'

Operation Phoenix had already been in existence prior to the Tet Offensive, but went into overdrive afterwards. Created as the Intelligence Coordination and Exploitation Program as part of the general Civil Operations and Revolutionary Development Support program (CORDS), it was quickly renamed Phoenix (or Phung Hoàng in Vietnamese). MACV Directive 381-41 of 9 July 1967 established it with the aim of attacking with a 'rifle shot rather than a shotgun approach to target key political leaders, command/control elements and activists in the VCI'. In essence, it was similar to previous CIA operations, a struggle for the hearts and minds of the

Vietnamese, so that they chose to turn against the Communists. It therefore needed to be carried out by the Vietnamese themselves.

Oversight committees operating at national, corps and district levels agreed the framework within which the Phoenix teams could operate, and set quotas. At the provincial level were teams, usually comprised of trained South Vietnamese soldiers, who would ascertain who was involved with the Viet Cong, and 'neutralise' them. This didn't necessarily mean they were killed: it was recognized that that sort of heavy-handed operation could be counter-productive, and of course, dead Viet Cong couldn't provide useful intelligence. According to a CIA report in 1969:

> The Provincial Reconnaissance Unit (PRU) Program in South Vietnam forms an investigative and paramilitary attack upon the covert communist apparatus in South Vietnam. PRU teams, currently totalling approximately 4,200 men, operate in 44 provinces of South Vietnam. PRU are based in their home areas and operate in teams of 15–20 men. They are presently advised and supported by 101 US military advisors and seven CIA personnel. CIA funds the PRU and retains overall administrative control of the project for the US Government.

The official remit of Phoenix was:

> ... the collection of intelligence identifying these members; inducing them to abandon their allegiance to the VC and rally to the government; capturing or arresting them in order to bring them before province security committees or military courts for lawful sentencing; and as a final resort, the use of reasonable force should they resist capture or arrest where failure to use such force would result in the escape of the suspected VCI member or would result in threat of serious bodily harm to a member or members of the capturing or arresting party.

The problem was that there were many occasions where those carrying out the Phoenix program went beyond their orders, leading to the belief that Phoenix was a cover for assassination (although obviously there was a grey area between targeted kills of Viet Cong operatives and assassinations.) Interrogations could be brutal – K. Barton Osborn, who was connected to Phoenix in 1968, described the techniques in graphic detail to a Congress subcommittee in 1971, and called Phoenix a 'sterile depersonalized murder program . . . I never knew an individual to be detained as a VC suspect who ever lived through an interrogation.'

The CIA wanted to pull out of the program and leave it in South Vietnamese hands as early as 1969, in part because it didn't really fit with their intelligence-gathering mission any more. The program was run by William Colby, who had been Chief of Station in Saigon; it officially came to an end shortly after he returned to Washington as Executive Director of the CIA in 1971 and Congress began investigating the abuses. As far as Colby was concerned, despite the problems that he acknowledged had occurred, it was a success; as he explained in a 1981 television interview: 'I have heard several references to North Vietnamese and South Vietnamese communists who account, who state that in their mind the most, the toughest period that they faced in the whole period of the war from 1960 to 1975 was the period from 1968 to '72 when the Phoenix Program was at work.'

The CIA was instrumental in assisting with information about prisoners of war being held during the Vietnam War. Future Vice-Presidential candidate James Bond Stockdale (yes, that really was his name) was shot down in September 1965 and spent the next seven years as a prisoner. During that time he developed a code that he used in letters home to his wife, which gave the identities of some of the men held with him. US Naval Intelligence originally handled communications with Stockdale, using a letter from his wife to secretly send him invisible carbon paper – although they warned him that if he was caught, he would be treated as a spy.

Stockdale was able to send back lists of potential targets, prisoners held and information on the camp's location, but when senior officers decided to back off from the project, noting that the POWs 'have got it tough enough right now . . . The last thing we need to do is make them spies', the Navy turned to the CIA. The Technical Service Department's Bruce Rounds came up with a new code which Stockdale's wife used for a letter in May 1967.

Although the communications would lead to Stockdale's brutal torture, they continued with other POWs, allowing families to find out about the fate of their loved ones. TSD agent Brian Lipton worked at night on the project which was kept secret from all but a very few at the CIA: it remained a classified secret even after the Vietnam War ended, with Lipton persuading now Rear Admiral Stockdale not to give up all the secrets in his autobiography. It was eventually revealed in a history of the Technical Services Division published in 2008, three years after Stockdale's death.

The other key element of the CIA's involvement in south-east Asia was Air America, the civilian airline owned by the Agency. This carried out multiple operations supporting the tribal groups, known as the Montagnards, who lived in the highlands between Vietnam and Laos, as well as mounting missions to rescue US pilots who had been shot down in North Vietnam. Between 1962 and 1975 Air America provided support to the Royal Lao Army and was used to transport anything and everything that needed to move around the area – from live pigs and cows during a famine, to Richard Nixon himself. According to some of its pilots, it was also involved in the opium trade (an accusation that gained credence with the release of a movie in 1990); it certainly was aware of the drugs trade, but its role was assisting in fighting the war against the communists, not policing narcotics.

Air America's own history points out that its crews were involved in many different varieties of mission:

> [They] transported tens of thousands of troops and refugees, flew emergency medevac missions and rescued downed airmen throughout Laos, inserted and extracted road-watch teams, flew night-time airdrop missions over the Ho Chi Minh trail, monitored sensors along infiltration routes, conducted a highly successful photo reconnaissance program, and engaged in numerous clandestine missions using night-vision glasses and state-of-the-art electronic equipment.

As the tide of the war in Laos turned against the Americans, Air America took heavy casualties. CIA Director Richard Helms decided to shut the operation down in 1972 once the war was concluded, but the final two years of service saw twenty-three Air America personnel killed. Although the operation's reputation has been attacked, it is still regarded by the CIA as one of its finest. A plaque to those who served was unveiled at CIA Headquarters at Langley in 1988: 'The aircrew, maintenance, and other professional aviation skills they applied on our behalf were extraordinary. But, above all, they brought a dedication to our mission and the highest standards of personal courage in the conduct of that mission.'

8

DISHONOUR

The seventies were a time of disillusionment in the Western world. In Britain, Edward Heath's administration struggled with industrial disputes, and his successor Harold Wilson believed that MI5 were organizing a coup against him. In America, the ignominious end of the Vietnam War came as a shock to the country's sense of self-belief. Matters were made worse when President Richard Nixon assisted in the cover-up of a break-in at the Watergate building in Washington DC, and would have to resign two years into his second term of office rather than risk being impeached. Worries about the CIA's links to that burglary, as well as revelations about operations apparently directed against the American people, prompted investigations into the agency's conduct, and a great deal of dirty linen being washed in public. West Germany's chancellor was forced to resign when his closest advisor was revealed as a Stasi spy. And at the end of the decade, the Soviet Army, assisted by the KGB, invaded Afghanistan.

Not everything was doom and gloom. The decade began

with a notable coup for MI5, who were able to arrange the expulsion of a ring of Soviet agents from the UK in Operation Foot, causing a major setback to Moscow Centre's plans, not just in Great Britain but throughout the non-Communist world. In all, 105 agents were removed, which resulted in Soviet intelligence operations being severely hampered in the UK for the rest of the seventies.

Operation Foot came about because of increasing concern on the part of MI5 through the sixties at the size of the Soviet intelligence set-up in the UK – even if some in government and the civil service seemed to think that the threat from the KGB was diminishing following the Cuban Missile Crisis. In November 1968, following pressure from MI5, the government restricted the size of the Soviet embassy, but the KGB and GRU simply added intelligence officers to the Trade Delegation. Sir Alec Douglas-Home, appointed Foreign Secretary in Ted Heath's cabinet following the June 1970 general election, raised the issue with his counterpart, Andrei Gromyko, only to be told: 'These figures you give cannot be true because the Soviet Union has no spies.'

After some persuasion, the new Home Secretary, Reginald Maudling, wrote a joint memo with Douglas-Home on 30 July 1971 to the prime minister, warning that there were at least 120 Soviet intelligence officers (from the KGB or GRU) in the UK, and that they were causing serious problems. 'If the cases of which we have knowledge are typical, the total damage done by these Soviet intelligence gatherers must be considerable,' they wrote. 'Known targets during the last few years have included the Foreign Office and Ministry of Defence; and on the commercial side, the Concorde, the Bristol "Olympus 593" aero-engine, nuclear energy projects and computer electronics.' On 4 August, Douglas-Home sent a final warning to Gromyko about 'inadmissible Soviet activities'.

Operation Foot would have taken place in October had it not been for the defection of KGB officer Oleg Lyalin on 3

September. Lyalin had been providing information to MI5 since the previous April, revealing his role as the senior representative of Department V, the KGB's sabotage and covert affairs section. According to the plans Lyalin was compiling, seaborne sabotage groups would land at Hayburn Wyke on the north Yorkshire coast (240 miles north of London) with airborne colleagues dropping in north of the Caledonian Canal to cause major problems for the British infrastructure. In addition, he had been the case officer for Sirioj Husein Abdoolcader, the KGB spy in the GLC motor licensing department; Abdoolcader was arrested two weeks after Lyalin's defection.

On 24 September, the Permanent Undersecretary at the Foreign Office, Sir Denis Greenhill, told the Soviet chargé d'affaires that ninety GRU or KGB officers were being expelled, and fifteen others who were in the Soviet Union at the time had their visas revoked. The following day Douglas-Home faced an angry Gromyko at the UN, who warned it was dangerous for Britain to threaten the USSR. Douglas-Home apparently burst out laughing and said, 'Do you really think that Britain can "threaten" your country? I am flattered to think that this is the case.' Gromyko complained about the 'hooligan-like acts of the British police' and expelled eighteen British diplomats, but the matter didn't escalate. The success of Operation Foot led to MI5's standing within the international intelligence community rising.

KGB operations were hampered but not stopped altogether – in fact their key operative in the UK wasn't affected by Operation Foot at all, since he was controlled from abroad. This was Geoffrey Prime, whose work at the British SIGINT headquarters at the Government Communications Headquarters (GCHQ) building in Cheltenham and elsewhere could have been much more damaging to British interests than it was, MI5 believed, had he been run by the KGB First Directorate, who handled most espionage operations. The

Third Directorate, to whom Prime reported, weren't used to handling such sensitive material. Even so, during his time at Cheltenham, the Russians suddenly changed their communications procedures, making them impenetrable to NSA and GCHQ analysts.

Prime had offered his services to the Russians while stationed with the RAF in West Berlin in 1968 – leaving a message at a Soviet checkpoint, asking Soviet intelligence to contact him – and was encouraged by them to apply for a post with GCHQ. He would later claim that he worked for the KGB 'partly as a result of a misplaced idealistic view of Russian Communism which was compounded by basic psychological problems'. Prime was a sexual pervert, whose interest in young girls would eventually lead to his arrest.

During his work at GCHQ, Prime had access to intercepts that he would pass through to his Soviet controllers, using his own judgement as to what was important. Like many spies before him, Prime suffered from stress because of his double life, exacerbated by his sexual problems, and eventually, in 1977, he resigned from GCHQ, and went on to work as a Cheltenham taxi driver. The KGB left him alone for three years, before trying to reactivate him in 1980, but although Prime provided them with material he had obtained during his final few months at Cheltenham, he wasn't willing to try to regain his old job. His espionage activities were only revealed after his arrest on child sex charges in 1982 when his wife handed over one-time pads and other spy equipment to the police. Prime was sentenced to thirty-eight years' imprisonment (thirty-five for spying, three for the sex offences), of which he served nineteen. In an echo of the Rosenberg case, Prime was told by the judges that if Britain had been at war with the Soviet Union, he would have been sentenced to death.

When the KGB began reactivating their agents, they discovered that one of their most important assets over the

years was no longer in a position to help them, since she had
retired! Melita Norwood's long service to Communism
passing over atomic secrets had been recognized with the
Order of the Red Banner in 1958; she eventually collected it
in Moscow in 1979. She had evaded detection by the Security
Service in the UK over the years ('a harmless and somewhat
uninteresting character' was the assessment in April 1966) and
had been instrumental in recruiting other agents including a
civil servant, code-named Hunt. He was reactivated in 1975
via a French agent, but according to KGB papers supplied by
Vitali Mitrokhin when he defected in 1992, Hunt's usefulness
was pretty minimal, and an MI5 investigation concluded that
it was unlikely that his activities caused any significant
damage. That assessment was also applied to three other
agents – a chemical engineer, a lab assistant, and an aeronautics
and computer engineer – who were brought back into the
KGB fold in the mid-seventies.

The Soviets were able to get useful information from some
agents during the decade. Code name Ace, aircraft engineer
Ivor Gregory, was recruited for cash by the London residency
in 1967, and was able to pass technical details on numerous
planes, including Concorde, aero-engines and flight simula-
tors, which enabled the Soviets to create their own versions.
He died in 1982, although his treachery wasn't discovered
until a decade later.

Michael John Smith, code-named Borg, was an electronics
engineer, who received security clearance when reports of his
earlier affiliation to the Communist party weren't cross-filed
properly. He started working for the KGB in May 1975 and
in the three years before his security clearance was revoked,
he was able to pass the Soviets vital information from his
employment at Thorn EMI defence contractors on the then
top-secret Project XN-715, developing and testing radar fuses
for Britain's free-fall nuclear bomb. His material was so good
that the KGB suspected he was a double agent, and went so

far as to test him with a non-contact polygraph during a trip to Vienna. However, the Soviets broke off contact after he lost his security clearance, until he changed jobs; then between 1990 and 1992, he supplied information from the General Electric Company. He was betrayed when his original case officer, Victor Oshchenko, defected in 1992; Smith was sentenced to twenty-five years' imprisonment, reduced to twenty on appeal. Since his release, he has campaigned 'to discover and expose the full story behind the conspiracy that led to my conviction of supposedly spying for the Russians in the early 1990s', according to his blog.

'It is hard to overstate the damage done to the intelligence service during the seventies,' CIA Director William J. Casey said in a speech in 1982. 'Unrelenting questioning of the Agency's integrity generated a severe loss of credibility.' Although the Church Committee and other assaults on the CIA certainly caused severe problems for the Agency, they were the cause of some of their own difficulties.

James Jesus Angleton, chief of counter-intelligence for the CIA from 1954 to 1975, has been seen by some as a scapegoat for the Agency's problems; to others, the way in which he was allowed to operate epitomizes what was wrong with the Agency during this period. Even the CIA themselves describe him as 'one of the most influential and divisive intelligence officers in US history'.

Angleton was recruited into the OSS in 1943, and served with the counter-intelligence branches in London and Rome, finishing the Second World War as chief of counter-intelligence operations in Italy. He remained there until 1947 and then became the liaison between the new CIA and other western counter-intelligence organizations, notably Shin Bet and Mossad, the agencies for the new country of Israel. In 1954 he was appointed to the role at CIA headquarters that he held until his departure. Although charming in a social context, in business he was described as 'arrogant, tactless, dismissive, and even threatening' to those who disagreed with him.

It was Angleton who managed to get hold of a copy of Nikita Khruschev's denunciation of Stalin in 1956, via his Israeli contacts, when no one else had been able to obtain it. Angleton was utterly convinced that the Soviet Union was implacably hostile towards the West and, on top of that, as far as he was concerned, international Communism was mono-lithic. He didn't believe that the Sino-Soviet split of 1960 was genuine, but was simply part of an elaborate disinformation campaign, and it was a firm tenet that the KGB had penetrated all of the Western agencies.

Angleton's interactions with two KGB spies informed this opinion. He had been friendly with Kim Philby during the forties: the two met regularly when Philby was stationed in Washington from 1949 onwards, to the extent that their weekly dinner meetings were known as 'The Kim and Jim Show'. When Philby's treachery became obvious after the defection of Guy Burgess and Donald Maclean in 1951, Angleton spent the next few years deconstructing his former friend's career, and realized that his various promotions had been part of a Soviet plan. If Philby could reach a situation where he was being seriously talked of as a future head of MI6, there could well be other agents. As a result, DCI Allen Dulles agreed to the establishment of the counter-intelligence section.

The other agent was Anatoli Golitsyn. While many re-garded him as – to put it politely – a fantasist, his tales of KGB infiltration of the entire Western intelligence operation (which he didn't start to mention until sometime after his defection) fit in precisely with Angleton's way of thinking. Golitsyn claimed that British prime minister Harold Wilson was a KGB agent; by the end of his time at the Agency, Angleton would add Swedish prime minster Olaf Palme and West German chancellor Willy Brandt to that list (Brandt of course wasn't the source of any leaks – it was his assistant Günter Guillaume).

In 1962, shortly after Golitsyn's defection, Angleton moved to the new CIA building at Langley and set up the Special Investigation Group (the SIG), searching for KGB influence within the Agency. To the surprise of many, Angleton accepted Golitsyn's claims at face value. It reached a point where the SIG would pass Golitsyn its case files for evaluation, and the Russian would 'finger' specific individuals as likely agents, a practice that later CIA officers found hard to credit.

This meant that when Yuri Nosenko defected, and his claims often contradicted Golitsyn (notably about the presence of a KGB spy within the CIA itself), the newcomer was ignored. The drastic treatment that Nosenko received at the CIA's hands was because Angleton and like-minded colleagues refused to believe he wasn't a KGB plant. Only when new DCI Richard Helms intervened and ordered a review of the evidence was Nosenko exonerated.

Angleton's methods antagonized his colleagues, and many believed that he was speculating about likely Soviet agents, rather than bringing actual proof. The case that Angleton made regarding one particular agent, interrogated in 1968, was described as 'the last piece of reasoning you would bring into a case where you already had evidence. But it's certainly not the kind of thing that you would start off a case with.' The paranoia that Angleton fostered even resulted in one of the counter-intelligence chief's analysts accusing Angleton himself of being a Soviet spy.

Golitsyn maintained that there was one specific spy at the heart of the CIA, code-named Sasha, prompting what became known as the Great Molehunt. (The connection to John le Carré's character George Smiley's most famous mission in the novel *Tinker, Tailor, Soldier, Spy* becomes more apt when one considers the description given of Angleton in 1980: 'If John le Carré and Graham Greene had collaborated on a superspy, the result might have been James Jesus Angleton.') Among the forty or so CIA officers who Angleton focused his suspicions upon was Richard Kovich (born Dushan Kovacevich) whose career was ruined by Angleton's actions – despite placing bugs in Kovich's home and finding nothing, Angleton still sought to prevent his promotion. After Angleton's enforced retirement, CIA analysts spent three years going through the papers he had compiled – he refused to allow his material to be computerised, or otherwise indexed – and found not one shred of hard evidence to back up his notion that there was a mole.

Angleton's suspicions extended to personnel in other countries' intelligence agencies as well. Welsh-born agent Leslie James ('Jim') Bennett had served in British intelligence in Istanbul alongside Kim Philby, as well as Melbourne, Australia, before heading to Canada, eventually becoming deputy chief of the counter-espionage branch of the RCMP. Although Bennett's service record wasn't particularly outstanding – he suffered various setbacks that he ascribed in part to the KGB having a spy within the RCMP – he was invited to be part of the team debriefing Golitsyn. However, when he started to disagree with Angleton, the CIA chief opened a file on him, with allegations mounting to such a level that Bennett had to resign in July 1972. After Angleton's departure from the CIA, no evidence was found against Bennett. Vitaly Yurchenko, a later defector, confirmed that the KGB spy had been Giles G. Brunet, not Bennett.

Much as Angleton's behaviour upset those he worked with – although his counter-intelligence section continued to provide the goods, which meant that successive DCIs backed him – the public revelation of two operations that his department carried out brought his career to an end, and contributed to the bad odour with which the Agency became surrounded in the mid-seventies.

An operation had begun in 1952 in an effort to see if Soviet agents were communicating with the USSR via the US mail, and whether there might be any Soviets writing to American citizens who could become potential assets for the CIA. Originally only copying addresses from envelopes, in 1955 the operation was renamed HTLINGUAL and the letters within the envelopes were opened – in contravention of American law, although some of the Postmasters General over the two decades were informed of the operation by the CIA. The FBI had been a party to HTLINGUAL initially, although they stopped taking an active role in 1966. A similar operation, code-named CHAOS, began in 1967 in response to President Johnson's desire to know if the anti-Vietnam War movement was being used by the Communists.

While Angleton and his counter-intelligence team regarded this work as 'foreign surveillance', the cold reality was that the post opened was travelling to and from American citizens. The CIA did not have a remit to operate domestically within the United States – its participation in 'internal security functions' was specifically prohibited by the National Security Act. Incoming DCI James Schlesinger shut CHAOS down when he learned in 1973 that it had yielded very few results; HTLINGUAL was stopped by Schlesinger's successor William Colby later that year. When *New York Times* journalist Seymour Hersh warned that he was investigating the projects in 1974, Angleton's time at the Agency was drawing to a close, and he finally retired, very reluctantly, in 1975.

Suspicions about the CIA's activities domestically had been circulating even before Hersh's warning. Howard H. Baker Jr., the vice chairman of the Senate Watergate committee investigating the break-ins at the Watergate building in Washington DC in 1972, said at the time that the role of the CIA in the scandal was like 'animals crashing around in the forest – you can hear them but you can't see them'. On 2 August 1973 the committee was told by former DCI Richard

Helms categorically that 'The CIA had no involvement in the break-in. No involvement whatever.' The fact that five of the seven burglars had previously worked for the CIA; that four of them had been involved with the Bay of Pigs fiasco in 1961; and that the two ringleaders, James W. McCord Jr. and E. Howard Hunt, had been career CIA officers prior to their involvement with the White House would seem to suggest that the committee's questions weren't unjustified.

If the committee had been aware of all the facts, then they might well have questioned Helms further. Although it was the letter sent by James McCord to Judge Sirica in March 1973 that would eventually expose the whole operation to public scrutiny, McCord had previously written to the CIA requesting assistance and was on the verge of exposing the operation, according to *Washington Post* reporter Bob Woodward, whose articles were instrumental in the cover-up's failure. However, this letter, written in August 1972, was not passed over to the FBI investigation, on DCI Helms' instructions. Nor did Helms see fit to share Howard Hunt's request a couple of months before the Watergate burglaries to the External Employment Assistance Branch to see if a 'retiree or resignee who was accomplished at picking locks' might be available for some work on behalf of the White House. Writing in 2007, Bob Woodward referred to the CIA's role in the Watergate scandal as 'one of the murkiest parts of the story'.

The committee's final report in June 1974 suggested that Congress 'should more closely supervise the operations of the law enforcement "community"', pointing out that it had produced evidence that the White House had 'sought and achieved CIA aid' for the burglars, and 'unsuccessfully sought to involve the CIA in the Watergate cover-up'.

By 1974, questions were also being asked about the CIA's involvement in Chile. Richard Helms had been forced to step down from the CIA in late 1972 by President Nixon (partly because he refused to let the CIA be involved in an active cover-up of the Watergate scandal), but that didn't mean that he stopped being loyal to the office that he had sworn to serve or protective of the men and women who had been under his care. As well as making his categorical statements regarding Watergate, he also perjured himself when called to give evidence in public before a Congressional committee over the CIA's involvement in Chile. 'Did you try in the Central Intelligence Agency to overthrow the government in Chile?' Senator Symington asked Helms. Unhesitatingly, the former DCI replied, 'No, sir.'

This was completely untrue. In 1970, the Marxist leader Salvador Allende Gossens finally won the presidency of Chile, on his fourth attempt, despite the CIA passing funds to opposition parties, and advising global company International Telephone and Telegraph (ITT) how to finance the opposition. According to its own internal review in 2000, the Agency had been active in Chile since 1962, initially supporting the Christian Democratic Party, and then providing assistance to anti-Marxist groups, both financially and with propaganda. On 15 September 1970, President Nixon informed Helms that an Allende regime in Chile would not be acceptable to the United States. Authorizing a budget of $10million, Nixon instructed the CIA 'to prevent Allende from coming to power or unseat him ... without advising the Departments of State or Defence or the US Ambassador in Chile'. The Agency tried to start a coup to oust Allende, working with three separate groups of plotters, before the Chilean Congress reaffirmed his victory. One group had 'extremist tendencies' so were dropped; military hardware was supplied to the second; the third, led by retired General Roberto Viaux tried to kidnap Army Commander in Chief René Schneider, but mortally wounded him. The CIA had already withdrawn their support by this stage and didn't proceed further following the strong reaction to Schneider's death.

On his departure from the CIA, Helms was appointed Ambassador to Iran, and underwent Congressional nomination hearings by the Senate Foreign Relations Committee. In both 1973 and 1975 he point blank denied that the CIA were involved in Chile. 'If the Agency had really gotten behind the other candidates and spent a lot of money and so forth, the election might have come out differently,' he said at the earlier hearing, although in 1975 he admitted that he might have made a mistake but pointed out that Allende was still in power at the time 'and we did not need any more diplomatic incidents or any more difficulties'.

Only a few months later, Allende would be gone, the victim of a coup by General Pinochet that took place in September 1973. Unlike similar operations in other countries, this wasn't orchestrated by the CIA, although even the Agency admits that 'because [the] CIA did not discourage the takeover and had sought to instigate a coup in 1970 [it] probably appeared to condone it'. Rather than accept an offer of safe passage, Allende stood his ground in the presidential palace, and, as a forensic report in 2011 showed, he committed suicide with an AK-47 given him by Fidel Castro.

When it became clear that Helms had lied to Congress, it seemed as if he was part of yet another cover-up by an associate of disgraced President Nixon. However, as far as Helms was concerned, 'I found myself in a position of conflict,' he told a court in November 1977, when pleading guilty to a charge of perjury. 'I had sworn my oath to protect certain secrets. I didn't want to lie. I didn't want to mislead the Senate. I was simply trying to find my way through a very difficult situation in which I found myself.' Passing sentence, Judge Barrington D. Parker said, 'If public officials embark deliberately on a course to disobey and ignore the laws of our land because of some misguided and ill-conceived notion and belief that there are earlier commitments and considerations which they must observe, the future of our country is in jeopardy ... You stand before this court in disgrace and shame.' As far as Helms was concerned, 'I don't feel disgraced at all. I think if I had done anything else I would have been disgraced.' His $2,000 fine was paid by CIA officers.

By the time Helms was facing the perjury charge, the tide in America had turned very definitely against the intelligence services. Seymour Hersh's article, 'Huge C.I.A. Operation Reported in U.S. Against Antiwar Forces, Other Dissidents in Nixon Years', appeared on the front page of the *New York Times* on December 22, 1974, and revealed the existence of a set of internal CIA documents called the Family Jewels. According to the compiler, future CIA DCI William Colby, these consisted of '693 pages of possible violations of, or at least questionable activities in regard to, the C.I.A.'s legislative charter'; that among the contents were 'bizarre and tragic cases wherein the Agency experimented with mind-control drugs'; and that accompanying them was 'a separate and even more secret annex' that 'summarized a 1967 survey of [the] C.I.A.'s involvement in assassination attempts or plans against Castro, Lumumba and [Dominican Republic dictator Rafael Leónidas] Trujillo [who was in fact killed by his officers of his own army]'. Certainly that material is in there, but the majority of the documents chronicle times where the CIA may have been acting outside their remit domestically – for example, in assisting a suburban Washington police department. The device they supplied may have helped prevent a policeman's death, but they shouldn't have been involved.

The article was yet another attack on the Agency, and prompted the formation of both a commission headed by Vice President Nelson Rockefeller and the United States Senate Select Committee to Study Governmental Operations with Respect to Intelligence Activities – chaired by Senator Frank Church, and known as the Church Committee. The headings of the latter's final report give an indication of the concerns it threw up: '(A) Violating and Ignoring the Law (B) Overbreadth of Domestic Intelligence Activity (C) Excessive Use of Intrusive Techniques (D) Using Covert Action to Disrupt and Discredit Domestic Groups (E) Political Abuse of Intelligence Information (F) Inadequate Controls on Dissemination and Retention (G) Deficiencies in Control and Accountability.'

While there were concerns that Senator Church was using the Committee to further his own political ends, it undeniably threw light on the CIA – as well as the FBI and the NSA – which the Agency didn't want. For example, at the first televised hearing, Church displayed a CIA poison-dart gun as a way of illustrating the committee's discovery that the CIA had directly violated a presidential order by maintaining stocks of shellfish toxin. Over the months it took evidence, many previously hidden CIA operations came to light – from the drug experiments of MKULTRA to the assassination plans against Castro and Patrice Lumumba; from the financial assistance for political parties in foreign countries to the support of indigenous populations during time of war.

Helms had been replaced as DCI by James Schlesinger, but Nixon soon tapped him to serve as Secretary of Defence. The attitude of his successor William Colby, was to reveal what needed to be revealed and create a working relationship with those who had been set up to monitor and investigate them. Unfortunately, there were those on all the various committees set up – as well as the Rockefeller Commission and the Church Committee, there was also the Pike Committee set up by the House of Representatives – who were determined to bring the various agencies to heel, and the hearings became power plays between the committee members, the CIA and even, at times, the White House.

Chairman Otis Pike did come out of the hearings with an improved respect for the CIA:

We did find evidence, upon evidence, upon evidence where the CIA said: 'No, don't do it.' The State Department or the White House said, 'We're going to do it.' The CIA was much more professional and had a far deeper reading on the down-the-road implications of some immediately popular act than the executive branch or administration officials. One thing I really disagreed with Church on was his characterization of the CIA as a 'rogue elephant.' The CIA never did anything the White House didn't want. Sometimes they didn't want to do what they did.

Colby was certain about the effect that the work of the various committees was having on the CIA: 'These last two months have placed American intelligence in danger,' he said in May 1975. 'The almost hysterical excitement surrounding any news story mentioning CIA or referring even to a perfectly legitimate activity of CIA has raised a question whether secret intelligence operations can be conducted by the United States.'

The end result of the various committees was that the CIA came under increased government scrutiny, not just operationally but also in terms of its budget. Its days of plausible deniability and acting at one remove from the president were gone. Thirty years after its creation, with a new DCI, future US President George H.W. Bush, the CIA was forced into a new role.

In addition to the openness being imposed on it by demands from the oversight committees, the CIA also had to deal with information being revealed publicly by one of their own former officers. Philip Agee, who had left the Agency in 1969, published *Inside the Company: CIA Diary*, an exposé of CIA practices, in Britain in January 1975. Supported by the KGB, it named 200 officers worldwide, and accused the CIA of corrupt practices: 'In the CIA we justified our penetration, disruption and sabotage of the left in Latin America – around the world for that matter – because we felt morality changed on crossing national frontiers,' Agee wrote. He added to his revelations in the extreme left-wing magazine *Counterspy* – and as a direct result, Richard S. Welch, the CIA station chief in Athens, was murdered in December 1975.

Agee willingly passed information to the KGB, who in return gave him more material: his books *Dirty Work: The CIA in Western Europe* and *Dirty Work: The CIA in Africa*, blowing the cover of a further 2,000 agents, were supplemented by the *Covert Action Information Bulletin*, which was able to publish secret CIA documents.

In 1980 the US Senate Intelligence Committee, set up in the wake of the Church and Pike committees, revealed how damaging Agee had been to the CIA. This led to the Intelligence Identities Protection Act (known as the 'anti-Agee' bill), which made it a federal crime to intentionally reveal the identity of a covert intelligence agent. (One of those who voted against the act was Barack Obama's vice-president, Joe Biden.) This curtailed Agee's activities considerably.

The general dismay within the Western intelligence world was not alleviated by the discovery of Gunther Guillaume at the heart of the West German government. The self-described 'partisan for peace' had become one of chancellor Willy Brandt's most trusted aides following the 1972 election. Even though Guillaume came briefly under suspicion the following year, the charges weren't taken seriously, particularly by Brandt, who later admitted he had overestimated his knowledge of human nature. Guillaume was able to pass over material sent to Brandt by President Nixon, as well as the many pieces of confidential NATO documentation that passed through the office. However, the West German counter-intelligence department was still suspicious, and in April 1974 Guillaume and his wife were arrested and admitted their guilt. Willy Brandt resigned the following month, something that the Stasi didn't really expect, or want, according to its former chief Markus Wolf. It was 'equivalent to kicking a football into our own goal' – a simile that could have applied to many other agencies' activities during that period.

9

REBUILDING

The late seventies would see both sides in the Cold War try to regain the ground that had been lost in the earlier part of the decade. New ideas were tried out, new agents recruited – although the KGB noted that it was much harder to gain ideological recruits during this time. The majority of agents were motivated by money.

One of the more unusual Soviet plans sought to gain intelligence on American military capabilities, but was derailed by the CIA's Operation Silicon Valley. Unlike the KGB scheme to ruin the area as seen in the 1985 James Bond movie, *A View to a Kill* (in which Soviet agent Max Zorin attempted to flood Silicon Valley), this was espionage by stealth.

Described by the CIA later as 'part of . . . a broad Soviet effort to acquire Western technology for military and commercial purposes', the Soviet plan, developed in 1973, was to buy banks that were financing developments in Silicon Valley, the heartland of American technological progress, and thereby gain access to their secrets. Three banks were targeted to be approached by their intermediary, apparently wealthy Hong Kong businessman Amos Dawe: the Peninsula National Bank in Burlingame, the First National Bank of Fresno, and the Tahoe National Bank in South Lake Tahoe. At the same time, Dawe's associate Y.T. Chou was trying to gain a half-interest in the Camino California bank in San Francisco.

The manager of the Singapore branch of the Moscow Narodny bank offered to finance Dawe's future plans if he would travel to the States to make the purchases. The KGB hoped to eventually gain control of twenty separate institutions, each worth around $100 million. The genius of the plan was that such a takeover wasn't illegal at the time under American law – once the sale had taken place, Dawe could appoint whosoever he wished to be his representative on the board. And, of course, that would have been a KGB agent.

A $1.8 million first down payment on the triple transaction was made before an astute agent at the CIA noticed a peculiar lending pattern by the Narodny branch: money was going from Singapore to the Pacific Atlantic Bank in Panama, to the Commerce Union Bank in Nashville, Tennessee, and, finally, by letters of credit, to Dawe in San Francisco. Rather than simply expose Dawe's actions, the CIA set up Operation Silicon Valley; in October 1975, the Agency leaked their information to the publisher of the Hong Kong financial newsletter, *Target*. As soon as the story was published, the Narodny bank withdrew its funds, leaving Dawe vulnerable and broke – and then the Soviets even tried to sue him for the return of the monies already supplied. Contrary to some reports, Dawe was eventually convicted of fraud in Hong Kong, and sentenced in 1985 to five years' imprisonment, serving only half. He disappeared after his release and his Hong Kong company was compulsorily wound up in 2009.

Similarly motivated by greed was one half of a pair of spies who would gain notoriety under their code names, the Falcon and the Snowman, particularly after a film of their exploits was made starring Timothy Hutton and Sean Penn as the eponymous KGB assets. Although the film was a fictionalized version of events, based on a book by journalist Robert Lindsey, many spy histories have treated it as a documentary.

'The Falcon' was Christopher John Boyce, who had taken up falconry as a hobby as a youngster; 'the Snowman' was Andrew Daulton Lee, whose nickname derived from his drug-dealing activities. While it was Boyce who found himself in a position to benefit the KGB, Lee was the one who walked into the Soviet embassy in Mexico City in April 1975 offering the secrets. The two had known each other since they were boys; Lee had drifted into drug-dealing while Boyce had been able to find a job working at the TRW Corporation in Redondo Beach, California. TRW had been at the forefront of development of America's first Inter-Continental Ballistic Missiles, as well as the Pioneer spacecraft for NASA. At the time Boyce was employed there, they operated the satellites in the Defence Support Program, and Boyce worked in the ultra-secret 'black vault' room, which housed the coding equipment for the CIA, his job being to change the ciphers daily.

Boyce accordingly had access to some of the most secret material in America, including details of the Rhyolite satellite and its planned successor, Argus, an essential part of the surveillance of both the Soviet and Communist Chinese. He would also see other 'chatter', including information regarding the CIA's alleged role in influencing the Australian labour unions against the then-prime minister Gough Whitlam. He therefore proposed to Lee that he would copy material which Lee could then take to the Soviets and sell – although Boyce would maintain that his primary purpose for his treason was his disgust at American behaviour: 'I have no problems with the label traitor, if you qualify what it's to,' he told an Australian reporter in 1982. 'I think that eventually the United States government is going to involve the world in the next world war. And being a traitor to that, I have absolutely no problems with that whatsoever.'

Although appalled at the lack of sense demonstrated by Lee in coming direct to the highly watched embassy in Mexico, the KGB realized that they had access to prime material. Over the next eighteen months they not only provided Lee and Boyce with around $77,000 for their efforts (of which Boyce only received around $20,000), but also trained Lee in basic tradecraft. Unfortunately, Lee's drug use increased with his available spending money, and he became more and more careless.

Boyce eventually travelled with Lee to Mexico, where their KGB handler proposed that Boyce leave TKW and go back to college, with a view to becoming a longer-term agent working for Moscow Centre. Boyce agreed to do one final job – photographing the technical drawings for TRW's new satellite, the Pyramider. This would net a further $75,000.

Lee missed his rendezvous with the KGB on 5 January 1977, and, in total breach of all tradecraft and common sense once more, threw a package containing the negatives of the designs into the Soviet embassy grounds the next day. He was instantly arrested by the Mexican police, and the films were developed. Lee eventually admitted he was a spy, but claimed he was working on a disinformation operation for the CIA.

Boyce was arrested a few days later. The two men were tried separately; Boyce claimed that the material on Pyramider had been over-classified, since the project didn't go ahead, and that Lee had blackmailed him into continuing with the treachery. He was found guilty and sentenced to forty years' imprisonment. He would later escape and go on the run, allegedly planning to fly from Alaska into the Soviet Union, but he was recaptured before he could try. Lee's lawyers maintained his story that he was part of a CIA disinformation plan, and that both he and Boyce had been abandoned by the Agency when they got into trouble. Lee was sentenced to life imprisonment.

* * *

As in Britain, during the seventies the KGB concentrated on scientific and technical espionage against the country they regarded as 'The Main Adversary' – the United States. Their attempts to penetrate the inner circles of the Nixon and Ford administrations met with little success, although Secretary of State Henry Kissinger was one of many policymakers to grant favoured access to Soviet ambassador Anatoli Dobrynin, much to the annoyance of the KGB, who wanted to cultivate their own 'back door' to the power players in Washington. They had slightly more luck with the United Nations, with KGB agents becoming personal assistants to the secretaries-general from U Thant to Javier Pérez de Cuéllar. However they had to admit in 1974 that 'For a number of years the Residency has not been able to create an agent network capable of fulfilling the complex requirements of our intelligence work, especially against the US.' When Jimmy Carter became president in 1977, attempts were made to capitalize on previous friendly relationships between Soviet officers and Secretary of State, Cyrus Vance, and National Security Advisor, Zbigniew Brzezinski. Neither succeeded. Valdik Enger and Rudolf Chernyaev, two KGB agents at the UN, were arrested by the FBI in May 1978 after accepting classified information about anti-submarine warfare from a US naval officer who was actually working for the FBI and the Naval Investigative Service (the forerunner of the NCIS, as featured in the popular TV show).

The KGB were far more successful recruiting scientists. The Falcon and the Snowman weren't the only TRW employees engaged by the KGB – a scientist, code-named Zenit, was recruited a year after Boyce's arrest. There were agents at IBM and McDonnell Douglas, and researchers at MIT, the Argonne National Laboratory and the US Army's Material Development and Readiness Command. Some of these agents were approached on a personal level by Soviet colleagues in the same field; others worked purely for cash.

Inevitably, some were caught. Dalibar Valoushek, a Czech border guard, had been placed under cover in Canada in 1957, and ten years later become the controller for the KGB's most important Canadian agent, Hugh Hambleton, whose access to research projects made him an ideal spy. However a year later, Valoushek was moved to New York and ordered to infiltrate the think tank, the Hudson Institute. When this proved unfeasible, Valoushek was removed from the assignment. In 1972, he told his son Peter of his double life, and recruited him into the KGB; Peter was trained in Moscow and sent to McGill University in Montreal and later Georgetown University, looking for students whose parents had government jobs, or other likely recruits. However in May 1977, Valoushek senior was arrested and turned by the FBI.

According to KGB files, for the next two years, Dalibar Valoushek tried to inform Moscow Centre that he was now a double, but no one took any notice. The FBI tried to use him to put pressure on Hambleton in 1980, but the latter was confident that he could not be arrested. 'A spy is someone who regularly gets secret material, passes it on, takes orders, and gets paid for it,' he said at the time. 'I have never been paid.' The RCMP and the Canadian Ministry of Justice tried to bring charges, but found insufficient evidence. Hambleton was eventually arrested when visiting London in 1982.

Three key KGB agents provided material throughout the seventies: two in the US, one in Europe. John Anthony Walker, Karl Koecher and George Trofimov were all busy during this period, passing classified information often in exchange for large sums of cash.

Walker had volunteered his services to the Soviets in 1967 when he was working in the communications room for the US Navy's submarine operations in Norfolk, Virginia: 'I'm a naval officer,' he told staff at the Soviet embassy in Washington. 'I'd like to make some money and I'll give you some genuine stuff in return.' The first item he stole was a key list for an old cryptographic machine – which, it was later suggested, led directly to the North Koreans' desire to capture the US spy ship, the USS *Pueblo*, a month later – and from there on photographed multiple documents, claiming sarcastically that 'K Mart has better security than the Navy'. Although Walker retired from the Navy in 1976, he had already recruited his friend Jerry Whitworth, and later brought in his own son and elder brother so that the work could continue.

Karl Koecher and his wife Hana, meanwhile, were actively working for the KGB from within the CIA. The pair were originally Czech StB agents sent across as illegals in 1965; they had broken off contact with the StB in 1970, but tried to build bridges with their former employers in 1974, a year after Karl had begun working in the CIA's Soviet division. This brought them to the attention of the Soviets, who took over their case. Highly sexually active (and apparently with all the allure of Mike Myers' spoof spy Austin Powers – 'a terrible lover' according to one report), Koecher was able to pass on compromising information on Washington officials, as well as classified Soviet and Czech material. Koecher went freelance in 1975 but continued to supply the KGB, passing on information that would compromise the CIA's Moscow asset Aleksandr Ogorodnik in 1977.

George Trofimov was a retired US Army colonel based in Germany as a civilian who in 1969 became Chief of the United States Army Element at the Nuremberg Joint Interrogation Centre, giving him access to very high levels of documents. He was recruited to the KGB by his boyhood friend, Igor Vladimirovich Susemihl, a bishop in the Russian Orthodox Church. This wasn't as unusual as it might sound: the KGB often used the church and its officials within its schemes. Throughout the seventies and eighties – and until his retirement in 1995 – Trofimov sent material to Moscow via

Susemihl, who continued to rise within the Orthodox Church, eventually achieving high rank as the Metropolitan of Vienna.

West Germany was a useful source of information for the Soviets. The 'secretaries initiative' continued to reap dividends. Margret Hîke passed on information from the office of the West German president from 1968 throughout the seventies, in exchange for 500 marks a month and expenses. Using a camera disguised as a tube of lipstick, she gave the KGB ten volumes of documents between 1968 and 1980, including mobilization plans, details on the government war bunker, and accounts of the president's meetings with foreign diplomats.

Heidrun Hofer, a secretary in the BND, was seduced by an East German illegal who claimed to be part of a neo-Nazi group of German patriots; she continued to spy even after deducing she was working for the KGB. She was arrested in 1977 and tried to commit suicide when her unsuspecting BND fiancé broke off their engagement as a result of her confession.

Elke Falk was equipped with a camera disguised as a cigarette lighter and a fake can of hairspray to put her films in. Working initially in the West German chancellor's office after her recruitment in 1974, she was transferred to the transport ministry in 1977 and then to the economic aid ministry two years later.

In France, the KGB's longest-serving agent, 'Jour', continued to impress, singled out for a large bonus personally approved by KGB chief Andropov between 1973–75. The cipher clerk at the Foreign Ministry was recruited by the Soviets at the end of the Second World War and allowed Moscow to read French SIGINT, including their discussions with their embassies during the Cuban Missile Crisis. New teleprinters installed in the French Embassy in Moscow over the winter of 1976 were bugged thanks to his information, and he continued to assist with recruiting new agents right to the end of his thirty-seven year career as a Soviet spy.

The Italian Embassy in Moscow was one of the KGB's key targets, and 'swallows' were used to honey trap key employees. Some of these, including a senior diplomat code-named both Artur and Arlekino, were then used as spies within Italy itself. The KGB also targeted scientific personnel, with code name Uchitel ('Teacher') able to pass valuable intelligence on military aircraft, helicopters and guidance systems, including information on the new Tornado plane being jointly developed by Germany, Italy and Great Britain.

One of the KGB's more successful agents travelled around Europe using seduction and romance as a weapon to gain information from unsuspecting targets. Ex-Metropolitan Police Detective Sergeant John Symonds had gone on the run in 1972 while awaiting trial at the Old Bailey on charges of corruption, and had approached the KGB via the Soviet embassy in Rabat. 'I was taught how to be a better lover,' he told the BBC in 1999. 'Perhaps I wasn't a very good one before, I don't know. But it was very pleasant. I was taught by two extremely beautiful girls. That was quite an interesting part.' After this training, he was sent to Bulgaria where he seduced the wife of a West German official; Africa, where he targeted women at the American and British missions; Moscow, India, Singapore, and Australia. Eventually when he could no longer turn his good looks to his advantage, he decided to surrender to British justice. He made no mention of his espionage activities, and was simply charged with corruptly taking £150 from a London criminal. Although he later tried to persuade the British authorities of his KGB work, he wasn't believed and his spying activities only came to light when Vasili Mitrokhin passed over his material from the KGB archives in 1992. However by then, he had been given immunity from prosecution in return for giving evidence in other cases. As of this writing, a movie based on his exploits is in pre-production.

*   *   *

Although the official policy of the KGB since the early sixties had been to use assassination sparingly as a weapon, there were times that it was deemed necessary. Moscow Centre assisted the Bulgarian secret service, the Duzhavna Sigurnost, with the murder of a particularly troubling dissident intellectual, Georgi Markov. The assassination has entered into folklore for its method: Markov was stabbed with poison concealed within the tip of an umbrella.

Earlier in his career, Markov had been a protégé of the Bulgarian President, Todor Zhivkov, but he had defected to Britain in 1969. Working for the BBC World Service, Radio Free Europe and German station Deutsche Welle, Markov verbally attacked Zhivkov. In early 1978, the head of the DS, General Dimitar Stoyanov, requested help from Moscow, and reluctantly KGB chief Yuri Andropov agreed that the KGB would provide the means for the assassination, but not the agent to carry it out. 'Give the Bulgarians whatever they need, show them how to use it and send someone to Sofia to train their people. But that is all,' he ordered the Operational Technical Directorate.

Rather than use a poisoned jelly rubbed on Markov's skin (which was tried unsuccessfully on another émigré), or a poison within his food, the KGB scientists decided to use a small ball containing ricin, which was derived from castor plant seeds. They created a pellet and inserted it in the tip of a specially modified umbrella – bought by the KGB residency in Washington, its American origins designed to place the Soviets one step further removed from the operation – and given to the agent chosen. Although there is some question over this, it is generally believed that Francesco Giullino, a Dane of Italian extraction who had been recruited as an agent in 1970, was responsible.

On 7 September 1978, as he was waiting at a bus stop on Waterloo Bridge in London to head to the BBC radio headquarters, Bush House, Markov felt a sting in his thigh.

Turning, he saw a stranger pick up an umbrella he had apparently dropped, then get in a taxi. That night Markov fell dangerously ill, and he died in hospital on 11 September.

A post-mortem examination by scientists at the Chemical Defence Establishment at Porton Down discovered the metal pellet that had contained the poison, but none had survived contact with Markov's blood stream. A process of elimination resulted in the deduction that ricin had been involved, based on the symptoms Markov presented and the toxicity of the tiny dose that the pellet would have contained. Another émigré, Vladmir Kostov, had been similarly attacked in Paris, but the pellet had failed to release the ricin.

Reeling from the effects of the various Congressional committees, the CIA underwent a period of retrenchment and reorganization in the late seventies. It was under considerably more scrutiny than previously. A new broom was required, and, as the CIA's own description of William Colby's replacement George H.W. Bush points out, 'Having as DCI a politically skilled leader who had served in Congress fit the unprecedented circumstances of the moment.'

Future president Bush senior was appointed as DCI in November 1975, and served until the arrival of the Carter administration in January 1977. Bush was not a career spy: 'I walked in [to the CIA in 1975] untutored in the arts of intelligence,' he recalled when opening the George Bush Center for Intelligence in 1999. 'You had every reason to be suspicious of this untutored outsider who had, though he came out of a non-political post in China, spent a lot of my time in partisan politics. I understood the anxiety and concerns on Capitol Hill about that. But this Agency gave me their trust from Day One.'

President Ford issued new executive orders that created a new command structure for foreign intelligence-gathering and was described by the White House as 'the first major reorganisation of the Intelligence Community since 1947'. He also imposed a specific ban on assassinations. A new Senate Select Committee on Intelligence was established, followed by a House committee during President Carter's tenure.

However, the new president brought in Admiral Stansfield Turner as DCI, who proved to be a divisive head, emphasizing technical intelligence and SIGINT over agents in the field. The 'Halloween massacre' in which 820 CIA employees were given notice was Turner's way of continuing the house clearing that had actually begun under James Schlesinger back in 1973, but this was far more drastic. Described as insensitive by some Agency observers, this saw 147 career officers take early retirement, seventeen sacked, and most of those who had served since the OSS days and the institution of the CIA in 1947 removed. Turner himself would come to regret the action: 'In retrospect, I probably should not have effected the reductions of 820 positions at all, and certainly not the last 17,' he wrote in 2005.

Although analysts and electronic intelligence would form the backbone of Turner's plans for the Agency, the CIA still used and needed spies. Dimitri Polyakov continued to be a highly effective asset for the Agency within the GRU until 1980, despite his cover being blown by traitorous FBI agent Robert Hanssen a year earlier when he first made contact with Soviet intelligence; the GRU simply refused to believe that such a high-ranking officer would commit treason. When Polyakov realized he was being investigated, he chose, albeit reluctantly, to retire.

Another recruit, Alexsandr Ogorodnik, would turn out to be one of the CIA's most useful agents within the Soviet Union itself, while the identity of his handler in Moscow would surprise many working for the KGB.

Ogorodnik was recruited while stationed in the Soviet Ministry for Foreign Affairs in Bogotá, Colombia, in 1973.

His dislike of the Soviet system, combined with a taste for the high life, as well as complications with his local mistress, made him a good choice as a spy. Rapidly trained in tradecraft before his recall to Moscow, Ogorodnik was provided with the latest in miniature cameras, the T-50. This was only an inch and a half long and three-eighths of an inch in diameter, and could shoot up to fifty exposures on its fifteen-inch film. Ogorodnik, now code-named Trigon, was given the camera within an expensive-looking pen, supplied to the CIA by a leading manufacturer working under secret contract.

Trigon's first assignment occurred while he was still in Bogotá, photographing a Soviet policy paper on China – the first time that a CIA agent had ever been able to do this within a Soviet residency. According to then-Secretary of State Henry Kissinger, it was 'the most important piece of intelligence he had read' while in office.

Ogorodnik was recalled to Moscow in 1975, and insisted on receiving a suicide pill from the CIA before he left. This was reluctantly agreed to by senior officials at Langley and concealed within another pen. Once back in the Soviet Union, Ogorodnik was subject to the usual scrutiny that any returning diplomat received from the KGB, but once this had become less rigorous, he began working for the CIA once more.

His handler was Martha D. Peterson, who became known as 'The Widow Spy', the first female CIA case officer ever posted to Moscow. The KGB used very few women as spies – they were useful as bait for honey traps or if they were already in position as secretaries with access to confidential material, but at various times there were specific prohibitions within the KGB against their recruitment as agents – so didn't consider that Peterson could be there as a CIA handler.

In spring 1977, communications between Peterson and Trigon broke down, and the Soviet failed to respond to a request for a meeting. However, there was a reply to an alternate signal, which indicated that Trigon would collect a package at a predetermined spot. On 15 July, Peterson headed to the Krasno Gluhovsky Bridge crossing the Moskva River and filled the dead drop with material for Trigon. As she left, she was arrested and taken to the Lubyanka for questioning. After a short time, she was released because of her diplomatic immunity, declared persona non grata and thrown out of the country.

Trigon was already dead. Karl Koecher had seen documents that indicated that a Soviet diplomat was working for the CIA, and informed the KGB. They had carried out a lengthy investigation, and eventually arrested Ogorodnik. He agreed to write a confession, but asked to use his own pen, as the interrogator's was too clumsy. Swiftly he removed the capsule, and was able to kill himself before the guard in the interrogation room could stop him.

MI6 were also running an agent within the Soviet Union by this stage. Oleg Gordievsky, whose files on the KGB would prove to be a treasure trove of information when he eventually defected, signed up in 1974. Embittered by the actions of the KGB during the Prague Spring in 1968, he noted in his autobiography that 'Until the early 1970s I clung to the hope that the Soviet Union might still reject the Communist yoke and progress to freedom and democracy.' He told the BBC in 2009, 'I was approached by MI6 but in a way I provoked that approach. I realised slowly that this was a state that was worse than Hitler's Germany.' Gordievsky was stationed in Denmark at the time and would become as useful to the West as Oleg Penkovsky had been in the previous decade – particularly when he was posted to London as the KGB resident in 1982.

The CIA and FBI ran an agent jointly based at the United Nations for over two years. Arkady Shevchenko was a senior Soviet diplomat who had risen to Under Secretary-General at the United Nations for Political and Security Council Affairs.

He had been seduced by the glamour of the West during his first posting to New York in 1958 but when he contacted the CIA in 1975 aiming to defect, he was persuaded to remain in position and act as a spy. Over the next three years, he passed over details of Soviet policy on every major issue, and as a lifelong specialist in arms control, he was able to provide key insight into Soviet negotiating strategy for the disarmament talks that were carried out by President Carter and Premier Brezhnev. Understanding the import of a summons back to Moscow in March 1978 for consultations and 'discussion of certain other questions', he was extracted by the CIA. During his debriefing he learned that his wife had been repatriated to Russia and had died in Moscow – he remained convinced until his death twenty years later that the KGB killed her.

The NSA had a notable success throughout the seventies with Operation Ivy Bells, a joint project between the agency and the US Navy. This was another cable-tapping similar to the operations in Vienna and Berlin during the fifties. However, rather than digging a tunnel beneath the roads of a busy metropolis, a pod was placed beneath the surface of the Sea of Okhotsk, between the Kamchatka Peninsula and Siberia, tapping into the cables that carried unencrypted traffic between the submarine base at Petropavlovsk to Soviet Pacific Fleet headquarters in Vladivostock. The operation came to a sudden halt in 1981 when a Soviet navy salvage ship lifted the pod off the seafloor, thanks to the information supplied by a former NSA operative, Ronald Pelton.

In 1974, Harold Wilson returned to 10 Downing Street as Prime Minister, and during the two years before he stepped down in April 1976, seemed to believe that he was the target of an operation by members of MI5. Although the idea was comprehensively dismissed at the time by his successor James Callaghan, the notion of the 'Wilson plot' gained some credence a decade later with the publication in 1987 of former MI5 officer Peter Wright's memoir, *Spycatcher* (although the credibility of that was itself knocked a year later by Wright himself).

'Is that man mad? He did nothing but complain about being spied on!' CIA Director George H.W. Bush said of Wilson after a meeting during the last few weeks of the prime minister's term of office. Wilson certainly was demonstrating paranoid tendencies during this time, seeing conspiracies against himself everywhere. According to MI5's official history these simply didn't exist. The Security Service were certainly concerned about some of Wilson's contacts – notably Joseph (later Lord) Kagan, who was actively being groomed by KGB officers prior to the mass expulsion of Soviet spies in 1971, and Rudy Sternberg, later Lord Plurenden, who many believed was a spy, although there was no concrete proof against him. MI5 of course had a file on Wilson, but this could only be accessed with permission from the Director-General of the Service, Sir Michael Hanley.

Part of Wilson's mistrust of MI5 stemmed from his discovery of the Fluency Committee's investigations of Sir Roger Hollis during the sixties, something of which he wasn't aware at the time, but felt with hindsight he should have been. The prime minister's relationship with Hanley deteriorated to such an extent that the Director-General considered resigning. By December 1975, Wilson's official biography notes that he was convinced there was a plot and he was 'reasonably certain that elements of MI5 were doing the donkey work, though at what level he did not know', and he began turning on all the taps in the lavatory before saying anything in there.

Things weren't improved when George Young, the former Deputy Chief of MI6, announced in March 1976 that three of Wilson's ministers were crypto-Communists, and it's possible that after Wilson was briefed about Young's right-wing connections, and links to journalist Chapman Pincher, he got his services confused and discussed a plot to discredit him by 'a very small MI5 mafia who had been out of the Service for some time who still continue their vendetta for no doubt very right wing purposes of their own'.

Wilson continued to protest he had been the subject of a conspiracy after his resignation, and cooperated with two journalists, Barrie Penrose and Roger Courtiour, preparing a story that they printed in the *Observer* newspaper, which attacked MI5, and included the fact that Wilson had turned to the head of the CIA for help investigating the plot against him. Prime Minister James Callaghan instituted an internal inquiry, then reported to the House of Commons that it was clear there was nothing to the allegations.

This might have been seen as nothing more than the early onset of the illness that would torment Wilson during his retirement had it not been for Peter Wright's book, in which it was claimed that thirty MI5 officers had given their approval to a plot against Wilson. Again, this was investigated, and then Prime Minister Margaret Thatcher categorically denied the allegations: 'No evidence or indication has been found of any plot or conspiracy against Lord Wilson by or within the Security Service.'

Talking on documentary programme *Panorama* in October 1988, Wright admitted that in fact there was probably only one other member of MI5 who wanted to get rid of Wilson, and that his book was 'unreliable'. However, that didn't get anything like the publicity of the *Observer* article, and there are still many who believe MI5 were actively plotting – the book and TV series *A Very British Coup* suggest how such a plot might have played out.

Faith in its country's security service was also lacking during this time in Australia, with the head of the Australian Secret Intelligence Service (ASIS), William T. Robertson, forced to resign over the use of an Australian agent in East Timor's affairs in 1975. ASIS had been established in 1952 as a collector of foreign intelligence, primarily in the Asian-Pacific region, and like MI6 in Britain, it did not officially exist. During the sixties and early seventies it monitored Communist groups and paramilitary groups in Indonesia.

In the build-up to Indonesia's invasion of East Timor in 1975, ASIS employed local businessman Frank Favaro to supply information on local political developments. However, he was quite unstable and in September 1975, ASIS fired him. Favaro wanted more money for the work he had done, and wrote to the Australian prime minister, Gough Whitlam, and the Foreign Minister, Don Willessee, who stated in Parliament that Favaro was a private citizen who didn't represent the Australian government in any capacity. When Whitlam realized that ASIS had indeed hired Favaro and risked a charge of interfering in another country's affairs, without obtaining his authority, he demanded Robertson's resignation. When Whitlam was removed from office by the Governor General in November 1975, the new prime minister, Malcolm Fraser, claimed that the Robertson sacking was 'a powerful argument that Whitlam was not fit to govern'.

'We are bogged down in a war we cannot win and cannot abandon,' one KGB general admitted privately a few years after the invasion of Afghanistan, noting that the 1979 action had led to their equivalent of the Vietnam War. And, although it wasn't said publicly, this was the KGB's fault.

As well as spying on the 'Main Adversary', the KGB was still charged with maintaining order around the Communist countries, and it became clear during 1979 that despite a Communist coup the previous April, the regime of Hafizullah Amin was precarious. The KGB residency in Kabul predicted that an anti-Soviet Islamic Republic (similar to that which had taken power in Iran the previous year) could well replace the regime unless Amin in Afghanistan went. Despite the best efforts of Lieutenant Colonel Mikhail Talebov to poison him, Amin survived.

On Christmas Day 1979 the Soviets invaded Afghanistan, with KGB Alpha Anti-Terrorist assault commandos at their head, disguised as Afghans. In an echo of CIA actions in the sixties, they broadcast radio messages purporting to come from the government, calling for Soviet assistance. This the Soviets duly provided, creating a new regime – and the KGB helped the Afghans to set up a more organized Security Service, the Khedamat-e Etela'at-e Dawltai (KHAD) 'to protect democratic freedoms . . . as well as to neutralise . . . the plots hatched by external enemies of Afghanistan'. In practice this meant the Soviets taught their new pupils the worst excesses of torture.

The KGB had anticipated that the invasion would go like earlier such incursions in Hungary and Czechoslovakia. Like many before – and since – they underestimated the will of the Afghan people. Instead of a quick and easy operation, KGB officers would be bogged down in Afghanistan for the next decade and as a result of the invasion, relations between East and West would hit a new low. Spies on all sides of the Cold War would be affected.

10

THE EMPIRES STRIKE BACK

The first half of the eighties was a time of mounting tension. The Soviet invasion of Afghanistan had led to the US and others boycotting the Moscow Olympics in 1980, and when the former Governor of California Ronald Reagan was voted into the White House later that year, the anti-Soviet rhetoric was dialled up.

In a speech to the National Association of Evangelicals in Orlando, Florida, in March 1983, Reagan made reference to an 'evil empire ... [who] preach the supremacy of the state, declare its omnipotence over individual man and predict its eventual domination of all peoples on the Earth. They are the focus of evil in the modern world.' The Soviet news agency TASS responded that Reagan 'can think only in terms of confrontation and bellicose, lunatic anti-communism'. The militaries in both West and East were built up. At the same time as the 'evil empire' speech, Reagan authorized the Strategic Defence Initiative (SDI) (commonly known as 'Star Wars' after the George Lucas film), which the new

Soviet leader Yuri Andropov said 'put the entire world in jeopardy'.

Politically, the Soviet Union went through major changes. Leonid Brezhnev died in 1982 and was succeeded by KGB Chief Andropov – but he too would die in office, a mere two years later. Konstantin Chernenko, a crony of Brezhnev's, followed for a short time, then on his death, Mikhail Gorbachev was appointed in March 1985. Although it wasn't clear to anyone at the time, Gorbachev's policies would lead to the end of the Cold War.

The stakes were raised for the intelligence agencies on either side of the Iron Curtain, with the CIA changing course once more and increasing the amount of HUMINT (human intelligence) on which they were relying (partly caused by the blows to SIGINT abilities following Ronald Pelton's defection in 1980). However 1985 would prove to be a watershed in the espionage game, with a series of recruitments and betrayals by both sides.

Ronald Reagan appointed a new DCI when he took office: William J. Casey, who had served as chief of secret intelligence in Europe for the OSS in World War II. He was the president's campaign manager, and was the first DCI to be given a seat as a fully participating Cabinet member. He and Reagan shared a similar view of the Soviet threat, and as DCI, Casey wanted to strengthen analysis, revive covert actions in the service of foreign policy, strengthen counter-intelligence and security, and improve clandestine espionage operations. The appropriations for the CIA rose by 50 per cent in the first three budgets of the Reagan administration, and Casey presided over a resurgence in HUMINT. He also took the Agency into areas that had been deemed dangerous during the seventies, with support for anti-Communist insurgent organizations in developing countries – leading to the Iran-Contra scandal that would dominate Reagan's second term of office.

One of the great successes of Casey's period in charge of the

CIA came from Operation CKTAW. This was a wiretap on the communications lines that ran underground between the Soviet Ministry of Defence in Moscow and the Krasnaya Pakhra Nuclear Weapons Research Institute, in the closed city of Troitsk, twenty-three miles from the centre of the capital. Phone, fax and teletype material could all be accessed from the cables.

The cable-laying was spotted by a KH-11 satellite pass in 1976, and over the next two years, CIA agents in Moscow identified a manhole along the Warsaw Boulevard as the best access point. At the same time, scientists from the Agency's Office of Development and Engineering created a collar that could be placed around the cable to tap the information. By 1979, they were ready to identify which was the best cable to access with the collar, and Office of Technical Services technician Ken Seacrest was sent to Moscow to enter the manhole. This required him to elude any watchers and risk standing thigh-deep in cold water for a couple of hours beneath the manhole as he tested the different cables. Once the line from the Weapons Research Institute was identified, a permanent tap was set up, which operated successfully until the spring of 1985.

This helped to make up for the sources of SIGINT that were betrayed to the Soviets by former NSA operative Ronald Pelton when he walked into the Soviet embassy in Washington in 1980, desperately in need of money to cover his growing debts. As well as giving up details on Operation Ivy Bells, he told them about the Vortex satellites that were intercepting microwave radio-relay systems; the amount of material coming from a joint NSA-CIA listening post in the Moscow embassy, code-named Broadside; and about the seven most highly classified intelligence operations that the NSA were currently working on. He even revealed the existence of fake tree stumps containing electronic bugs which were placed by CIA operatives near Soviet military installations. Worst of all, he gave them details of every Russian cypher machine that the NSA had been able to crack – leading to the Soviets changing their systems.

CKTAW itself was revealed to the Soviets by a former CIA employee, Edward Lee Howard, who had been dismissed from the Agency in May 1983 after failing a polygraph test prior to taking up a new posting in Moscow. Unfortunately, by that stage he was already privy to a considerable amount of information about CIA activities in Russia, including CKTAW – one of the reasons for his firing was that he admitted to cheating during exercises regarding access to the manhole. That summer, he wrote to the Soviet embassy in Switzerland proposing a meeting with a KGB officer to hand over 'interesting' information. The KGB turned him down. In October that year, he considered whether to volunteer information directly to the Soviets at the Washington embassy, but ultimately decided against it. He moved to Santa Fe, New Mexico, where he became involved in a major fight and was put on probation for five years. Around the same time, the KGB reconsidered his application, and he was advised to travel to Vienna to meet a handler. Despite a probation prohibition on leaving the States, he went to Europe, where he passed on documents and information on CIA operations in September 1984 and then again in April 1985. Howard was himself betrayed by a defector from East to West, Vitaly Yurchenko that year, but he managed to evade the FBI, fleeing to Moscow, where he died in 2002.

Howard was also responsible for the end of the life of a major CIA asset in Russia, scientist Adolf Tolkachev. In an odd mirror of the career of his betrayer, Tolkachev also tried unsuccessfully to approach the other side's intelligence agencies before being taken seriously. Describing himself as a 'dissident at heart' (to the extent that at one point he discussed with the CIA the possibility of passing some of his salary from the Agency to the dissident movement in Russia), Tolkachev was a systems engineer at the Scientific Research Institute of Radio who had a top-secret clearance and decided to offer his services to the opposition. His first attempt in January 1977 – dropping a letter into an American's car – failed because by chance he had chosen the head of the CIA station in Moscow, and his offer seemed too good to be true. He tried on three more occasions, but each time he was ignored. That December he passed through a note containing some details on Soviet aircraft; that calling card proved to be effective, and in February 1978 communications were begun. A risky personal meeting between Tolkachev and CIA handler John Guilsher took place on New Year's Day 1979 and over the next eighteen months, a system was established. Tolkachev was provided with a camera and was able to supply hundreds of rolls of 35mm film to his CIA contacts, sometimes even taking documents home to photograph them when security was less stringent, other times taking the chance of filming them at his office.

Despite KGB suspicions about leaks from the Institute, Tolkachev refused to stop his activities, and his case officer noted, 'This is indeed a man who is driven to produce, by whatever means he deems necessary, right up to the end, even if that end is his death.' On more than one occasion, he had to ditch his spy equipment because the KGB seemed to be closing in, but then he would return to work as normal. In January 1985, he had his last meeting with his handlers, where he passed over what he said was information on a new Soviet fighter aircraft. The pictures were unreadable. The next meetings were abandoned because of surveillance, but on 13 June, the case officer went to the meeting, and was arrested by the KGB. Tolkachev had been in their hands since April; he was executed at some point between then and September 1986.

A memo in March 1979 to then-DCI Stansfield Turner described Tolkachev's material as 'of incalculable value'. At the time of his death, the *Washington Post* called him 'one of

[the] CIA's most valuable human assets in the Soviet Union'. Perhaps the best indication of his effectiveness as a spy is that it took five years after his death for all of the information he passed back to Langley to be fully evaluated.

Tolkachev wasn't the only spy within the KGB run by Western intelligence during this period. Code-named Farewell, Colonel Vladimir Ippolitovich Vetrov, who claimed that he hated the Soviet leadership for its 'vulgarity, corruption, brutality, unrelenting self-advancement and failure to help the Russian people', was able to supply over four thousand documents to French intelligence during the summer of 1981. This led to one of the more ingenious counter-espionage operations of the eighties.

Vetrov was a technical officer at the KGB, charged with evaluating Western technology that was obtained by Section T. The information that he passed on included the names of Soviet agents in American and European laboratories, government agencies and factories, as well as details of many other agents in place. Most helpfully for the West, it listed the technological requirements that these agents were seeking to fulfil.

French President Mitterand passed details of Vetrov to President Reagan in July 1981 and CIA DCI Casey suggested preparing faulty equipment that the Soviet agents could obtain. A cooperative effort between the CIA and the FBI led to major problems for the Soviets with the Trans-Siberian Pipeline, resulting in a huge explosion, as well as many bugs within other projects, such as stealth aircraft, space defence and tactical aircraft. Even the Soviet Space Shuttle was based on a rejected NASA design. Finally, once the fake information had been passed back to Moscow, the CIA informed the relevant governments of the agents' existence, and over two hundred were detained.

Vetrov himself was arrested in February 1982 after murdering a stranger in a Moscow park and attempting to kill his mistress, a KGB secretary. His espionage activities were discovered during the investigation, and he was executed.

Ronald Reagan wasn't the only new leader in the Western world. May 1979 saw the arrival in 10 Downing Street of Britain's first female prime minister, Margaret Thatcher. One of her earliest encounters with the spy industry came with the public revelation of Anthony Blunt's treachery. Blunt had confessed his role to MI5 in 1964, but was granted immunity from prosecution and had naively believed that he would hear no further about it. He, perhaps unwisely, tried to prevent the publication of Andrew Boyle's book *The Climate of Treason*, which detailed his activities under the pseudonym Maurice; *Private Eye* magazine revealed his legal action, and ten days later, Mrs Thatcher made a statement to the House of Commons, confirming Blunt's treachery. Literally within minutes of the announcement, Blunt's knighthood was stripped from him. He died in 1983, a year after Oleg Gordievsky had told the British that John Cairncross was the Fifth Man, although that information wouldn't become public knowledge until Gordievsky's history of the KGB was published in 1990.

Gordievsky's importance in the early eighties cannot be underestimated. He had been passing information to MI6 since 1974, while continuing to rise in the KGB. He had come very close to discovery in 1978 when Kim Philby was asked to look over a file regarding the arrest of a KGB asset in Norway, elderly secretary Gunvor Haavik, whom Gordievsky had told MI6 about while stationed in Copenhagen. Philby's reaction was that there must be a mole within the KGB, but luckily for Gordievsky the topic was not pursued.

In January 1982, a visa request was sent by the Soviets for Gordievsky to enter Britain as a 'counsellor' at the embassy – in fact, he was a senior KGB political officer at the residency. Once in Britain he was handled jointly by MI5 and MI6, and was able to pass over details of a new joint KGB-GRU operation set up by KGB chief Yuri Andropov in May 1981, code-named Ryan (derived from the Russian acronym for the phrase Nuclear Missile Attack). The Soviet Politburo fervently believed that the United States and NATO were preparing for a surprise nuclear first strike against the Soviet Union, and Operation Ryan was set up to collect intelligence on these plans. According to Gordievsky, while many residencies and KGB officers did not believe that such plans existed, they weren't willing to say as much to Moscow, so exaggerated the importance of events, which in its turn prompted requests for more information. Thatcher and Reagan's rhetoric was making the Soviets even more paranoid than they already were. The importance attached to Operation Ryan reports by the Kremlin gave Gordievsky, and thus the West, an indication of how threatened the Soviets felt at any given time.

With access to a lot of the relevant documentation regarding the London residency's operations, Gordievsky was able to provide information on current KGB agents in the UK. He noted that union leader Jack Jones, who had been regarded as an agent by the Soviets between 1964–1968, as well as MP Bob Edwards were both now regarded as of little significance. The KGB were interested in supporting peace movements, such as the Campaign for Nuclear Disarmament, and trying to gain influence over it, but MI5 operations over the next few years would demonstrate that, much as they might wish to try to run the CND, the Soviets were only really able to create a confidential contact with the 94-year-old peace activist and founder of the World Disarmament Campaign, Lord Brockway, who was in no position to give them any practical assistance.

Former GCHQ employee Geoffrey Prime's treason came to light in 1982 when he was arrested for sexually abusing under-age girls and his wife handed police his spying equipment. This was followed the next year by the arrest of

Michael Bettany, an MI5 officer who put a parcel of top-secret information through the door of the KGB Resident, Arkadi Guk, on Easter Sunday, 3 April 1983. This included information explaining exactly why three members of the Soviet staff had been declared persona non grata the previous month (although it unsurprisingly didn't mention that Igor Titov had been removed from the UK in order to allow Gordievsky to be promoted), as well as an offer of further secrets. Guk, a paranoid alcoholic described by Gordievsky as 'a huge bloated lump of a man, with a mediocre brain but a large reserve of low cunning', believed this was an entrapment by MI5 and ignored the letter.

In June, the residency received a document listing the KGB and GRU staff in London. When Gordievsky revealed this to his British handlers, they realized that there was a mole within MI5; Guk still believed it was an MI5 plot and didn't make any moves towards Bettany. MI5 set up a molehunt, code-named ELMEN, which quickly focused on Bettany, who was acting increasingly strangely. Taking a risk, since they could not prevent him leaving the country if he resigned from the Security Service, the ELMEN team (nicknamed the Nadgers) brought Bettany in for questioning. After a day and a half of interrogation, Bettany elected to confess.

There was little time for congratulation though, since Gordievsky had been reporting that Operation Ryan was reaching a peak. In February 1983, KGB staff had been given twenty tasks to monitor British preparations, which included whether the price paid to blood donors had increased (they're actually unpaid), and how many lights were being left on at night in government buildings. In August, further tasks were added.

The relationship between East and West seriously faltered after the Soviets shot down a civilian 747, Korean Airlines flight KAL 007, on 1 September 1983, killing all 269 people aboard, including US Congressman Lawrence McDonald.

The NSA radio facility at Hokkaido in Japan intercepted the transmission from fighter pilot Major Osipovich stating, 'I have executed the launch ... the target is destroyed.' This recording was released to the public, ratcheting up the rhetoric.

However, this intercept only told part of the story. When the entire conversation was reviewed, it showed that the Soviets thought that they were tracking an American RC-135 reconnaissance aircraft, not a Boeing 747, and that the Korean pilots hadn't responded to tracer bullets fired in front of the airplane. President Reagan went on US television on 5 September to accuse the Soviets of a crime against humanity. The next day the US ambassador to the UN, Jeanne Kirkpatrick, accused them of mass murder. The dispute overshadowed a meeting of foreign ministers in Madrid on 8 September, with Andrei Gromyko suggesting 'the world situation is now slipping towards a very dangerous precipice'. On 28 September, Yuri Andropov gave a speech from his sick bed that accused the Reagan administration of 'imperial ambitions' and wondered 'whether Washington has any brakes at all preventing it from crossing the point at which any sober-minded person must stop'.

Their fear was magnified by the NATO exercise ABLE ARCHER 83, which was held between 2 and 11 November. Its stated aim was to practise nuclear-release procedures, but the Soviets genuinely believed that it would be used as a cover for a real first strike. According to Sir Geoffrey Howe, then British Foreign Secretary, Gordievsky 'left us in no doubt of the extraordinary but genuine Russian fear of real-life nuclear strike'. It was clearly time to tone down the rhetoric: reassuring signals were sent by Washington and London to Moscow. Yuri Andropov's death in February 1984 no doubt helped alleviate the tension (his successor, Chernenko, wasn't quite so paranoid about a first-strike).

The publicity given to the KGB resident Arkadi Guk as a

result of Bettany's trial in 1984 gave MI5 the excuse to declare him persona non grata, and aid Gordievsky's elevation a stage further (the downside was that the British head of station in Moscow was kicked out from the Soviet Union). Gordievsky continued to pass information through to MI6, assisting with Margaret Thatcher's preparations for Mikhail Gorbachev's visit to Britain at the end of the year. It seemed as if Gordievsky's star was still in the ascendant, particularly when the KGB decided to appoint him as Guk's successor in January 1985. However, his luck was about to run out.

While much of the free world's intelligence agencies were concentrating on the heightened level of Soviet activity, the Australian Secret Intelligence Service found themselves once more the subject of some unwanted publicity.

On 11 November 1983, the final day of ABLE ARCHER 83, the ASIS began training a team in various elements of tradecraft, including close-quarters combat, surveillance, medical skills and methods for illegal entry. As an exercise, the team were instructed to carry out an armed rescue of a supposed defector, John, and his brother Michael. It all went badly wrong, ending up in an operation that was described in an official report as 'poorly planned, poorly prepared and poorly coordinated'.

To begin with, guns were removed from a secret armoury without authorization. Then the trainees lost contact with John and the supposed foreign agents with whom he was consorting. They had to be told to go to the upmarket Sheraton Hotel in Melbourne, where they exceeded their instructions by using a sledgehammer to break down the door of the room in which John and his colleagues were meeting. When the hotel manager, Nick Rice, investigated, the trainees' team leader got in a fight with him in the elevator – whereupon Rice called the police. The team leader then released the supposed foreign agents, who had been handcuffed as part of the exercise, and raced to meet the rest of his team who were 'abducting' John from the hotel. The Sheraton staff were not impressed, and although the trainees and John claimed they were from ASIS, took the car licence number and reported it. Police stopped the car and arrested the occupants.

The resultant publicity led to local paper the *Sunday Age* revealing the names of five of the agents involved in an article headlined 'The Sheraton Shambles', which provoked a court case over whether the government had the right to release agents' names (it was effectively agreed that they did indeed have the right, but shouldn't exercise it). ASIS Director-General John Ryan refused to cooperate with the police enquiry, but he resigned after being held responsible by a Royal Commission for authorizing the operation. In the end, no charges were brought against any of the agents. The Federal government paid over A$300,000 in settlement to the Sheraton and its staff.

The Australians weren't the only ones to bungle during this time. The case of Richard Miller once again demonstrated that not everything in the spy world goes according to plan.

Miller has the distinction of being the first KGB spy to be caught within the FBI, and possibly the most incompetent agent within either agency. He joined the Bureau in the early sixties, and quickly gained a poor reputation, trying to obtain goods from stores by showing his FBI badge, and even stealing and selling information from the Bureau on behalf of a local private investigator. According to a scything attack on the FBI in *Washington Monthly* in 1989, by 1982, Miller had 'a personnel file filled with doubts about his job performance ... A psychologist examined Miller and told the FBI that he was emotionally unstable and should be nurtured along in some harmless post until retirement.'

This harmless post turned out to be with the counter-intelligence unit in Los Angeles, where in 1984 he came to the attention of low-level KGB agent Svetlana Ogorodnikova, a Russian émigré. Miller was seduced and asked to find out the location of Soviet defector Stanislav Levchenko. This he was unable to do, but he did pass across an FBI manual stating the sorts of intelligence that the Bureau was looking for. Ogorodnikova was known to the FBI, and they began watching Miller to see if there was potential to use him as a double agent.

That October, Ogorodnikova wanted Miller to travel to Europe with her, to meet with her KGB superiors, and at this point Miller approached his superiors, saying he was trying to infiltrate the Soviet network. The Bureau believed that he only did this because he had spotted the surveillance, and fired him – then arrested him for espionage, as well as Ogorodnikova and her husband. They pleaded guilty to conspiracy to commit espionage; Ogorodnikova was sentenced to eighteen years in prison, her husband to eight. Miller claimed he was working on behalf of the Bureau to penetrate the spy ring; the jury disbelieved him and he was sentenced to two consecutive life terms. A mistrial was declared on technical grounds and at a second trial in 1990, he was found guilty again and sentenced to twenty years, reduced to thirteen. Ogorodnikova spent years battling deportation to Russia before escaping to Mexico with a new husband.

Although Miller's low-scale treason would be regarded as a blot on the FBI's record, it became increasingly unimportant as the events of 1985 unfolded – a year described by the American press as 'The Year of the Spy'.

11

THE YEAR OF THE SPY

'We should begin by recognizing that spying is a fact of life,'
President Ronald Reagan told the American people during his
radio address to the nation on 29 June 1985. 'The number and
sophistication of Soviet bloc and other hostile intelligence
service activities have been increasing in recent years ...
During the seventies, we began cutting back our manpower
and resources and imposed unnecessary restrictions on our
security and counter-intelligence officials. With help from
Congress we've begun to rebuild, but we must persevere.'

Reagan's call to arms followed the arrest of John Anthony
Walker, the retired Naval officer whose spy ring had been
passing material to the Soviets for eighteen years. It was the
first openly acknowledged move on the American side in
The Year of the Spy, but the following twelve months would
see both parties in the Cold War discover agents within their
own borders – sometimes as a result of new assets being
developed within the opposition. The problems the Americans faced on that front were compounded by the discovery

of agents working against them on behalf of China, Ghana and Israel.

'This has been an extraordinary year in the international espionage trade,' Maria Wilhelm wrote in an October 1985 article for *People* magazine. The Walker case shocked America, partly because it seemed to demonstrate an incompetence on the part of the country's counter-intelligence services in failing to apprehend him – or his brother Arthur, son Michael, and friend Jerry Whitworth, all of whom were part of the group – over such a long period. Certainly the Walker ring was one of the most useful sets of assets that the Soviets possessed within the United States – according to Vitaly Yurchenko, whose own defection from and subsequent rapid return to the KGB was another of the year's key events, the information that they provided over the years enabled the Soviets to decipher over a million top-secret messages.

Walker's spying activities were brought to an end in part thanks to a tip-off from his own ex-wife, Barbara. She had been aware of his spying for the Soviets for many years, and had threatened to expose him on countless occasions, but had never taken the final step. Eventually, when their marriage came to an end (and possibly in annoyance that Walker had tried to recruit their daughter into the spy ring), she contacted the FBI in April 1985. Former KGB agent Victor Cherkashin denied that her report triggered the arrest, and suggested that an FBI spy within the KGB based at the Washington residency, Valery Martynov, overheard discussion about Walker's activities during a trip home to Moscow, and reported this back to his handlers.

Whatever prompted the FBI to begin the surveillance, Walker was arrested on 20 May when he dropped a number of documents for collection by the Soviets; his handler, embassy official Alexei Tkachenko, was posted back to Moscow a few days after the arrest. His colleague Jerry

Whitworth, brother Arthur and son Michael were also arrested. John Walker agreed to testify against Whitworth in return for his son receiving a lesser sentence; he, Whitworth and Arthur Walker were sentenced to life imprisonment, Michael receiving a twenty-five year term.

Around the time that Walker's wife was informing the FBI about her husband's spying, CIA counter-intelligence officer Aldrich Ames was beginning his treasonous career for the KGB, which would last for the next nine years. Initially using the alias Rick Wells, Ames requested $50,000 from the Soviets in return for information on CIA operations, which, once they saw what he was willing to provide, they gladly gave. Victor Cherkashin was put in charge of handling 'Wells', and quickly deduced that they had potentially struck gold: not only did 'Wells' have access to good material, but he was actually the CIA's chief of Soviet counter-intelligence!

Ames had joined the CIA in 1962 as a trainee, and served at the Ankara station, as well as in Mexico, where he was one of those who handled Aleksandr Ogorodnik's training. In New York he helped look after Arkady Shevchenko, before transferring back to the Agency's headquarters at Langley, where his job was to meet with Soviet embassy officials to look for potential defectors. This gave him the perfect cover for visiting his new paymasters – so long as the meetings didn't attract attention by being too long.

In June 1985, Ames passed over a list of virtually every CIA asset within the Soviet Union; as a direct result, thanks to this confirmation of Edward Lee Howard's earlier information, Adolf Tolkachev's fate was sealed. Major-General Dmitri Polyakov had retired from the GRU in 1980 to his dacha in the countryside; following Ames' list, he was arrested, and, as he had predicted to one of his CIA case officers, his eventual resting place was a 'Bratskaya mogila', an unmarked grave. He was executed on 15 March 1988.

Ames' information also ended the career of Valery Martynov, who was working for both the FBI and the CIA within the KGB's Washington residency. A target of the FBI's Operation Courtship, which was set up to recruit Soviets in the capital during the early eighties, Martynov was able to pass disinformation back to his Soviet bosses and give the Americans accurate data on the Soviet activities within the residency. Although he had come under suspicion during 1984, there was insufficient evidence for the KGB to act against him until Ames included him in his list. He was sent back to Moscow, ostensibly as a guard for the returning defector Yurchenko, and taken straight to Lefortovo prison. He was executed around September 1987.

Another American agent within the Soviet residency was also betrayed by Ames: Sergei Motorin, who had already been rotated back to Moscow. Motorin had been turned by the FBI after he was photographed trying to pay for some electronic equipment with cases of vodka in a Maryland store in 1980, and, like Martynov, was used to feed the Soviets false information. Arrested in Moscow, he was shot.

Among the others Ames betrayed, Colonel Leonid Polishchuk had originally been enlisted by the CIA in 1974 when stationed in Nepal; he had dropped out of contact for many years before being assigned to Lagos, Nigeria, in February 1985, where the Agency approached him once more. After being named by Ames, he was arrested when he went back to Moscow to arrange the purchase of an apartment; in a successful effort to misdirect the CIA, the KGB claimed that they had stumbled on a CIA officer loading a dead drop in Moscow, and they had arrested the man who went to collect the money from it.

A GRU officer working for the CIA escaped the same fate. Colonel Sergei Bokhan had been employed by the Agency for a decade, while based in Athens, Greece. He had informed them about various attempts to sell military secrets to the

Soviets, including the manual for a spy satellite and the plans for a Stinger missile. Summoned back to Moscow in May 1985, a month after Ames' initial contact with the KGB, supposedly because his son was having problems at the military academy, he defected to the US.

GRU Lieutenant Colonel Gennady Smetanin, codename Million, was 'a shining example of the CIA's professional handling', according to Victor Cherkashin, but the Agency was powerless when his details were passed to the KGB by Ames. Based in Lisbon, Portugal, he and his wife Svetlana worked for the CIA from 1983 onwards. They weren't particularly useful agents at this point in their careers, but were an investment for the future – which was short-lived. In August 1985, Smetanin was ordered back to Moscow for an early home leave, and he and his wife were arrested on arrival.

Ames was also able to pass over details of various intelligence-gathering operations within the Soviet Union, including CKTAW, already revealed by Edward Howard, and Operation Absorb, an ingenious scheme to monitor the movement of nuclear warheads by tracking the tiny amounts of radiation that they emitted.

One agent who Ames is often accused of betraying is Oleg Gordievsky – even the defector himself says that Ames 'received his first payment, of $10,000, for putting the KGB on my trail'. However, according to Cherkashin, who was handling Ames, this wasn't the case: Ames was only asked about Gordievsky at their meeting in June, as corroboration. Whether this was disinformation and Ames did pass over the name a month earlier, or there was another KGB spy within the CIA whose identity has still yet to come to light, Gordievsky's career as an MI6 agent came to an end in May 1985.

Unexpectedly called back to Moscow, apparently for high-level briefings about his new position as KGB resident in London, Gordievsky was suspicious when he wasn't met at the airport as he would have expected. He then realized that the KGB had broken into his flat, after a lock that he never used (because he had lost the key) had been engaged. Discussions about high-level agent penetration in Britain turned into an interrogation, but Gordievsky revealed nothing, even when the KGB insisted that they had information about him, commenting, 'If only you knew what an unusual source we heard about you from!' He was allowed to remain at liberty, so that the KGB could gain further evidence against him, and eventually decided to defect, knowing that he was facing execution. With the aid of future MI6 chief John Scarlett, Gordievsky made his escape across the Russian/Finnish border in the boot of an MI6 car.

As a result of the information Gordievsky was able to provide in a complete debriefing once in Britain, thirty-one Soviet agents were declared persona non grata and removed from the UK; a similar number of British personnel were sent back from the embassy in Moscow. Over the coming years, Gordievsky would continue to brief the British and Americans on the Soviets' likely response to situations, such as the American line in the arms reduction negotiations, and give them an insight into the Soviet mindset.

As Oleg Gordievsky was plotting his escape from Moscow, CIA operative Sharon Marie Scranage was counting the cost of passing sensitive information to her boyfriend, Michael Soussoudis, an agent for Ghanaian intelligence. Scranage was the CIA Operations Support Assistant in Accra, and had given Soussoudis details of agents and informants. The CIA noted that 'damaging information on CIA intelligence collection activities was passed on to pro-Marxist Kojo Tsikata, Head of Ghanaian Intelligence, by Soussoudis who shared it with Cuba, Libya, East Germany and other Soviet Nations'.

According to a report in the *Washington Post* on 12 July 1985, Scranage had failed a polygraph test on her return to the

US and agreed to cooperate with the FBI to entrap Sous-soudis. In November both were found guilty of committing espionage; Scranage was also convicted of violating the Intelligence Identities Protection Act, set up following Philip Agee's activities. She served two years; Soussoudis was given a twenty-year sentence suspended on condition he left the US immediately. The Ghanaian agents whose identities were compromised were stripped of their nationality and sent to America. According to female CIA operatives, in the years following, Scranage's disgrace was regularly held up to them as an example of how easy it is to fall for a honey trap.

The 12 October 1985 *People* article about the various comings and goings in the spy world that were public knowledge at that point described the previous season as 'The Spy World's Frantic Summer'. At the time, it couldn't have guessed at the outcome of one of the stories it covered, which turned out to be one of the oddest events of the year. Vitaly Yurchenko, described as one of the KGB's most powerful spymasters, defected to the CIA on 1 August – and three months later defected back to the Soviet Union.

Whether he was a genuine defector who changed his mind, or a plant used to throw the CIA off the scent of the KGB's newest recruit Aldrich Ames, has never been totally explained. Victor Cherkashin, in charge at the Washington residency throughout Yurchenko's sojourn in the West, believed the former, and that rather than shoot Yurchenko for his crimes when he returned to the Soviet Union, the KGB elected to use his survival to confuse the CIA.

The possible reasons for Yurchenko's change of heart after his defection were multiple. He believed that he was dying of stomach cancer, and hoped for treatment in the US; he was also in love with the wife of another Soviet official, who was now stationed in Montreal. On both counts, he received surprising news: medical investigations revealed that he only had a stomach ulcer; while the woman he loved told him that she'd loved a KGB colonel, not a traitor, and wanted nothing further to do with him. He also asked that his defection was kept quiet, to protect his wife and children back in Moscow; to his intense annoyance the CIA leaked the story to the *Washington Times*, eager for some good publicity.

Yurchenko had served in the KGB for a quarter of a century, and was privy to a lot more information than he passed over to the CIA. However, he did give them enough to identify both Edward Lee Howard and Ronald Pelton as Soviet spies, and passed on a warning regarding the danger facing Oleg Gordievsky (not realizing that he was already safely in Britain). Although Pelton was arrested and sentenced to life imprisonment, Howard evaded his FBI surveillance and reached Moscow. He died in slightly mysterious circumstances in 2002.

The last straw for Yurchenko was the release of information he had passed over regarding Nicholas Shadrin, aka Nikolai Artmanov, a former Soviet Baltic Fleet captain who had defected to the West in 1959, and eventually ended up as a triple agent. Realizing his treachery, the KGB had kidnapped Shadrin in Vienna in December 1975, but unfortunately he died during transportation behind the Iron Curtain. His widow filed a suit against the US government, and Yurchenko's revelations about Shadrin's real fate – his work for the CIA had been public knowledge since 1978 – were included in the Agency's papers handed over as part of the court case, which were then released to the media.

On 2 November, Yurchenko persuaded his CIA handler to take him shopping, during which time he called the KGB residency at the embassy. He then went for a meal and asked his handler if the agent would shoot him were he to get up and walk out. 'We don't treat defectors that way,' the CIA man replied. Yurchenko left the table and went straight to the Soviet embassy.

Although the KGB knew exactly what Yurchenko told the CIA during his debriefing, since Aldrich Ames was one of those involved in his interrogation, they allowed him to claim that he had been kidnapped and drugged, and not been a willing party to anything. Public denunciations of the CIA followed; the Agency retaliated by claiming that Yurchenko had been executed, and his family charged for the bullets. Yurchenko promptly appeared in an interview from Moscow with German television to point out he was 'live and kicking'. All that was certain was that, in the words of a *Life* magazine article from the following September, the questions raised by his defection and return 'threatened to again pry open a Pandora's box of suspicions and troubles' within the CIA.

Defections went both ways during the summer of 1985. Three weeks after Yurchenko crossed from East to West, Hans Joachim Tiedge, a top West German counter-intelligence officer went the other way. The alcoholic officer – whose deputy at the Bundesamt für Verfassungsschutz (West German counter-intelligence) was also a spy for East Germany – defected 'because of a hopeless personal situation, but of my own free will', according to the handwritten note he released shortly afterwards. Tiedge had been searching for East German and Soviet moles in West Germany, but instead had been in a position to tip them off that they were under investigation. At least three agents fled to the East in the weeks before Tiedge's defection, and one of Chancellor Kohl's secretaries, Herta-Astrid Willner, would follow a few weeks later, believing that she would no longer be protected. On 23 August, four days after Tiedge took a train to the East, East German authorities claimed that they had arrested 170 West German spies in East Germany as a result of information supplied by Tiedge.

According to Stasi spymaster Markus Wolf (who claimed in 1997, rather disingenuously, that Tiedge hadn't worked for the

GDR prior to his defection), Tiedge had a computer-like memory, despite his alcoholism, and was able to pass on copious details on plans, personnel and operations. According to one official estimate, between his time in the West, and the information he gave during his debriefing, he compromised 816 different operations. Unsurprisingly, an atmosphere of mistrust grew between the West Germans and the other Western intelligence agencies as a result, even after Heribert Hellenbroich, Tiedge's boss, was fired shortly after the defection for keeping Tiedge on the job despite his evident problems.

Tiedge fled from East Germany to Moscow in 1990, shortly before German reunification, and despite the statute of limitations for his crimes expiring, did not return to the former West Germany before his death in April 2011.

As well as the embarrassment caused by the re-defection of Vitaly Yurchenko, November 1985 saw the revelation of the activities of naval intelligence officer Jonathan Jay Pollard, who was arrested outside the Israeli embassy after his spymasters there refused to help him. Sentenced to life imprisonment, his case became a cause célèbre in Israel, leading to tension between Washington and Tel Aviv. However, the case is not as clear-cut as many would like it to be.

Pollard's superiors in the intelligence community, four retired Navy admirals, pointed out in an article in the *Washington Post* in December 1998 that:

> We, who are painfully familiar with the case, feel obligated to go on record with the facts regarding Pollard in order to dispel the myths that have arisen from this clever public-relations campaign aimed at transforming Pollard from greedy, arrogant betrayer of the American national trust into Pollard, committed Israeli patriot.
>
> Pollard pleaded guilty and therefore never was publicly tried.

Thus, the American people never came to know that he offered classified information to three other countries before working for the Israelis and he offered his services to a fourth country while he was spying for Israel. They also never came to understand that he was being very highly paid for his services – including an impressive nest egg currently in foreign banks – and was negotiating with his Israeli handlers for a raise as he was caught. So much for Jonathan Pollard, ideologue!

Pollard initially applied to work for the CIA in 1977, but was turned down because of drug use at university. Two years later he began working for the US Navy Investigative Service and despite lying repeatedly about his background and his abilities, he was given a high security clearance. This was downgraded after concerns were expressed about his behaviour, but he threatened legal action to have it restored. The Commander of Naval Intelligence himself, Admiral Sumner Shapiro, wanted Pollard fired or at the very least have his security clearances revoked, but Pollard was able to persuade a psychiatrist that he was OK. He was returned to the high classification in 1982.

According to NCIS investigator Ronald Olive, Pollard tried to sell secrets around this time to Pakistan and South Africa; during Pollard's trial, an Australian Royal Navy officer, who had been part of a personnel exchange, alleged that the American had tried to pass him confidential documents, although Pollard denied this. What is certain is that in 1984 he became friendly with Israeli Air Force colonel Aviem Sella, and began passing information on to him (in exchange for cash and jewellery), including satellite imagery and details on new weapons systems in Egypt, Jordan and Saudi Arabia. Photos of Palestine Liberation Organisation residences were also passed across, which were very helpful to the Israelis during their September 1985 attack on the terrorist organization. A forty-six-page document was prepared for Pollard's trial by

Caspar Weinberger, the US Secretary of State for Defence, detailing what Pollard had given to the Israelis, including analysis of twenty key documents, one of which was a complete guide to American SIGINT.

Pollard's espionage activities came to light when co-workers noticed that he was leaving the office with packages of materials, and his supervisor found files on his desk that didn't correlate with the work he was meant to be doing. During the questioning that followed, Pollard was able to get a message to his wife Anne that told her to remove any classified documents from the house before it was searched. She gave these to a next-door neighbour, who, unfortunately for the Pollards, grew suspicious and contacted Navy Intelligence. Pollard was followed to the Israeli embassy, where he tried to gain asylum but was turned away; the FBI arrested him. Anne Pollard managed to alert Colonel Sella, who left the US with his team of agents before the FBI could capture them. Anne Pollard was arrested; Pollard agreed to cooperate in a plea bargain for a lesser sentence for his wife. She served three years of a five-year term; he remains incarcerated.

Although the Israelis originally claimed he was part of a rogue operation, they have subsequently admitted he was working for them, and urged his release. However, the American government remains committed to his imprisonment: as naval intelligence legal adviser Spike Bowman wrote in *The Intelligencer* in their Winter/Spring 2011 issue, '[Pollard] was neither a US nor an Israeli patriot. He was a self-serving, gluttonous character seeking financial reward and personal gratification. Without doubt, he is intense and intelligent, but also arrogantly venal, unscrupulous and self-obsessed.'

The other big surprise for the American public in The Year of the Spy was the arrest in November of Larry Wu-Tai Chin, a translator for the CIA, who had been spying for the People's

Republic of China (PRC). The PRC's activities in the US are less well-known than those of their Soviet counterparts, but they were also interested in military and technological advances.

Chin was one of two spies within Western intelligence who were exposed by one of the few agents that the CIA managed to gain within the PRC. Yu Zhensan was the adopted son of Kang Sheng, the Soviet-trained head of the PRC Ministry of State Security Foreign Bureau (MSS), and began providing information to the Agency in 1984. He revealed the existence of a PRC spy within the CIA but the only clue he had was that on one occasion, the agent, of Asian origin, had been delayed prior to a flight to Hong Kong to meet a handler. This was enough for the FBI, who were able to trace the specific flight and identify Chin from the passenger list.

From 1952 to 1981 Chin was an employee of the CIA, working in the Foreign Broadcast Information Service; he had spent the previous decade with the US Army liaison office in China, where he had come to the attention of the MSS. In 1952, he received his first payment from the MSS for information concerning the location of Chinese POWs in Korea and the type of intelligence information that American and Korean intelligence services were seeking from the POWs. Between then and his retirement in 1981, Chin was able to pass over thousands of secret documents to the MSS from his posts in Okinawa (Japan) and California, and at the CIA Langley headquarters. Between 1976 and 1982, he was providing photographs to MSS couriers in Toronto, Hong Kong and London and continued travelling to the Far East to meet handlers up until March 1985.

No hint of suspicion attached itself to him – he was even awarded a long and distinguished service medal in 1980 – because he was very careful over the money he was given by the PRC, purporting to be a gambler for high stakes and investing in property in Baltimore to explain his income. He is believed to have been paid over a million dollars during his career. Chin was found guilty in February 1986 of spying for China and tax evasion, but before sentencing he committed suicide in his cell.

While Aldrich Ames was a useful asset for the Soviets within the CIA, the other recruit who joined the KGB during the tail end of 1985 would prove to be one of their best agents, giving them access to the FBI's counter-intelligence efforts periodically between then and his capture in 2001. Robert Philip Hanssen was described by David Major, the former director of counter-intelligence at the US National Security Council and Hanssen's direct superior from 1987 onwards, as 'diabolically brilliant ... He knew everything we knew about what the Soviets did – and we knew a lot about how they operated. He also knew what we did. So he could operate within the cracks.'

Hanssen joined the FBI in 1976, and three years later was assigned to the New York field office helping to create an automatic database to track Soviet intelligence officers – and promptly became one himself, volunteering his services to the GRU via their front organization, AMTORG. In return for cash, he provided the Soviets with information regarding Dmitiri Polyakov's espionage activities for the CIA (which the GRU chose to ignore), as well as a list of Soviets that the FBI suspected were spies in the US.

His work for the GRU came to an end in 1981 after he was caught by his wife writing to the Soviets; he confessed to his priest, and passed the monies the GRU had given him to charity. Hanssen was transferred to Washington that year, where he headed up a unit analysing the FBI's data on Soviet activities, and coordinating projects against them.

Hanssen returned to New York in 1985 as supervisor in counter-intelligence, operating against the Soviet mission at the UN, as well as the consulate. Ten days after his arrival in the Big Apple, he wrote to Victor Degtyar, a middle-level intelligence officer at the Washington residency. He enclosed a letter for KGB resident Victor Cherkashin, in which he asked for $100,000 for a box of documents of classified and top-secret material that would shortly be delivered to Degtyar's private address, and revealing the names of three spies (all of whom, although he was unaware of it at the time, had already been betrayed by Aldrich Ames). When Cherkashin received the promised documents, they showed how valuable this anonymous spy would be.

Because he knew so much about both American and Soviet tradecraft, Robert Hanssen wasn't prepared to fall in line with the usual KGB methodology regarding dead drops and rendezvous. He dictated how they would be handled, operating, as David Major noted, 'within the cracks'. He made the KGB come to dead drops near his own home so that their actions were minimised – as Cherkashin admiringly notes in his autobiography, 'All we had to do was drop our package and make a signal.' He also refused to reveal his identity – the first time Cherkashin knew Hanssen's name was when he was arrested in 2001.

Money didn't seem to be his underlying motive (although he would tell his interrogators something different after his capture); Cherkashin considered that Hanssen liked showing off his expertise, and 'was either unhappy with his job or simply bored'. He certainly didn't see this – at that stage at least – as a long-term arrangement: 'Eventually, I would appreciate an escape plan. (Nothing lasts forever.)', Hanssen wrote shortly after making contact. Hanssen deliberately avoided communication with Cherkashin through the spring and early summer of 1986 after becoming overly suspicious of a mention of the KGB resident in a defector's debriefing, and dropped in and out of contact over the next fifteen years. It would be a long time before he might need an escape plan. As it transpired, Robert Hanssen was only five weeks away from retirement when he was eventually caught.

12

THE LONG TWILIGHT STRUGGLE

In June 1985, President Ronald Reagan told the American people that they were 'in a long twilight struggle with an implacable foe of freedom'. Very few people would have predicted at the end of The Year of the Spy that within six years the KGB would be no more, the Cold War would be over, and the intelligence services of the West would find their future role under discussion.

During the late eighties, the KGB continued its policy of misinformation, planting propaganda stories that would influence other countries' views of America and the CIA. The CIA's involvement in the Iran–Contra affair suggested that the dark times of the sixties might be returning. The game of Spy vs Spy seemed to be at its height, with the trade-offs of the Daniloff affair equivalent to some of the ill-matched spy swaps of the earlier decades. But Mikhail Gorbachev's reforms – coupled with some genuine accidents, such as the one that led to the end of the Berlin Wall – meant that the era of the Soviet Union's domination of Eastern Europe was drawing to a close.

* * *

Spreading lies and disinformation about the Main Enemy was not a new tactic for the KGB; through front organizations and receptive writers, they had propagated many false theories over the years, such as Soviet agent Joachim Joesten's book *Oswald: Assassin or Fall-Guy*, published in 1964 about the assassination of John F. Kennedy. In 1982 Moscow Centre had tried to discredit the US Ambassador to the United Nations, Jeane Kirkpatrick, with a story planted in the British *New Statesman* magazine which suggested strong ties between her and the then-pariah South African regime (although the documents backing this up hadn't been checked properly – the spelling of the word 'priviously' (*sic*) was a giveaway.) This was written by journalist Claudia Wright, who would later push other Soviet propaganda lines, such as her statement in the Dublin *Sunday Tribune* in 1989 that KAL 007 'the Korean Airlines jumbo jet, shot down by the Soviet Air Force six years ago today, was on a spy mission for the US'.

These operations, known as 'active measures', became more prevalent in the late eighties, despite Chairman Gorbachev's claim in July 1987 that 'We tell the truth and nothing but the truth.' In one of Yuri Andropov's last decrees as Chairman of the KGB in 1982, he stated that it was the duty of all foreign intelligence officers, no matter which department they were part of, to participate in active measures. It was an area that was often 'sub-contracted' to satellite states, such as East Germany. As Colonel Rolf Wagenbreth, director of Department X (disinformation) of East German foreign intelligence, once said, 'Our friends in Moscow call it "dezinformatsiya". Our enemies in America call it "active measures", and I, dear friends, call it "my favourite pastime".'

After attempts were made to blacken the name of Polish Solidarity leader Lech Walesa before he was awarded the Nobel Peace Prize in 1983, Pope John Paul II, himself a Pole, came under attack. The KGB had been treating him as an enemy since 1971 for his anti-Communist tendencies, and in December 1984 they began further measures designed to tar him as a reactionary. President Reagan's speech to the European Parliament in May 1985 was heckled as an active measure. Forged letters were used to bolster the impression of an out-of-control American government: CIA director William Casey apparently planned to overthrow Indian prime minister Rajiv Gandhi in 1987; in January 1988 documents suggested President Reagan gave instructions to the NSA to destabilize Panama. South African Foreign Minister Pik Botha referred to a secret and sinister agreement with the US in a letter he supposedly sent in 1989.

The most potentially damaging active measures were stories about medical experiments carried out by the Americans. The story that the Aids virus was manufactured during a genetic engineering experiment at Fort Detrick, which had been the home of the US biological weapons' programme, first appeared in a pro-Soviet Indian newspaper, *Patriot*, in 1983, but was really ignored until it was magnified in the Russian *Literaturnaya Gazeta* in October 1985. This new version was then followed by a report from a retired East German biophysicist (and Stasi informant), Professor Jacob Segal, which 'demonstrated' that the virus had been artificially synthesized. Segal genuinely believed his theory, despite it being discredited, and pushed it until his death in 1995. His hypothesis was reported as fact by British newspapers the *Sunday Express* and the *Daily Telegraph* the following year, and indeed continues to be quoted to this day by conspiracy theorists.

In August 1987, Soviet officials formally denied that they considered Aids to be an American creation, but by then the story had become established, particularly in the Third World. In March 1991, a letter to the Zimbabwean *Bulawayo Chronicle* stated that not only had the United States invented Aids, but that the CIA had exported 'Aids-oiled condoms' to other countries in 1986!

A later variant of the same Aids story suggested that it had been created as an ethnic bioweapon by the Americans, targeting non-whites. This was partly a continuation of the KGB's attempts to foment racism at the 1984 Los Angeles Olympics where offensive letters supposedly from the Ku Klux Klan were sent to African and Asian countries promising their athletes 'a reception you'll never forget'.

One particular active measure gained some recognition from the European Parliament, who passed a motion condemning trafficking in 'body parts' in which Latin American children were butchered to provide organs for sick Americans. Even the Jehovah's Witnesses were taken in by this one, publishing the story in their magazine *Awake* in 1989 to an audience of eleven million people in fifty-four languages. Although far more is known about active measures now than at the time of the Cold War, perusal of the world's papers today indicates that the KGB's successor, the SVR, is still hard at work peddling skewed versions of reality.

The sometimes byzantine nature of the spying game in the late eighties is amply demonstrated by the Daniloff case from August-September 1986, which saw the Soviets falsely accuse Nicholas Daniloff, an American journalist, of spying in Russia mere days after one of their own agents at the UN was arrested by the FBI, in what *Time* magazine described as 'a risky game of tit for tat'. Played out against the backdrop of the plans for the first summit meeting between President Reagan and Mikhail Gorbachev in Iceland later that year, the affair saw the eventual swap of Daniloff for Gennady Zakharov (even if neither side would admit that that is what it was at the time).

The Soviet agent, a physicist working at the United Nations, had been cultivating a Guyanese resident of New York, known only as CS or Birg, who worked at a defence contractor. What Zakharov didn't realize was that Birg had been working with the FBI for three years, ever since the initial contact. When he handed Birg $1,000 in exchange for three classified documents, the FBI were waiting. A few days later, Daniloff, who had spent the previous five and a half years as a correspondent for the *News & World Report*, met with a friend, Misha, in the Lenin Hills of Moscow; Misha gave him a sealed packet with some press clippings in – or so Daniloff thought. In fact, as he discovered when the KGB arrested him on the street and took him to Lefortovo prison, they were photos of soldiers and tanks in Afghanistan. As one paper at the time explained, 'The KGB has trumped up a case against [Daniloff] that is literally a mirror image of the case against Zakharov.' Although Daniloff and Zakharov were released after a fortnight into the custody of their respective embassies, the threat against the American continued; when Zakharov faced charges of spying, so did Daniloff.

Part of the problem was that the KGB did have some very slight cause for concern about Daniloff. A letter had been passed to him by a dissident Russian Orthodox priest back in January 1985 for onward transmission to CIA DCI William Casey. Daniloff had given it to the Second Secretary at the US Embassy. According to the KGB, this was proof that he was working with the CIA.

After many days of tense discussions, during which the summit due to be held in Reykjavík in mid-October looked likely to be cancelled if the stalemate wasn't resolved, and the US threatened to send home two dozen Soviet delegates from the United Nations, the Soviets finally agreed to release Daniloff on 30 September. The same day, Zakharov was allowed to leave America, having pleaded no contest to the charges. While the summit went ahead, the twenty-five Soviet delegates were still expelled; in retaliation, on 19 October, the Soviets kicked out five US diplomats. Two days later, the US sent home fifty-five more Soviets – allegedly to bring about parity between the size of the respective missions in the countries. A day later the Soviets expelled five more Americans.

But the rules of the game meant that nobody would admit the reality of what had happened. Daniloff was quite clear that he had not been swapped since as far as he was concerned there was no comparison between the two situations. 'In my case, the investigation into the charges against me was concluded,' he stated bluntly. 'There was no trial, and I left as an ordinary free American citizen. In Zakharov's case, there was a trial, and he received a sentence. I do not believe that these two things are in any way equivalent.' Although some dissidents were released in the Soviet Union at the same time as Zakharov left the US, it was clear to all neutral observers that this was as much a swap as the handovers between KGB and CIA in Berlin had been during the sixties.

Both John Walker and Jonathan Pollard had targeted the Navy; other branches of the US military fell victim to Soviet agents during the late eighties. In 1987, United States Marine Corps Sergeant Clayton J. Lonetree was the first marine convicted of spying against the US; two years later, Warrant Officer James W. Hall III, who described himself as 'a traitorous bastard, not a Cold War spy', was found guilty of betraying hundreds of secret documents to both the Stasi and the KGB.

When writing to support a reduction in the thirty-year prison term to which Lonetree was sentenced, his commanding officer, General Alfred M. Gray Jr., wrote that the young marine wasn't motivated by 'treason or greed, but rather the lovesick response of a naive, young, immature and lonely troop in a lonely and hostile environment'. Lonetree had fallen for the charms of Violetta Sanni, a Russian girl who worked as a translator at the US Embassy in Moscow, where he was posted as a guard. Despite rules prohibiting fraternization with members of the opposite sex in a Communist country, they began an affair.

Lonetree fell head first into the honey trap, and began providing Violetta's 'Uncle Sasha' (KGB agent Alexei Yefimov) with photographs and floor maps of the embassy, as well as details of American agents. When he was posted to Vienna in mid-1986, he continued to supply information willingly to Uncle Sasha. That December though, he reconsidered what he was doing, and after contemplating suicide, confessed. Although it seemed at the time as if his actions had led to the deaths of around twenty CIA agents, it later transpired that the names he passed had already been supplied to the Soviets by Aldrich Ames. Lonetree's thirty-year sentence was reduced to fifteen and he was freed on parole in 1996.

James W. Hall III was a very different proposition. His career as a spy for both the Stasi and the KGB was brought to an end following the debriefing of an East German defector, Dr Manfred Severin, who mentioned an American soldier who had provided multiple documents. Hall admitted his guilt to Severin and an FBI agent posing as a Soviet contact in December 1988, bringing to an end a six-year period working for the Communists.

Hall was recruited to the Stasi in 1982 by Huseyin Yildirim, an auto-mechanic at the US Field Station in Berlin, although he had made contact with the KGB a couple of weeks earlier. He would claim later that his motives were purely financial: 'I wasn't terribly short of money,' he told the FBI agent who arrested him. 'I just decided I didn't ever want to worry where my next dollar was coming from. I'm not anti-American. I wave the flag as much as anybody else.'

During his time in Berlin, and later Frankfurt, Hall provided documents regarding electronic eavesdropping operations carried out by the Americans to Yildirim or KGB officers, and was paid in dollars or German marks. There was concern at the time of his arrest that Yildirim might have been running a spy ring out of the Berlin Field Station: 'We are looking at the potential – and it's so far just potential – that this could be the Army's Walker case,' one investigating officer said, during preparations for Yildirim's trial; current assessments agree that Hall caused as much damage during his six years as Walker did in eighteen.

Hall admitted that he delivered between thirty and sixty documents to his handlers, which led to a programme designed to exploit a Soviet communications vulnerability uncovered in the late seventies being rendered useless, as were plans to disrupt electronic commands and surveillance. 'Without commenting on the specifics, it appears that Hall did very serious damage,' Senator David Boren, chairman of the Senate Intelligence Committee, said at the time. Some of the material he provided, such as the National SIGINT Requirements List, enabled Stasi spymaster Markus Wolf to 'take relevant countermeasures' against American plans.

Hall was court-martialled and sentenced to forty years' imprisonment; Yildirim received a life sentence, with the FBI telling his lawyer in 1997 that they 'think it is not inappropriate for him to rot in prison. They say his work might not have caused physical harm to Americans, but he hurt a lot of Americans by contacting them, so that they lost security clearances and ruined their careers.' He was, however, released in 2004, and on his return to Turkey, boasted of his affairs during his spying missions.

Huseyin Yildirim was by no means the first spy to brag about his career after retiring or being forcibly removed from the game. Robert Hanssen claimed that he was inspired as a child by Kim Philby's interesting take on his career in his book *My Secret War* (although this was clearly another of Hanssen's fabrications: he was actually twenty-four when the KGB spy's book was published). Some career retrospectives have become the authoritative sources on events – Victor Cherkashin's book on handling Ames and Hanssen provides perspective that no one else could have had; Oleg Gordievsky's account of his interrogation shows the way in which the KGB operated against one of their own. One book, however, became the cause of considerable problems for the British government.

MI5 officer Peter Wright's *Spycatcher* attracted considerably more attention as a result of the government's actions than its not particularly well-written pages deserved. After his retirement in 1976, embittered at being awarded a lower pension than he felt he deserved, the former MI5 agent moved to Tasmania and cooperated with British writer Chapman Pincher's exposé of British intelligence in *Their Trade is Treachery*, published in 1981. This rehearsed Wright's beliefs that Sir Roger Hollis had been a KGB agent. He then appeared in a *World in Action* television documentary on 16 July 1984, publicly accusing Hollis. Both were in breach of his obligations under the Official Secrets Act and an agreement on his retirement 'never to disclose anything I knew as a result of my employment, whether classified or not'.

Wright worked on his own book, and although some publishers were put off by warnings from the government, Heinemann decided to put the book out through their Australian subsidiary. Determined to stop it by whatever legal means necessary, the Attorney General, Sir Michael Havers, began proceedings in Australia. This unfortunately meant that Havers had to admit, solely for the purposes of the court case, that Wright's allegations were accurate. This undermined the case for publication not being in the public interest, particularly since Hollis had helped to set up the Australian security service, the ASIO.

The government's case wasn't helped by its official position that it still refused to acknowledge the existence of MI6 – which led to a surreal moment where Sir Robert Armstrong had to agree that the service had existed while Sir Dick White was head of it (since he had volunteered that information in an earlier answer), but could not admit it had any prior or subsequent existence! Many agreed with Wright's co-author, *World in Action* director Paul Greengrass' assessment of the case: 'It became a great set-piece encounter – conflict, really – trying to define where the boundaries lay between the government's desire to protect national security and our right as citizens to know what is done in our name.' Unsurprisingly, the government lost the battle, and *Spycatcher*, with its allegations about a plot against Harold Wilson, and considerable manipulation of the facts, was published in Australia and America.

Apart from allowing an insight into the mindset of some of those employed by MI5 during the height of the Cold War, the *Spycatcher* Affair did have one very important consequence: it was clear that it was impossible for the government to continue maintaining that the security services MI5 and MI6 didn't exist. The Security Service Act of 1989 was the first in a number of Acts of Parliament that eventually put both services on a full constitutional footing.

Greengrass later went on to great fame in the fictional spy world as director of the second and third films based on Robert Ludlum's spy Jason Bourne, as well as the drama documentary *United 93*, about the third plane involved in the 9/11 hijackings.

The first major Eastern bloc spy captured in Britain after the expulsion of the twenty-five Soviet illegals identified by Oleg Gordievsky was Dutchman Erwin Van Haarlem. He only came to light when MI5 followed a member of the Soviet Trade Delegation whom they (probably wrongly) suspected of being a GRU officer and saw him behave furtively on Hampstead Heath before entering a local pub. Half an hour later a second man searched an area of ground on the heath before entering the same pub. MI5 followed this other man and identified him as Van Haarlem, a self-employed art dealer, who was actually in Britain working for the Czech secret service.

Special Branch raided Van Haarlem's flat on 2 April 1988, and caught him red-handed, in the middle of receiving a transmission from Prague. He admitted he was Czech, and produced his one-time cipher pads. One of the main witnesses at his trial was future MI5 head Stella Rimington (referred to as Miss J) who explained that MI5 believed Van Haarlem was a sleeper agent, ready for a front-line role in time of war.

It turned out that Van Haarlem wasn't the spy's real name, even though an Erwin Van Haarlem had been abandoned in Prague, aged six weeks, in 1944. The baby's mother had tracked the man down using that name in 1978 and he had pretended to be her son. However, DNA testing proved that they were not in fact related: the spy had adopted the name prior to leaving Czechoslovakia in 1974.

The judge at his trial, at which he was found guilty of committing an act preparatory to espionage, noted, 'I address you by the name Van Haarlem, although I am convinced it was not yours at birth,' adding, 'I have not the least doubt you are a dedicated, disciplined and resourceful spy and I have equally no doubt that had you not been caught you would in future years have done whatever your Czech controllers required you to do, however harmful that might have been to our national interests. Those interests and freedoms we must jealously guard.' He was sentenced to ten years in prison in 1989, but was deported to Prague after serving five. MI5 discovered his true name was Václav Jelinek; the real Van Haarlem was eventually reunited with his mother, unaware that his identity had been stolen after he had changed his own name some years earlier.

As far as the CIA is concerned, the eighties was the era of DCI William Casey and the Iran-Contra affair, a convoluted saga of deals involving arms shipments to Iran in exchange for the release of hostages which actually made a profit – and was then illegally used to support the Contra faction in Nicaragua, in direct violation of the law. In the middle of the explosive revelations about the actions of the National Security Council (NSC) and the CIA, DCI Casey was diagnosed with a brain tumour, which effectively incapacitated him at a time when the Agency needed strong leadership.

The Congressional Committees investigating the affair pointed out the fundamental problem at the heart of the Iran-Contra situation: 'The common ingredients of the Iran and Contra policies were secrecy, deception, and disdain for the law ... the United States simultaneously pursued two contradictory foreign policies – a public one and a secret one.'

In 1979 the Sandanistas took power in Nicaragua, and despite receiving aid from President Carter, the regime allied itself with the Soviet bloc via Cuba, receiving guns and other material from the Communists. The Nicaraguan Democratic Force (aka the Contras) were created in 1980, and as the Sandanistas started supporting the rebels in El Salvador, the US began to provide support to the Contras, although armed action was prohibited by the president. When President Reagan took office in 1981, he cut all aid to the Sandanistas, and on 1 December, signed an order permitting the CIA to support the Contras with arms, equipment and money. The NSC organized publicity stunts to ensure there was support domestically within the US for the aid to continue.

However, not everyone in Congress was in favour of the CIA's involvement, which led to Massachusetts Representative Edward P. Boland's first Amendment in 1982, which barred 'the use of funds "for the purpose of" overthrowing the government of Nicaragua or provoking a war between Nicaragua and Honduras'. This left a loophole which was quickly exploited – third-party funds could be solicited, and general aid could still be provided to the Contras. The CIA assisted with covert actions in Nicaragua, destroying fuel tanks and mining the harbour. After their role was revealed by the *Wall Street Journal*, Representative Boland pushed through a second Amendment in 1984:

> During fiscal year 1985, no funds available to the Central Intelligence Agency, the Department of Defense, or any other agency or entity of the United States involved in intelligence activities may be obligated or expended for the purpose or which would have the effect of supporting, directly or indirectly, military or paramilitary operations in Nicaragua by any nation, group, organization, movement or individual.

Although this was designed to stem the flow of support, it failed. Third-party donations could still be obtained, and the NSC could oversee other activities, since technically they didn't fall under the definition of prohibited agencies in the Amendment. Colonel Oliver North, on loan to the NSC from the Marine Corps, was placed in charge.

Around the same time, clandestine negotiations were going on with Iran. The fundamentalist Islamic regime that seized power in January 1979 had taken American hostages at various times – but also needed support in their war against Iraq, so required some way of dealing with The Great Satan (as they dubbed America). A communications pipeline was opened via the Israelis in July 1985 so that thirteen days after President Reagan vehemently denounced any idea of giving reward to terrorists – like those in Iran – he was informed of a plan to exchange a hundred anti-tank missiles for some of the American hostages being held. (There are multiple contradictory versions of how much he knew about this and exactly when.) The deals began to go through, and profits from the second were channelled to a front company, known as the Enterprise.

This second deal, in November 1985, was the one that caused the CIA major headaches, as Oliver North involved them to assist with some logistical problems. What the CIA knew about the nature of the flight and the contents of the shipment that they were helping to supply became the focal point of the discussions. Most within the CIA were unaware that it involved the transport of weapons (which at that point was technically illegal).

In light of the second flight's problems, it was decided that the arms would be sent directly from the Enterprise to Iran, and President Reagan signed a Presidential Finding authorising such shipments on 17 January 1986. Shortly afterwards, someone came up with the idea of diverting the profits from the arms sales to the Contras – or at least, whatever proportion of the profits that the private businessmen involved would allow to be passed across. Many believe that the scheme was devised by DCI Casey, others that it was Oliver North's brainwave – a memo North wrote on 4 April 1986, which he failed to shred during his mass destruction of documents when the Iran-Contra affair became public later that year, spells out specifically that monies would be diverted to the Contras. North certainly maintained that he believed that President Reagan was aware of this plan, and approved it.

When news of the covert shipments leaked in November 1986, the main concern at the CIA was over the November 1985 deal, since it took place before the Presidential Finding that gave the Agency permission to assist with an arms deal. DCI Casey – probably already suffering the effects of the brain tumour that would remove him from power before the end of the year – was uncharacteristically lapse in his preparation for the questions about the Agency's role in an illegal covert action. This wasn't helped by Oliver North's attempts to disassociate the NSC from that shipment, or Casey's inability to recall whether he specifically knew that there were Hawk missiles in the cases that were dispatched with CIA aid, rather than oil-drilling bits, per the manifest. Many in Washington believed that DCI Casey intended to perjure himself to the Congressional Oversight Committee over this, although this may stem from a draft wording that Casey appended to a document during a meeting the day before the hearing – according to CIA sources, he never approved anything that specifically cleared the NSC or CIA of knowledge.

The CIA's concern increased when details of the diversion of funds to the Contras became public knowledge a few days later, since William Casey had made no mention of it in his testimony to Congress. There were many calls for his resignation, but in what appeared to be a combative interview with *Time* in early December (those present suggest that the DCI was in fact quite ill by this point), Casey made it clear he had told Congress all he knew. He knew nothing about diversion of funds, and the CIA had been simply providing support to the NSC. 'A lot of people are trying to put responsibilities on us that we didn't have,' he concluded. This stance was contradicted by a discussion Casey had two months later with reporter Bob Woodward, in which the reporter said Casey admitted that he was aware of the diversion scheme.

The Iran-Contra affair rolled on throughout 1987, with emphasis switching from the role of the CIA to what knowledge President Reagan had of the deal. His National Security Advisor at the relevant time, Admiral Poindexter, claimed that he had shredded a document signed by Reagan authorizing the deal. Oliver North wrote: 'Ronald Reagan knew of and approved a great deal of what went on with both the Iranian initiative and private efforts on behalf of the contras and he received regular, detailed briefings on both . . . I have no doubt that he was told about the use of residuals for the Contras, and that he approved it. Enthusiastically.'

As had happened a dozen years earlier in the aftermath of the Watergate scandal and the publicity attached to the release of the incriminating 'family jewels', throughout the rest of President Reagan's time of office the CIA underwent a period of retrenchment in an attempt to restore its battered image. Highly respected former FBI director Judge William H. Webster became DCI, and brought Richard F. Stoltz out of retirement to act as head of covert operations, replacing Clair E. George, who had been forced to resign after the Iran-Contra details became public. All the while, Aldrich Ames was passing information to the KGB from the CIA, while Robert Hanssen was doing similar from the FBI.

The CIA was heavily involved with the resistance to the Soviet occupation of Afghanistan, which was justifying the pessimistic description of it as Russia's Vietnam. The Agency was operating covertly out of Pakistan's capital city Islamabad, mandated by President Reagan in 1985, to assist the Afghan resistance to push the Soviets back into Uzbeki-stan, using the new Stinger missiles. By the following year, even some of the Politburo in Moscow were starting to query the Soviet involvement, particularly after the resistance scored a stunning success, destroying an ammunition dump at Kharga, just outside Kabul, on 26 August 1986, using CIA-provided technical equipment, and then followed it up with an attack on three helicopters at Jalalabad the following month. At a meeting in November, Mikhail Gorbachev made it clear that Soviet troops should be out within two years, and leave behind a regime friendly to Moscow – without letting the Americans enter. Negotiations began in Geneva, while the CIA agents on the ground continued to assist the resistance to maintain pressure on the Soviets.

Following the losses in The Year of the Spy caused (although they didn't know it at the time) by Ames and Hanssen, the CIA was keen to gain new assets on the other side of the Iron Curtain. In May 1987, KGB officer Aleksandr Zhomov, code-named Prologue by the Agency, approached CIA case officer Jack Downing on the Red Arrow express – the overnight train between Moscow and Leningrad – and appeared to be offering access to a new counter-intelligence campaign by the KGB designed to disrupt the CIA's operations in Moscow. He also provided a list of CIA agents who had been arrested and executed since 1985, and revealed the names of double agents who were going to falsely offer their services to the Agency.

Conventional wisdom held that the KGB didn't use their officers in this way (an operation known as 'dangling'), but in fact Prologue really was too good to be true. When it finally became time to exfiltrate him from the Soviet Union in July 1990, it became clear that Zhomov's loyalty had been to Moscow Centre the entire time. After the fall of the Soviet Union, Zhomov became head of the American Division of the FSB, the Russian continuation of the KGB, and according to CIA veteran Milt Bearden, he became obsessed with finding out who betrayed Aldrich Ames and Robert Hanssen to the Americans.

Hanssen was responsible for foiling plans to capture another double agent in 1989. State Department diplomat Felix Bloch had become a person of interest after he received a telephone call in April from Reino Gikman, a KGB illegal in Vienna, by the CIA. Bloch had already come under suspicion because he had a taste for expensive sadomasochistic sex with prostitutes, which he would not be able to afford on his salary. Because Bloch was working in America, the CIA passed the case to the FBI. When Bloch flew to Paris in May, French counter-intelligence placed him under surveillance at the request of the Bureau, and photographed Bloch and Gikman (who Bloch would later claim he knew as Pierre Bart) meeting and passing over a bag. Eight days later, Hanssen informed the KGB that Bart/Gikman and Bloch were under investigation.

Gikman and Bloch met again in Brussels at the end of May,

but then at the start of June, Gikman disappeared from Vienna, and on 22 June, Bloch received a phone call from someone he later identified as Bart/Gikman. He told Bloch that he was calling 'in behalf of Pierre' who could not see him in the near future because he was 'sick', adding that 'A contagious disease is suspected.' He rang off after telling Bloch, 'I am worried about you. You have to take care of yourself.' The FBI were bugging Bloch's phone, and as far as they were concerned, this was a clear warning off. He was interrogated by the FBI, and placed under further surveillance – which was exacerbated when ABC News revealed the investigation in July, and the public took to referring to Bloch as 'Mr Spy'. However, the surveillance proved fruitless: Bloch ceased any activities for the Soviets, and thus the FBI were deprived of gaining any clue as to who warned the KGB to tip him off. Bloch was dismissed from the State Department and eventually wound up as a bus driver.

Later that year, Hanssen betrayed another major secret to the Soviets – Project Monopoly, a tunnel that had been dug underneath their new embassy in Washington. Although many still doubt the existence of the tunnel, it does seem to have been constructed to allow the NSA and FBI access to the Soviet secrets. However, according to Hanssen's biographer David Wise, since the buildings were only used by families during the eighties, little useful knowledge was gained. Because of a dispute over the bugs discovered in the American embassy in Moscow, the building in the capital wasn't used for business purposes until 1994, which meant that, as at least one senior FBI official maintained, 'There was no information of any kind' emanating from the expensive equipment that had been installed.

By this point, events behind the Iron Curtain were developing their own momentum. The final Soviet troops withdrew from Afghanistan in February 1989. In May, Gorbachev suggested that force was no longer a viable way to keep the Warsaw Pact together; the same month, the Hungarians started to tear down parts of the iron curtain of barbed-wire along the Austro-Hungarian border that had been in place for forty-three years. In June, they acclaimed Imre Nagy, the leader of the 1956 uprising, as a national hero; Solidarity, the Polish non-governmental trade union, led by Lech Walesa, gained a majority in the Polish parliament at the same time. That September, a non-Communist government was approved by the Polish parliament. The Hungarian Communist party reformed as a Socialist Party in October, with legislation created later that month that led to the creation of the Republic of Hungary.

Across the summer of 1989, thousands of East Germans fled to Hungary to gain access to the West, before travel restrictions were imposed. Barred from Hungary, they then headed to Czechoslovakia where a huge encampment of defectors sprang up in the West German embassy compound in Prague. After the deposing of GDR chancellor Erich Honecker in October, the new leader Egon Krenz found that protests were increasing – and was informed that Moscow wouldn't provide support to keep his regime in power. New rules regarding travel between East and West were meant to be announced by unofficial GDR spokesman Günter Schabowski, noting that journeys via a third country could be permitted, but in a press conference on 9 November, the Politburo member made an historic error and stated that East Germans could travel *directly* to West Germany – and that these new rules were coming into force immediately. The Berlin Wall began to crumble metaphorically within minutes, as the checkpoints were opened, and was eventually physically dismantled over the ensuing months.

The Western intelligence agencies had to learn all about it from television news channel CNN. Markus Wolf's Stasi had been very effective in locating and removing any potential assets that the Agency might accrue in the GDR, so diplomats in Washington, desperately trying to keep pace with events, were forced to turn to their televisions rather than their intelligence briefings.

Over the coming months the CIA would try to turn as many former East German operatives as they could – a procedure they would also try, with limited success, in the Soviet Union as that headed towards break-up. It wasn't always successful: some former Communist officers felt that all they had left was their honour, and asked to be left alone. Others, like Markus Wolf himself, listened politely, but ultimately turned the Agency down. There were so many defectors in the end that the CIA eventually had to tell some to simply apply through normal channels for travel to the West.

However, the many new agents gained the CIA and other Western agencies access to materials they couldn't have hoped for before, including the new SA-19 surface-to-air missile (SAM) that the Soviets had been developing. What they were not able to get – at that stage anyway – were the Stasi files, even though the East German security headquarters in East Berlin had been ransacked. Many of them had in fact been transferred to Moscow for safekeeping. Former enemies became allies, as the Czech agency, the StB, began cooperating with both the CIA and MI6.

There were those within the CIA who believed that the KGB was becoming toothless, as the power of the Communist state dwindled with the rise of independence movements in various Soviet republics during the start of 1991. Former head of operations in America Oleg Kalugin publicly criticized the KGB for its behaviour, noting that Gorbachev's reforms would never amount to anything until the KGB's power was reined in. The KGB tried to curb the independence movement in Lithuania around the time of the first Gulf War, when Saddam Hussein invaded Kuwait and was repelled, but this caused an outcry in Moscow and the CIA began hearing about a potential recall for some Army officers to preserve the Soviet Union. On 18 August 1991, two months after the election of Boris Yeltsin as Russian President, and as Gorbachev prepared to sign a New Union Treaty, which some believed would mean the end of the Soviet Union as they knew it, the KGB, led by Vladimir Kryuchkov, made its final move.

Mikhail Gorbachev was cut off from the outside world at his vacation home, as tanks began to line the streets of Moscow. Russians hurried to the parliament building, the White House, as Boris Yeltsin declared that a coup had taken place. Some of the military backed Yeltsin and a battle of wills ensued – with Yeltsin undoubtedly the eventual winner. The coup was defeated, and Gorbachev, who had been effectively side-lined during the crisis, resigned as Communist Party secretary, remaining as president until Christmas Day. In perhaps the most symbolic gesture, the statue of Felix Dzerzhinsky, the first leader of the Communist secret police, was torn down from in front of the KGB headquarters at the Lubyanka. The KGB limped on for a few more weeks under General Vadim Bakatin, but as the Soviet Union dissolved, so too did the KGB's power. Its successors in the new Russia were the Foreign Intelligence Service (SVR), the Federal Security Service of the Russian Federation (FSB), and the Federal Protective Service (FSO).

At CIA headquarters, the Christmas party was promoted with a button that read 'The Party's Over'. And to an extent, it was – but the end of the Cold War would lead to major questions for all the world's intelligence agencies, ones that would only really gain a full answer when two planes were piloted into the World Trade Center in New York City, and one into the side of the Pentagon, on September 11, 2001.

13

PRELUDE TO WAR

Although President Bush's 'War on Terror' would not be officially declared until after the horrific events of 9/11, intelligence agencies had been involved in counter-terrorism operations for many years. The CIA and the FBI had been taking an interest in Osama bin Laden's organization, al-Qaeda, since its formation in August 1988 during the tail end of the Soviet occupation of Afghanistan. The Israelis had exacted revenge on the Palestine Liberation Organisation (PLO) and other terrorist groups. The British continued to wage an undeclared war on the Irish Republican Army (IRA) and the many other cadres in Eire and Northern Ireland, as well as dealing with Middle Eastern terrorists. Eastern Bloc countries such as the German Democratic Republic had spied on their own citizens on the pretext of preventing 'terror' attacks by capitalist forces. In South Africa, the Bureau for State Security (often referred to as BOSS) and its successor the National Intelligence Service dealt with perceived threats to the status quo, and, like the Stasi, often turned its attentions perhaps too closely on its own people.

On its website, the new South African State Security Agency (SSA) explains its remit, defining terrorism as 'deliberate and premeditated attempts to create terror through symbolic acts involving the use or threats of lethal force to create psychological effects that will influence a target group or individual and translate it into political or material results'. Counter-terrorism agents often encounter attempts at subversion, which the SSA calls 'activities directed at undermining by covert unlawful acts or intended ultimately to lead to the destruction or the violent overthrow of the constitutionally established system of the government'. It's really irrelevant whether the motives of the terrorists are religious (as with the fundamentalists of al-Qaeda), or political (such as the PLO), or a quasi-mixture of the two (the IRA, whose creed is partly based on getting the British out of Ireland, and partly involved with the schism between Protestants and Roman Catholics); the definitions equally apply.

Terrorism as it is generally referred to today saw a resurgence at the end of the sixties. In Ireland, the IRA had ended its previous campaign in 1962, citing public indifference. However trouble flared in Northern Ireland again in the summer of 1968. An MI5 report commissioned by Home Secretary James Callaghan, pointed out that 'In basic terms the security problem in Northern Ireland is simple. It springs from the antagonism of two Communities with long memories and relatively short tempers.' Although historically, the IRA had been the responsibility of the Special Branch of the Royal Ulster Constabulary (RUC) – and the Special Branch of the Metropolitan Police for offences committed on the mainland – MI5 began to take a more active role, particularly after the UK government sent troops into Ulster on 14 August 1969.

Intelligence matters regarding the province remained confused over the next few years, with the odd division of responsibilities occasionally leading to costly failures. The

Provisional IRA attack on the Parachute Regiment headquarters in Aldershot, Surrey (33 miles south-west of London), on 22 February 1972 led directly to the establishment of
an Irish Joint Section (IJS) by MI5 and MI6. Arms shipments
to the IRA from other countries were monitored and
prevented where possible. Despite this, the IJS were unable to
provide information that would deal with the IRA's worst
attacks on the mainland in 1974, in which forty-four people
died. However, they were instrumental in setting up a back
channel between the IRA and the Northern Ireland Office:
this led to the Christmas 1974 ceasefire which then continued
into 1975. By the time the IRA ended the ceasefire with a
further campaign in London's West End later that year, the
counter-terrorism element of the intelligence agencies was
working much more efficiently, with the IRA's chief of staff
Joe Cahill later admitting that 'In many ways the Brits'
strategy was working and the movement had been caught
flat-flooted.'

Numerous agents were run within the IRA over the next
twenty years by both MI5 and MI6, but their identities, and
successful operations, remain classified: there are still those
who would take action against them, despite the 1998 Good
Friday Agreement that brought a degree of peace to the
province. The British Army and the IJS were also able to turn
various members of the IRA, although this inevitably meant
that they were, to an extent, condoning murder, since senior
IRA men, such as Freddie Scappaticci, code-named Stakeknife, had to maintain their cover. MI5 took responsibility for
targeting Loyalist paramilitary groups, assisting in the arrest
of various members of the Ulster Defence Association.

However, towards the end of the seventies, the IRA began
their campaign again; they attacked a barracks in Germany,
and set multiple bombs in English cities in December 1978. A
new campaign in England seemed under way but fizzled out.
But then an offshoot Marxist group, the Irish National

Liberation Army, scored a success, blowing up Conservative MP Airey Neave as he drove out of the House of Commons in May 1979. The IRA equalled this with the murder of the Queen's cousin, Lord Mountbatten, and three others at Sligo, north-west Eire, as well as detonating bombs that killed eighteen soldiers on 27 August 1979.

The IRA continued to be a threat to security throughout the eighties; the IJS, now run by MI5, provided intelligence that helped counter their activities. MI5 also cooperated with the FBI in an effort to combat American financial aid to the IRA via the Irish Northern Aid Committee (NORAID) and the less well-known Clan na Gael, a secret Republican society. In 1984, the IJS was wound up, and its operations brought totally in-house at MI5. Although the counter-terrorism forces had some successes, they were not able to prevent spectacular coups by the IRA, such as the bombing of the Grand Hotel in Brighton on 16 October 1984 that nearly took the life of Prime Minister Margaret Thatcher.

MI5 did assist with the tracking of an IRA Active Service Unit across Europe in 1988 that culminated in the deaths of three of its members on Gibraltar on 6 March (although the subsequent media controversy over an alleged shoot-to-kill policy did none of the intelligence or army agencies any favours). This was indicative of an increased pan-European policy against the IRA that was spearheaded by the Security Service, while the FBI assisted with the arrest of an electronics expert in the US who had been helping the IRA with their technical requirements.

As borders opened within Europe during 1990, the IRA began a fresh campaign, and in February 1991 they fired a mortar bomb at the Cabinet Room at 10 Downing Street. In November that year, Prime Minister John Major agreed that MI5 should now take over responsibility for all counter-terrorism matters; that decision became formal six months later. The IRA's campaign in the UK continued unabated, with one explosive device at the Baltic Exchange in the City of London in April 1992 leading to around £800m of insurance claims – although back channel contacts between the IRA leadership and the British Government, which would eventually lead to the Good Friday agreement, were reopened for a time.

The Republicans' campaign suffered a major setback when their key operatives Rab Fryers and Hugh Jack were arrested in July 1993, together with the material for six car bombs. MI5 reported that over the following twelve months, eighteen out of thirty-four IRA mainland operations were frustrated. A ceasefire was declared in August 1994 which lasted until February 1996; bombs planted in spring 1996 at Canary Wharf and Manchester's Arndale Centre were not as devastating as the IRA had hoped. An Active Service Unit comprising some of the IRA's most able members was put under surveillance by MI5 and arrested in July before they could disrupt London's power supply.

The ceasefire came back into effect three weeks after the Labour party's electoral victory in Britain in May 1997; less than a year later, Prime Minister Tony Blair said it wasn't the day for sound bites, but he felt 'the hand of history on his shoulder', as he prepared to sign the Good Friday Agreement.

America also faced domestic terrorists. Although counterterrorism wouldn't become the official fourth priority for the FBI until 1982, they dealt with various high-profile cases before then. These included the bombing at the University of Wisconsin-Madigan on 24 August 1970, in which an Army think tank, the Mathematics Research Center, was attacked by radicalized students protesting the Vietnam War; and the campaign waged by the Weather Underground Organisation (better known as the Weathermen). Their manifesto, Prairie Fire, claimed in 1974 that their intention was 'to disrupt the empire . . . to incapacitate it, to put pressure on the cracks'.

They carried out over two dozen bombings, including one at the State Department in Washington DC in January 1975. Those responsible were tracked down by the FBI over many years and brought to justice.

The FBI also tried to capture the Unabomber, Theodore Kaczynski, who sent explosive devices over a period of seventeen years from 1978. He was only caught after he sent a 'manifesto' to the FBI in 1995 explaining why he was carrying out his attacks; when it was printed, his brother David provided convincing proof that Ted was responsible.

The Bureau spent five years hunting down Eric Rudolph, who had been responsible for a bomb at the Centennial Olympic Park in Atlanta during the 1996 Summer Olympics. He planted further devices over a two-year period at abortion clinics and gay-friendly meeting places in Alabama before disappearing into the Appalachian wilderness and living rough. He was eventually caught while searching for food in a dumpster.

They were rather quicker tracking down the Oklahoma Bomber, former soldier Timothy McVeigh, whose homemade device killed 168 and injured hundreds more on 19 April 1995 – partly because he had actually been arrested for carrying a concealed weapon a mere ninety minutes after the blast. Nearly a billion pieces of information were reviewed in preparation for McVeigh and his co-conspirators' trial. McVeigh was executed on 11 June 2001. Suggestions that he had connections with Middle Eastern terror groups have never been proven.

When papers wrote about Middle East terrorists in the forties, they were usually referring to the Zionist extremists who were seeking to set up the state of Israel. However, with the arrival of the Popular Front for the Liberation of Palestine (PFLP) in 1968, the emphasis switched to the Arabs, and once al-Qaeda started to make a name for itself with various terrorist attacks during the nineties, the volatile region became the focal point for agencies worldwide.

With the exception of the Israeli security agencies, notably their secret service Mossad, most of the world's intelligence agencies weren't particularly pro-active in their attitude to potential terrorist threats emanating from the Middle East during the seventies and eighties. The terrorists of the PFLP, guided by Dr Wadi Haddad, devised a new strategy: hijacking aircraft. The first, in July 1968, was an El Al Boeing 707 bound for Tel Aviv (the one and only time an aircraft belonging to the Israeli national airline would be successfully hijacked). Haddad was eventually recruited as a KGB agent, giving the Soviets some control over the PFLP's actions. The terrorist group's actions escalated culminating in the attempted capture of four aircraft on 6 September 1970 with a fifth following three days later. Known as the Dawson's Field hijackings after the RAF base in Jordan to which the planes were flown and then blown up, this resulted in King Hussein of Jordan taking violent action against the newly formed Palestine Liberation Organisation led by Yasser Arafat.

While most intelligence agencies were focusing on securing airports and aircraft, the Israelis went a step further. When a Sabena aircraft was diverted to Lod airport in Israel by the PFLP in May 1972, they sent in special forces disguised as airport workers and recaptured the plane. This escalated the situation. Three weeks later, members of the Japanese Red Army Faction, working for the PFLP, massacred twenty-six passengers at Lod. And on 5 September, Black September, an offshoot of the PLO, killed two Israeli athletes and took nine hostages at the Munich Olympic Games. A firefight at the airport led to the death of all the hostages. With the help of assets that they had within the PLO, Mossad tracked down those responsible for the attack, and executed them (regret-tably killing some innocents along the way, notably in Lillehammer, Norway, in July 1973, when Ahmed Bouchiki was murdered in the belief he was Ali Hassan Salemeh. According to Mossad chief Zvi Zamir:

> We are accused of having been guided by a desire for vengeance. That is nonsense. What we did was to concretely prevent in the future. We acted against those who thought that they would continue to perpetrate acts of terror. I am not saying that those who were involved in Munich were not marked for death. They definitely deserved to die. But we were not dealing with the past; we concentrated on the future.

The PFLP's final reported hijacking resulted in West German forces storming the plane when it was on the ground at Mogadishu airport in 1977. The British took similar strong action when terrorists seized hostages at the Iranian Embassy in London in April 1980. When a hostage's body was pushed through the front door after the terrorists lost patience with the authorities, Prime Minister Margaret Thatcher gave permission for the SAS to attack. All bar one of the hostage-takers were killed; all bar one of the remaining hostages were released safely. In all such similar situations, intelligence agencies provided information on the hijackers and their causes and assisted with the planning of operations.

Libya, under Muammar Gaddafi, became an increasing threat to the West during the eighties, not simply because of his financial support of terrorist organizations. Regarding those who opposed his regime as 'stray dogs' who needed putting down, Gaddafi launched various waves of assassination attempts against émigrés, and assets within his People's Bureau were able to provide MI5 with information to prevent these. In April 1984, Gaddafi personally ordered Libyans within the London Bureau to fire on demonstrators outside (a fact MI5 learnt from Oleg Gordievsky, who had been passed it from Moscow Centre), which led to the death of WPC Yvonne Fletcher. Diplomatic relations were cut with the regime, and sixty of Gaddafi's spies were expelled from Britain.

America similarly had problems with Gaddafi. In July 1981, despite a warning from the CIA not to proceed, President Reagan had ordered a naval exercise in the Gulf of Sidra, which Libya considered its territorial waters. The NSA were able to read most of the Libyan diplomatic and intelligence cyphers and intercept Gaddafi's personal phone calls, which showed the depth of the Libyan leader's anger and the retaliatory action he ordered against Americans.

The conflict in Lebanon, in which American troops tried to protect a ceasefire between Druze and Shi'ite Muslim militias and the mainly Christian Lebanese army, saw two major setbacks for the CIA. In April 1983, a bomb at the embassy in Beirut killed most of the Agency's station staff, including the CIA's top Middle Eastern expert, Robert Ames. A few months later, when the NSA intercepted a message indicating that 'a spectacular action' was shortly to take place against American marines, they sent out an urgent warning – but it was ignored. In a horrible foreshadowing of the intelligence mess that would see warnings about 9/11 not passed on because no one put the pieces together in time, the notification was either not taken seriously, or became lost within the bureaucracy. On 23 October, a huge explosion at Beirut International Airport killed 241 marines and sailors.

In 1986, Reagan stepped up the pressure on Gaddafi's Libya with further exercises in the Gulf of Sidra. After the Navy destroyed a Libyan SAM battery and two guided missile patrol boats, Gaddafi ordered all Bureaus to target American servicemen. On 5 April a bomb went off in a disco in West Berlin, killing three and wounding 230, which the Libyans believed 'would not be traceable to the Libyan diplomatic post in East Berlin'. Perhaps unwisely, Reagan revealed two days later that they had proof of Libyan involvement in the bombing; the Libyans immediately changed all their codes.

On 14 April a huge attack was launched against Tripoli and Benghazi – although most of the information about its success derived from CNN rather than from spies on the ground.

The FBI's counter-terrorism program was assisted by the Omnibus Diplomatic Security And Antiterrorism Act of 1986, which allowed them to conduct investigations in a foreign country where crimes had been committed against American citizens, with that country's permission. The first to feel the effect of this was Hezbollah terrorist Fawaz Yunis, responsible for the hijacking in 1985 of a Royal Jordanian aircraft that was carrying four Americans. In 1987 Operation Goldenrod went into effect, in which, according to the court record, 'Undercover FBI agents lured Yunis onto a yacht in the eastern Mediterranean Sea with promises of a drug deal, and arrested him once the vessel entered international waters.' Yunis was sentenced to thirty years, of which he served sixteen and was then deported.

The most horrific terrorist incident prior to 9/11 was the bombing of Pan Am Flight 103, which exploded over the Scottish village of Lockerbie on 21 December 1988. Despite a massive investigation by all the various intelligence agencies affected, there remains considerable doubt over exactly who was involved with this – Abdelbaset Ali Mohmed al-Megrahi, an agent for Libyan intelligence, the Jamahariya Security Organization, was found guilty in 2000, but until his death in 2012 persistently maintained his innocence (he only dropped his appeal against his sentence in exchange for being returned to Libya in 2009 when allegedly he only had weeks to live). Libya accepted responsibility for the explosion in 2003, but this may have been a method of gaining readmission to the international community. About all that the court in the Netherlands could say for certain was that 'the cause of the disaster was the explosion of an improvised explosive device, that that device was contained within a Toshiba radio cassette player in a brown Samsonite suitcase along with various items of clothing, that that clothing had been purchased in Mary's House, Sliema, Malta, and that the initiation of the explosion was triggered by the use of an MST-13 timer'. Even some of those findings have subsequently been thrown into doubt.

Initial investigations focused on the PFLP and Syrian involvement, particularly since the PFLP had warned in 1986 that 'There will be no safety for any traveller on an Israeli or US airliner.' One of their cells in Germany was working on similar – although not identical – bombs, and it is alternately possible that after the cell was arrested in October 1988, thanks to the efforts of a Jordanian spy who posed as their bomb maker, the PFLP bosses subcontracted the bombing to the Libyans in the same way that they used the Japanese Red Army at Lod. Former FBI Special Agent Richard A. Marquise, the Chief of Terrorist Research and Analytical Center at FBI headquarters in the eighties, noted in 2008: 'Did Iran contract with the PFLP-GC? Probably! But it cannot be proven in court. Did Iran ask Libya and [Palestinian terrorist] Abu Nidal ... Perhaps, but that too cannot be proven and never will be unless a reliable witness or two comes forward with documentary evidence.'

However, the major terrorist threat of the next twenty years, until the assassination of its leader in May 2011, was only just coalescing into existence when Pan Am 103 fell from the sky. Al-Qaeda was formed by the Saudi Arabian-born Osama bin Laden around 1988 from elements of the international Muslim brigades opposed to the 1979 Soviet invasion of Afghanistan. According to the 9/11 Commission, that investigated the attacks on the World Trade Center and the Pentagon, bin Laden 'built over the course of a decade a dynamic and lethal organization' whose aims are simple: it wants to eliminate Western influence from Muslim countries, and dispose of what it regards as 'corrupt' regimes.

Bin Laden never made any secret of his aims: 'The US

knows that I have attacked it, by the grace of God, for more than 10 years now ... Hostility toward America is a religious duty, and we hope to be rewarded for it by God,' he told *Time* Magazine in 1998. 'To call us Enemy No. 1 or 2 does not hurt us. Osama bin Laden is confident that the Islamic nation will carry out its duty. I am confident that Muslims will be able to end the legend of the so-called superpower that is America.'

In the early nineties, having been thrown out of Saudi Arabia, bin Laden moved to Sudan, where he set up training camps for warriors in a 'jihad'. One of the first attacks linked to the group was that on the World Trade Center in 1993, when six people were killed and more than a thousand injured by a 500 kg bomb planted in the parking lot. Behind that attack was Ramzi Yousef, the nephew of Khalid Sheikh Mohammed, who in turn claimed to be the instigator of 9/11. (A British security expert based at the World Trade Center, Rick Rescorla, had reported that the parking lot was an obvious target for terrorists two years earlier; this was ignored, as was his subsequent report that the WTC would be attacked from the air. Rescorla lost his life escorting people out of the South Tower on 9/11.)

Al-Qaeda was linked to the downing of two Black Hawk helicopters in Somalia in 1993, as well as the June 1996 bomb at the Khobar Towers, an American military housing complex near Dhahran in Saudi Arabia, which killed nineteen Americans. Shortly before this, bin Laden moved from Sudan to Afghanistan and in September 1996, called on his followers to 'launch a guerrilla war against American forces and expel the infidels from the Arabian Peninsula'. A further fatwa (an Islamic legal pronouncement) was issued on 22 February 1998, by bin Laden and four of his associates in the name of the 'World Islamic Front for Jihad Against Jews and Crusaders', calling for the killing of Americans, saying it is the 'individual duty for every Muslim who can do it in any country in which it is possible to do it'. Six months later, 225 people were killed, and over four thousand wounded, when bombs were driven into American embassies in Kenya and Tanzania, which led to airstrikes by the US against al-Qaeda positions in Afghanistan and Sudan. Bin Laden was indicted in the US courts for these attacks. In October 2000, two suicide attackers rammed a boat carrying explosives into the USS *Cole* near the Yemeni port of Aden, killing seventeen sailors and wounding forty others.

Those weren't the only attacks linked to al-Qaeda in the nineties by the world's intelligence services. The 1992 bombing of the Gold Mihor Hotel in Aden and the Luxor Massacre of November 1997 were both al-Qaeda funded operations, while a triple strike planned for January 2000 was foiled by the arrest of the Jordanian cell responsible for one part; the destruction of a skiff planned to sink USS *The Sullivans* in Yemen; and the arrest of the bomber who was going to set off a device at Los Angeles International Airport.

All this came at a time when the role of the intelligence agencies worldwide was being questioned. The sudden and dramatic end of the Cold War had left many wondering if countries needed secret services such as the CIA or MI6. In Britain, it was decided that the existence of MI6 would be revealed publicly, which, as the then-head of service Sir Colin McColl pointed out, many believed would be the start of a 'slippery slope ... Our work is about trust; trust between government and people running the service; and the service and people all over the world working for it,' he told a BBC Radio documentary celebrating a hundred years of MI6 in 2009. In the end, what the Intelligence Services Act in 1994 did was simply confirm the services' existence, but didn't go into any form of operational detail. A team of management consultants were brought into MI6, who slimmed the service down considerably.

Similar events were happening at MI5, with the first female

Director-General, Stella Rimington, taking a much more public role. Consideration was given in 1994 to amalgamating the two services, but this was not implemented. A disaffected MI5 officer, David Shayler, tried to emulate Peter Wright with revelations about the service's activities (even appearing on light-entertainment programme *Have I Got News For You*) but like Wright, showed more about his own deficiencies and faults than those of MI5.

President Clinton's incoming DCI R. James Woolsey, who succeeded Robert Gates, told his confirmation hearings in 1992 that he was considering alternate activities for the CIA, such as possibly sharing their business intelligence with private companies. As he pointed out, the West had 'slain a large dragon', but still lived 'in a jungle filled with a bewildering variety of poisonous snakes'. There was more intelligence sharing with old enemies – particularly over such issues as the whereabouts of nuclear missiles and other materiel that might have fallen into terrorists' hands after the breakup of the Soviet Union. 'We are partners now,' the chief spokesman of the FSB, the Russian Foreign Intelligence Service, Yuri Kobaladze said in an interview, 'although it will take some time to find the right way to deal with each other. We have universal problems like proliferation and international terrorism. These are our enemies. That's why we have to cooperate with the US and the rest of the world.'

For spies, the ground rules had changed. During the Cold War, spies operating undercover in a foreign country could normally expect interrogation and imprisonment followed by the likelihood of exchange (although of course there was always the chance of execution). Former Deputy DCI Admiral Bobby Ray Inman explained in 1993 that terrorists and the drug-traffickers didn't play by those 'gentlemanly' rules. 'When you try to penetrate them and they suspect you, they don't put you in jail. They shoot.'

* * *

CIA morale was hit by the cost-cutting insisted on by the administration – although the plans were only for it to revert to the size it had been during the Carter presidency – and even more by the revelation of Aldrich Ames' treachery. Despite the KGB being wound up when the Soviet Union was dissolved, Ames' loyalty had continued to be to his Russian paymasters, and he gladly provided material to the SVR.

The CIA had suspected there was a mole as early as 1986, and Jeanne Vertefeuille (often likened to John le Carré's fictional obsessed researcher Connie Sachs from *Tinker, Tailor, Soldier, Spy*) was placed in charge of the investigation, although it was given no priority. Ames was posted to Rome between 1986 and 1989, and did not have a very distinguished career. When he returned, he was assigned to the counter-intelligence centre and was therefore able to pass Moscow all the details of the CIA's actions against the KGB and then the SVR. Suspicions about his spending habits had been voiced and eventually a joint task force was set up with the FBI. The Bureau took over the case in May 1993 and arrested Ames in February 1994. (Ames' handler Victor Cherkashin believes that Ames and later Robert Hanssen were actually betrayed by a CIA spy within the SVR.)

R. James Woolsey came in for a great deal of criticism over his attitude to the discovery – although verbal reprimands were issued to eleven key staff members (some of whom were retired), no one was fired over the Ames affair. However, the Senate Intelligence Committee called this response 'seriously inadequate' for a 'disaster of unprecedented proportions'. Woolsey resigned in December 1994. He was replaced by Deputy Defence Secretary John Deutch, who continued Woolsey's policy of declassifying documents relating to the Cold War, and trying to broaden the Agency's personnel base with more women and minorities (a class action case had been brought against the Agency by various female employees during Woolsey's time). For the first time since William

Casey's tenure, the DCI was a member of the cabinet, giving him more access to the president. He also brought in new management, in an effort to spring-clean the Agency.

The CIA's public image suffered further during the mid-nineties when it was revealed that they were continuing to supply aid to Guatemalan military intelligence, despite an instruction in 1992 to sever ties, and were possibly complicit in the deaths of two Americans; this was seen as a continuation of now-outdated Cold War policies and further evidence that the Agency wasn't moving with the times – as one former agent told *Time* magazine: 'If you were going to pick a place where the CIA still has a cowboy mentality, it's there.' An internal probe found that the Agency had indeed covered up the deaths.

Other internal investigations launched by Deutch criticized the way in which material supplied by known double agents was passed up the chain of command, often without the relevant warnings attached. This practice was something that would come to haunt intelligence agencies in 2003 when the erroneous information regarding Saddam Hussein's weapons of mass destruction (WMDs) was given far more credence than it would have been had it been flagged correctly. Earlier operations against Saddam gave the Agency another knock when their spies in Northern Iraq, who had been trying to bring Kurdish and Iraqi dissidents together against Saddam, had to make a hasty exit in August 1996, leaving behind many of those who had trusted them. 'It may be that the CIA actually made tremendous efforts to protect its people,' a leading Iraqi expert said at the time, 'but the perception among Iraqis is that having anything to do with Americans is dangerous to your health.'

In November 1996, another Russian spy was found in the CIA ranks. Harold James Nicholson was carrying exposed film and a computer disc with confidential Agency documents when he was arrested by the FBI. For the previous two years

he had been working as a teacher at Camp Perry, known as
'The Farm', the Agency's training centre for new agents; prior
to that he had been posted to Kuala Lumpur, where he was
turned by an FSB officer who Nicholson had claimed he was
trying to persuade to work for the CIA – ironically around
the time that Aldrich Ames was arrested. Nicholson's moti-
vation was financial – after he was seen trying to beat a
standard polygraph test in 1995, the FBI began investigating
his finances, and discovered large sums of money. He
eventually pleaded guilty to receiving $180,000 from the
Russians and to one specimen charge of espionage, although
he had blown the cover of the agents passing through The
Farm during his tenure there. Nicholson was a well-regarded
agent and many at the Agency believed that he was on the way
to becoming 'a big spy' for the Russians.

Around this time, the FBI discovered that they too were
being betrayed to the Russians – although it wasn't Robert
Hanssen whose treachery had come to light. Earl Edwin Pitts,
a senior agent, had contacted the KGB in 1987 when stationed
in New York, and for the next five years passed documents to
his handler, Rollan G. Dzheikiya. Unfortunately for Pitts,
Dzheikiya defected after the fall of the Soviet Union, and
became part of a sting operation run by the Bureau to capture
Pitts. On his arrest in December 1996, the American claimed
he was motivated by rage at the FBI, partly because of his low
pay. An investigation into Pitts' activities made some suspicious that the Russians must have another mole within the
Bureau, since they never asked Pitts for anything major. Pitts
himself suggested that Robert Hanssen might be a spy.
Neither lead was properly followed up, and Hanssen remained undetected.

In a rare demonstration of cooperation between the FBI and
the CIA, the two organizations worked together on a
four-year manhunt for Aimal Kansi, who had killed two CIA
employees outside Langley in 1993. He was eventually

tracked down to Pakistan, whose administration allowed the joint task force agents to enter the country to capture him.

John Deutch resigned as DCI in December 1996, and was replaced by his deputy, George Tenet, who, unusually, remained in place after President George W. Bush succeeded President Clinton in 2000 – changes of party in the White House usually led to a new DCI. This provided an element of continuity when major changes were needed following 9/11. Tenet and the CIA would be accused of intelligence failures – and while the criticisms were justified, the Agency did far more in the build-up to 2001 than they have sometimes been given credit for. If information had been shared properly though in the three years before 9/11, the history of the first decade of the twenty-first century would have been very different.

14

THE WAR ON TERROR

It's easy to be wise after the event. Everyone has 20/20 hindsight, and there has probably been more 'Monday morning quarterbacking' regarding the work of the intelligence agencies in the years leading up to 11 September 2001 than any other event in recent history.

In June 2012, many of the key documents relating to what the CIA knew were finally released after a Freedom of Information Act request by the National Security Archive, a private business. These were referenced, but not quoted, in the 9/11 Commission's Report, and, even in a heavily redacted form, show a trail of missed opportunities and interagency bickering that would have catastrophic consequences. Perhaps most worrying of all is the CIA's own Inspector General report from August 2001, which praised the Counterterrorism Center's performance for 'coordinating national intelligence, providing warning, and promoting the effective use of Intelligence Community resources on terrorism issues' and even noting that the relationship with the FBI was better than it had been in 1994 – mere days before that was conclusively proved to be false.

One of the biggest problems that the CIA and the other intelligence agencies faced when trying to deal with al-Qaeda was the religious fanaticism of its members, which meant it was far harder to infiltrate them. As Agency veteran Robert Dannenberg explained, al-Qaeda operatives weren't like Soviet agents, who might be persuaded that the American way of life was better by showing them supermarkets 'because they were driven by many of the same things that we're driven by: success and taking care of our families'. They did get lucky early on though: Jamal Ahmed al-Fadl, described by some as one of the founding members of al-Qaeda, walked into the US Embassy in Eritrea in spring 1996. He had embezzled $110,000 from al-Qaeda and was desperate to defect.

This came shortly after a designated bin Laden unit had been established within the CIA, the first time that the Agency had set up a group specifically to target one person or organization. This 'virtual station' operated out of Langley, and was run by Michael Scheuer, previously head of the CTC's Islamic Extremist Branch, with a predominantly female team. From January 1996 onwards, their aim, according to DCI George Tenet, was 'to track [bin Laden], collect intelligence on him, run operations against him, disrupt his finances, and warn policymakers about his activities and intentions'. Al-Fadl's information gave them vital leads regarding al-Qaeda's plans and hopes. SIGINT operations were put in motion; allies were sought. But even then, not everything was as smooth as it should have been: the NSA and CIA didn't cooperate over jurisdictional issues.

Following the embassy bombings in 1998, Tenet significantly increased the attention on bin Laden. The CTC carried out a review of strategy, which led to Scheuer's departure as unit leader and the development of a comprehensive plan of attack against al-Qaeda. Unfortunately, much as what was known as

'The Plan' called for a united campaign by the CIA, FBI, NSA and others, this didn't happen in practice. FBI agents working with the CIA's bin Laden unit were not allowed to pass relevant information back to the Bureau; the NSA left intercepts of phone calls to the FBI, fearful of going beyond their remit, but the Bureau didn't obtain the phone records for those who had already been identified as potential hijackers until after 9/11. A briefing by Counterterrorism 'Tsar' Richard Clarke briefed representatives of the various agencies about the al-Qaeda threat – but these weren't passed back properly, and indeed Clarke would suggest the threat wasn't so pressing at the start of August. In an effort to cope with all the information flowing to the Unit, a new Strategic Assessments Branch was set up – but its new chief only reported for duty on 10 September 2011.

The CIA's own internal report, following the 9/11 Commission's verdict that the intelligence community had failed the President, noted that:

> Agency officers from the top down worked hard against the al-Qa'ida and Usama Bin Ladin targets. They did not always work effectively and cooperatively, however . . . If Intelligence Community officers had been able to view and analyse the full range of information available before 11 September 2001, they could have developed a more informed context in which to assess the threat reporting of the spring and summer that year . . . That so many individuals failed to act in this case reflects a systematic breakdown.

Threats certainly were reported up the chain of command but no one was certain whether the attack would be within the United States or on American interests elsewhere in the world. In June, a briefing suggested 'operatives linked to Usama Bin Ladin's organisation expect the near-term attacks they are planning to have dramatic consequences'. A briefing for the

President on 6 August was headlined 'Bin Ladin Determined To Strike in US', but wasn't treated with the urgency it required, as 9/11 Commissioner Bob Kerrey later told CNN. 'You were told again by briefing officers in August that it was a dire threat,' Kerrey said of Bush's claim that he would have moved heaven and earth if he had been aware ahead of time of the al-Qaeda threat. 'And what did you do? Nothing, so far as we could see on the 9/11 Commission.'

Other agencies around the world similarly received information that confirmed bin Laden was planning a major operation against US targets. MI6 had warned the Americans in 1999 that al-Qaeda was considering using commercial aircraft in 'unconventional ways . . . possibly as flying bombs'. Egyptian President Mubarak claimed that his country's intelligence service had penetrated al-Qaeda and warned of an attack using 'an airplane stuffed with explosives', although the target appeared to be the G8 talks held in spring 2001. An MI5 report on 6 July 2001 noted that 'UBL and those who share his agenda are currently well advanced in operational planning for a number of major attacks on Western interests', although it thought the most likely location 'is in the Gulf States, or the wider Middle East'. Mossad sent warnings to their CIA counterparts over the summer of 2001 citing 'credible chatter' that their agents had picked up in Afghanistan, Pakistan and Yemen – the CIA forced one paper who reported this to print a retraction. Even the Taliban Foreign Minister Wakil Ahmed Muttawakil tried to pass on a warning, although this wasn't taken seriously.

On 11 September 2001, two hijacked planes were flown into the World Trade Center in New York; a third hit the Pentagon in Washington DC. A fourth was hijacked but was retaken by its passengers; it crashed in Pennsylvania killing all on board. There were 2,753 victims at the World Trade Center including 411 emergency workers; 184 died at the Pentagon, and forty were killed in the Pennsylvania crash. The world's intelligence agencies had failed to read the signs in time. Everything would have to change.

The CIA's DCI George Tenet refused to accept that the Agency had failed in its duty, blaming the FBI for the shortcomings that allowed the terrorists to enter the United States and get into position to hijack the aircraft. As far as he was concerned, the fact that he was able to present President Bush with a plan for retaliation within four days indicated that the CIA was on top of the situation, even if others were not.

Even while the attacks were continuing, the CTC was beginning to track down information from all their sources, and within hours Tenet told the president that the attacks 'looked, smelled and tasted like bin Laden'. Four days later, Tenet's plan, which included 'a full-scale covert attack on the financial underpinnings of the terrorist network, including clandestine computer surveillance and electronic eavesdropping to locate the assets of al-Qaeda and other terrorist groups' and his 'Worldwide Attack Matrix', a plan for covert action in eighty countries, was presented to the president and his advisers at Camp David. On 17 September, Bush signed a Presidential Finding authorizing the CIA to hunt down, and if necessary, kill the leaders of al-Qaeda: 'I want justice,' he told reporters that day. 'And there's an old poster out West, I recall, that said "Wanted, Dead or Alive".' (The CIA had requested this authority in July, but had not yet received it.) He also authorised an extra $1 billion funding for the Agency.

President Bush declared his War on Terror in a speech to Congress on 20 September, stating bluntly that 'Our war on terror begins with al-Qaeda, but it does not end there. It will not end until every terrorist group of global reach has been found, stopped and defeated.' Among the rhetoric, he announced the creation of the Department of Homeland Security, adding, 'We will come together to give law enforcement the additional tools it needs to track down terror here at home. We will come together to strengthen our intelligence capabilities to know the plans of terrorists before they act and to find them before they strike.' The phrase 'war on terror' was adopted around the world, although the British stopped using it, partly, as former MI5 head Elizabeth Manningham-Buller pointed out, because the 9/11 attacks were 'a crime, not an act of war'.

The Taliban refused to hand bin Laden and the al-Qaeda leaders over to the Americans, leading in October to Operation Enduring Freedom, the invasion of Afghanistan. During the preparation for the war, the CIA worked inside Afghanistan, trying to create rifts between al-Qaeda and the Taliban, even proposing to assist a coup from within the Taliban if it meant al-Qaeda were handed over. When these efforts failed, the invasion was launched and within a few weeks, bin Laden was forced to flee to Tora Bora, in the east of Afghanistan, from where (probably with the aid of Pakistani intelligence, even though they were ostensibly assisting the Americans), he was able to escape into Pakistan. For a long time, it was believed he was dead until a video recording was released in late 2002.

Interrogation of detainees has always been a useful source of intelligence for spies across the centuries, but it was taken to a new level in the aftermath of the attacks on the World Trade Center. The arguments for and against 'enhanced' interrogation – using such techniques as waterboarding (where water is poured onto a cloth over a suspect's face, making him believe he is drowning) and sensory deprivation – have been rehearsed many times: can evidence produced that way be trusted, or has the suspect said what he thinks the interrogators want to hear in order to prevent the torture from recurring?

The CIA was given wide latitude in its hunt for the terrorist suspects. José Rodriguez, who became head of the National Clandestine Service, in charge of the interrogations, defended their actions, pointing out, 'We did the right thing for the right reason. And the right reason was to protect the homeland and to protect American lives.' The CIA took over responsibility for the interrogations in early 2002 and began 'rendition' of the suspects – removing them secretly to 'black sites' in foreign countries, places where the Agency could have control over the interrogations without supervision from others in the US administration or the media. Abu Zubaida, believed at the time to be one of the senior members of al-Qaeda, was rendered to Thailand after his capture in Faisalabad, Pakistan, in March 2002, However, both George Tenet, in his book about his time as DCI, and Rodriguez maintain that they were careful to check the legality of their moves (what Rodriguez calls 'get[ting] everybody in government to put their big boy pants on and provide the authorities that we needed') before proceeding.

A series of techniques was approved in what became described as the 'Torture Memo', an eighteen-page document dated 1 August 2002 sent by the Assistant Attorney General to the CIA's General Counsel. This set out in considerable detail the methods by which the processes would be applied, and how the use of them could not be classified as torture within the definition of Section 2340A of title 18 of the United States Code. (It would be further clarified by three memoranda in 2005 totalling 106 pages.) Speaking in April 2012, Rodriguez claimed: 'This program was about instilling a sense of hopelessness and despair on the terrorist, on the detainee, so that he would conclude on his own that he was better off cooperating with us.'

The FBI carried out the initial interrogation of Zubaida, during which he identified Khalid Sheikh Mohammed (KSM) as the mastermind behind the 9/11 attacks, and revealed plans to attack American apartments with bombs, as well as an assault on the Brooklyn Bridge. According to Ali H. Soufan, the FBI officer in charge of the interrogation of Zubaida and other al-Qaeda members, Zubaida gave up nothing further of use during the enhanced interrogation – and indeed he and his Bureau colleagues refused to have anything to do with them.

It is perhaps telling that Rodriguez authorized the destruction of the CIA tapes which chronicled the interrogation of Zubaida, although he claims that he did so after the revelation of the torture of Iraqi prisoners at Abu Ghraib by Army personnel following the 2003 invasion. 'I was concerned that the distinction between a legally authorized program as our enhanced interrogation program was, and illegal activity by a bunch of psychopaths would not be made,' he told a CBS documentary in April 2012.

The enhanced interrogation techniques were applied to KSM when he was captured; again, their efficacy is dubious. KSM was deprived of sleep for over seven days; he was waterboarded 183 times; his diet was manipulated. Yet he was still able to try to put his interrogators on the wrong track of the courier who was serving Osama bin Laden, and claimed more responsibility for some of al-Qaeda's activities than he could have had in an effort to stop the interrogation.

MI5 became embroiled in the rendition and torture controversy when they hit the headlines in 2010. The *Guardian* ran a story entitled 'Devious, dishonest and complicit in torture – top judge on MI5', based on a draft judgement in the case of Binyan Mohamed, who had been arrested in Pakistan, based on information supplied by Zubaida prior to his enhanced questioning, and interrogated by the CIA in Morocco as part of the War on Terror. Mohamed claimed that British officers were present during his interrogation and were passing questions to the interrogators, fully aware that he was actually being tortured. In 2006, MI5 said that Mohamed had only been questioned in Pakistan, where he was arrested, and the officer involved had seen no evidence of torture – although they had not sought assurances from the Americans regarding future treatment.

A 2009 civil case became embroiled in a row over what

sensitive materials could be revealed in public, but what the courts saw was sufficient for the Attorney General to recommend that the police investigate MI5. Eventually, Keir Starmer, the Director of Public Prosecutions, announced in January 2012 that there was not enough evidence to prove that the security services provided information about Mohamed when they knew he was at risk of torture, effectively clearing them.

Another case of the British services assisting with rendition wasn't so easy to dismiss. Abdelhakim Belhadj, who would later lead the Tripoli Military Council during the uprising against Gaddafi, was rendered to Libya by the CIA with British help, then incarcerated and tortured in the notorious Abu Selim jail in southern Tripoli. The documents confirming this were discovered in an abandoned government building after the fall of Gaddafi's regime, with MI6's Sir Mark Allen writing to Gaddafi's head of intelligence, Moussa Koussa, 'I congratulate you on the safe arrival of Abu Abdullah al-Sadiq [the name used by Belhaj]. This was the least we could do for you and for Libya to demonstrate the remarkable relationship we have built over the years.' Belhadj is suing the British government and Sir Mark Allen for damages, and the Metropolitan Police is investigating the allegations.

The hunt for Osama bin Laden and other key al-Qaeda members would stretch across the next decade, but that wasn't the Bush administration's highest priority. Whether there was a genuine belief that Saddam Hussein's Iraq was a party to 9/11, or whether there were those in the American government – notably Defence Secretary Donald Rumsfeld – who saw the terrorist attack as an opportunity to deal with more than one menace at a time, the focus quickly turned to Saddam. While they were busily engaged searching for al-Qaeda, the CIA was also tasked with investigating Iraq, and particularly whether Saddam Hussein was developing weapons of mass destruction.

According to the report prepared by the Commission on the Intelligence Capabilities of the United States Regarding Weapons of Mass Destruction, set up by President Bush following the invasion: 'The Intelligence Community's performance in assessing Iraq's pre-war weapons of mass destruction programs was a major intelligence failure. The failure was not merely that the Intelligence Community's assessments were wrong. There were also serious shortcomings in the way these assessments were made and communicated to policymakers.' At the same time the Butler Report, set up in the UK for the same purpose, noted that the Joint Intelligence Committee's judgement that Iraq was 'conducting nuclear related research and development into the enrichment of uranium' was based on two new agents' reports, and 'those reports were given more weight in the JIC assessment than they could reasonably bear'. It pointed out that the judgement 'went to (although not beyond) the outer limits of the intelligence available' but that there was 'no evidence of deliberate distortion or of culpable negligence'.

Whether the evidence was sufficient to justify the various administrations' desire to create regime change in Iraq or not, there were allegations that the dossier of information had been 'sexed up' before it was revealed to the British parliament and media. Major General Michael Laurie told the Chilcott Inquiry into Iraq: 'We knew at the time that the purpose of the dossier was precisely to make a case for war, rather than setting out the available intelligence, and that to make the best out of sparse and inconclusive intelligence the wording was developed with care.' Tony Blair's communications chief Alastair Campbell has consistently denied the accusation, claiming that he only assisted with the presentational aspects of the dossier. He told Lord Chilcott:

At no time did I ever ask [Joint Intelligence Committee head Sir John Scarlett] to beef up, to override, any of the judgements that he had. At no point did anybody from the prime minister down say to anybody within the intelligence services, 'You have got to tailor it to fit this judgement or that judgement.' It just never happened. The whole way through, it could not have been made clearer to everybody that nothing would override the intelligence judgements and that John Scarlett was the person who, if you like, had the single pen.

There were two key elements to the accusations against Saddam: that he was gaining uranium from Niger which could be enriched to produce weapons of mass destruction – that could potentially be prepared for use within 45 minutes, according to the British dossier; and that he was also preparing biological WMDs. 'We have first-hand descriptions of biological weapons factories on wheels,' Secretary of State Colin Powell told the United Nations Security Council, as they debated a resolution over Iraq's future. 'The source was an eye witness, an Iraqi chemical engineer who supervised one of these facilities. He actually was present during biological agent production runs. He was also at the site when an accident occurred in 1998. Twelve technicians died from exposure to biological agents.'

The problem was that he wasn't. The evidence for the latter relied on Iraqi informant Rafid Ahmed Alwan al-Janabi, code-named Curveball, who was comprehensively proved to be a liar – and who eventually admitted to the *Guardian* he had manipulated his handlers within the Germany intelligence agency, the BND. 'I had the chance to fabricate something to topple the regime,' he said in 2011. 'I and my sons are proud of that and we are proud that we were the reason to give Iraq the margin of democracy.'

Although by no means all the information regarding Curveball has yet been released into the public domain, the story that has emerged backs up the assertion made by Sir Richard Dearlove in a meeting at Downing Street on 23 July

2002. A leaked memo indicates he reported on his recent meetings in Washington that 'Bush wanted to remove Saddam, through military action, justified by the conjunction of terrorism and WMD. But the intelligence and facts were being fixed around the policy.'

Al-Janabi entered Germany in late 1999 on a tourist visa, and then applied for asylum, claiming that he had embezzled Iraqi government funds and faced imprisonment or death if he returned. Once he was in the German refugee system, he began talking about his work as a chemical engineer, which immediately attracted the attention of the BND. (In his interview with the *Guardian*, Janabi later claimed that he didn't mention his work until he was granted asylum in March 2000; the BND says that he actually ceased active cooperation after his asylum was granted in 2001.) He revealed that he had been part of a team that equipped trucks to brew bio-weapons, and named six sites that were already operational. Refusing to talk directly to American intelligence, the newly (and as it turned out, appropriately) code-named Curveball provided reams of material to the BND, enough to furnish ninety-five reports to Langley. There analysts evaluated the information, spy satellites checked out the sites named and drawings of the trucks were prepared. The problem, of course, was that without direct access to Curveball, no one could be absolutely sure that they were interpreting what he said correctly.

Curveball's information was nowhere near as concrete as its use to back up Powell's speech would suggest. 'His information to us was very vague,' one of his supervisors at the BND told the *Los Angeles Times* in 2005. 'He could not say if these things functioned, if they worked ... He didn't know ... whether it was anthrax or not. He had nothing to do with actual production of [a biological] agent. He was in the equipment testing phase. And the equipment worked.' He admitted that he had only personally visited one site, where he said that he understood that there had been an accident in

1998 – the source of the alleged 'eye witness' account referred to by Powell.

Why was he taken seriously? Curveball's information tallied with what the CIA analysts had anticipated, and, worse, seemed to be backed up by other information. When those sources were discredited, Curveball wasn't immediately disregarded. Warnings were sent by MI6 and the BND to Washington regarding Curveball's credibility. 'Elements of his behaviour strike us as typical of individuals we would normally assess as fabricators,' MI6 noted in April 2002. But by September 2002, DCI George Tenet was reporting that they had 'a credible defector who worked in the programme' for biochemical weapons. Despite the reservations of some within the CIA (which Tenet later vehemently denied being aware of), Curveball's information and drawings were included in Powell's speech – although, as was pointed out at the time by one congressional staffer, 'a drawing isn't evidence – it's hearsay'. The BND assumed that the CIA had other sources to corroborate Curveball's story, but it became clear that his testimony was the lynchpin around which the case was built.

Despite massive searches by the UN Inspectors and the Iraqis themselves, no trace of the trucks that Curveball talked about could be found in the weeks between Powell's speech and the invasion. Hans Blix, the chief inspector, told the Security Council on 7 March 2003 that they had found 'no evidence', but of course many simply thought that meant Saddam had hidden it, as he purportedly had with his other WMDs.

The aftermath of the invasion of Iraq, and the subsequent discovery that Saddam did not have WMDs, continues to affect intelligence agencies and governments, with further official inquiries on-going. One aspect that became crystal clear, though, was that Curveball had lied. His family said that he had no problem with Americans; he had come near the bottom of his engineering class, not top as he had claimed. He was a trainee engineer, not the project manager that the CIA had made him out to be. Worst of all, he had been fired in 1995 – three years before the supposed accident, and just at the time when he claimed he started work on the WMD transports. A year after the invasion, the CIA was finally allowed access to Curveball directly, and took his story apart piece by piece.

Despite this, al-Janabi tried to stick to his guns, until he finally admitted the truth to the *Guardian* in February 2011, although he maintained that he only had sketchy dealings with the BND. In response, George Tenet posted a statement to his website noting that 'the latest reporting of the subject repeats and amplifies a great deal of misinformation about the case'. Amidst his further attempts at self-justification, he did make one key point: 'The handling of this matter is certainly a textbook case of how not to deal with defector provided material.' Few would disagree.

The perceived intelligence failures both prior to 9/11 and in the build-up to the war in Iraq led to one of the biggest shake-ups of the American intelligence community in half a century – or, at least, it should have done. The aim of the various reforms was to create an intelligence community fit for purpose in the twenty-first century. According to the Office of the Director of National Intelligence's (ODNI) website:

> The United States Intelligence Community must constantly strive for and exhibit three characteristics essential to our effectiveness. The IC must be *integrated*: a team making the whole greater than the sum of its parts. We must also be *agile*: an enterprise with an adaptive, diverse, continually learning, and mission-driven intelligence workforce that embraces innovation and takes initiative. Moreover, the IC must *exemplify America's values*: operating under the rule of law, consistent

with Americans' expectations for protection of privacy and civil liberties, respectful of human rights, and in a manner that retains the trust of the American people.

DCI George Tenet resigned unexpectedly, stepping down from the CIA in July 2004, shortly before the release of the report by the 9/11 Commission. This recommended the establishment of a National Intelligence Director who would not only take responsibility for the safety of the United States, but also have effective powers to control the seventeen different intelligence agencies. This didn't go down well with the government, or the various agencies that would be affected, and what many regarded as a typical Washington fudge and compromise ensued. Secretary of Defence Donald Rumsfeld, in particular, didn't want the Pentagon's various intelligence agencies answerable to the Director of National Intelligence (DNI); the FBI wanted to keep their autonomy. At the time, historian and journalist Fred Kaplan described the final bill as 'not reform in any meaningful sense. There will be a director of national intelligence. But the post will likely be a figurehead, at best someone like the chairman of the Council of Economic Advisers, at worst a thin new layer of bureaucracy, and in any case nothing like the locus of decision-making and responsibility that the 9/11 commission had in mind.'

Tenet's successor at the CIA was Porter Goss, who would be the last CIA chief to act as head of the intelligence community; one of the many clauses of the Intelligence Reform and Terrorism Prevention Act prevented a DNI from serving as head of the CIA or any other agency at the same time. The first DNI, appointed in 2005, was former US Ambassador to the UN and Iraq, John D. Negroponte; his successor in 2007 Admiral Michael McConnell also served for two years. Neither really was in a position to force through the changes that were needed within the intelligence community. By the end of November 2008, even the DNI's own Inspector General noted that the office was not providing effective leadership, which was 'undermining ODNI's credibility and fuelling assertions that the ODNI is just another layer of bureaucracy'.

Goss probably didn't expect to become DCI. A few months before Tenet's surprise resignation, in his capacity as Chairman of the House Intelligence Committee, Goss wrote to the Agency saying:

> After years of trying to convince, suggest, urge, entice, cajole, and pressure [the] CIA to make wide-reaching changes to the way it conducts its HUMINT mission [the] CIA continues down a road leading over a proverbial cliff. The damage to the HUMINT mission through its misallocation and redirection of resources, poor prioritization of objectives, micromanagement of field operations, and a continued political aversion to operational risk is, in the Committee's judgment, significant and could likely be long-lasting.

This damaged his relationship with senior staff at the Agency, many of whom would resign during his tenure.

Goss was succeeded by former NSA head, and Deputy DNI, Michael Hayden, who served from 2006 to 2009. During that time, the Agency was actively involved in (still-classified) missions in Pakistan, assisting with the removal of al-Qaeda's leadership. 'We gave President Bush a list of people we were most mad at, in the tribal region of Pakistan, in July 2008,' he said in 2010. 'By the time I left office, more than a dozen of those people were dead . . . What the Agency did to dismantle the al-Qai'da leadership . . . I'm most proud of that.' The CIA also helped with the identification of a nuclear reactor that was being built in Syria with North Korean assistance. Hayden was an advocate of confirming the intelligence publicly after the event – not earlier, since the Syrians 'might do something stupid if they were publicly embarrassed' – in order to ensure that people were aware of the Korean involvement during the discussions over nuclear proliferation.

British intelligence agencies were also actively involved with counter-terrorism operations after 9/11. As the bombings in London on 7 July 2005 (known as 7/7) which killed fifty-two people proved, they weren't always as successful as they might have liked, but as the public portions of the trials of terrorist suspects who have been arrested show, MI5 and MI6 have been responsible for preventing further atrocities. Errors have of course occurred – such as the shooting of innocent Brazilian electrician Jean Charles de Menezes on 22 July 2005, in the aftermath of an attempted second wave of bombings the previous day.

The attempt by Richard Reid to blow up a transatlantic jet just before Christmas 2001 was an indication to the British agencies that this form of terrorism could be home-grown. Over the next decade, MI5's budget and personnel were increased, and they were able to monitor a larger number of suspects. Operation Crevice led to the arrest of a terrorist cell in 2003 shortly before they began a campaign against nightclubs, shops and pubs using ammonium nitrate bombs – although unfortunately two men with whom they briefly had contact were not monitored. They went on to cause carnage in London on 7/7. Operation Rhyme, which took place in 2004, prevented Dhiren Barot from carrying out his planned attacks in London underground car parks. Operation Hat stopped the failed bombers of 21 July 2005 from trying again. Kazi Rahman was arrested trying to buy weapons in November 2005 after a police and MI5 sting operation – his name had been passed to MI5 by the FBI after they were able to turn al-Qaeda operative Mohamed Babar the previous year.

Operation Overt was aimed against Abdullah Ahmed Ali, who planned to rival the scale of the 9/11 attacks using suicide bombers inside multiple aircraft departing from Heathrow.

He and his co-conspirators were arrested in August 2006, shortly before they became operational; the way they intended to explode the devices is the reason why security measures regarding liquids being taken on board aircraft were tightened up immensely that summer. The nine members of a plot to create havoc at Christmas 2010, with targets including the Stock Exchange, Big Ben, Westminster Abbey, the Palace of Westminster and the London Eye, were arrested four days before they planned to set off their first device. On 1 July 2012, a plot by al-Qaeda in the Arabian Peninsula to explode a bomb during the London Olympics was foiled; a few days later, a suspected al-Qaeda terrorist was arrested after visiting the Olympics site in East London five times in one day, in contravention of the control order he was under.

As Eliza Manningham-Buller pointed out in a TV documentary about the war on terror, there never is just one plot being investigated. At any one time, dozens are under investigation.

Probably the highest-profile intelligence operation of the past few years has been the hunt for, and eventual assassination of al-Qaeda's leader Osama bin Laden. While Khalid Sheikh Mohammed (KSM) may have been in charge of the details of the 9/11 plot, it was bin Laden who was its instigator and mastermind, making him the ultimate target of all the American intelligence activities in the decade following the destruction of the Twin Towers in New York.

US Navy Seal Team Six entered the compound at Abbottabad, Pakistan, and carried out the mission that eliminated bin Laden in May 2011, but they weren't alone – members of the US Army's 160th Special Operations Aviation Regiment (Airborne) and the CIA were there beside them. Surprising as it may seem, even on the day that President Barack Obama gave the authorization for the mission to proceed, no one had ever captured a photograph of bin Laden at the compound or

been able to get a recording of the mysterious male figure who
occupied the building's top two floors.

Billions of dollars were expended by the US during the first
decade of the twenty-first century on electronic surveillance.
But it was through information gained through old-fashioned
means – interrogating prisoners – that bin Laden was finally
tracked down. The key to finding him turned out to be his
trusted courier, Abu Ahmed al-Kuwaiti, aka Ibrahim Saeed
Ahmed. Numerous leads had been followed up since bin
Laden disappeared from Tora Bora in 2002, following the
American invasion. All had turned out to be dead ends. Many
of the al-Qaeda hierarchy had been tracked down and
eliminated, as the CIA struck with Predator and Reaper
drones, but not bin Laden himself. Every aspect of the tapes
that he issued was analysed, whether it was the shape of the
rocks in the background or the birdsong briefly audible. Large
rewards were offered for information, but bin Laden's almost
messianic position as the perceived saviour of true Islam
meant that there were no takers.

Al-Kuwaiti's name was one of those mentioned by Mohammed al-Qahtani, an al-Qaeda operative who was originally
groomed as a twentieth hijacker for the 9/11 attacks. Captured
by the Pakistanis in December 2001, he was interrogated at the
American base at Guantanamo Bay in Cuba, where he
admitted, after weeks of abuse, that KSM had introduced him
to al-Kuwaiti, who had given him instructions in secret
communications. When KSM himself was captured, he told
his Pakistani interrogators that al-Kuwaiti had helped bin
Laden to escape from Tora Bora, although he later told his
American questioners that al-Kuwaiti was retired. This
information was divulged after his extreme interrogations, and
seems to have been a deliberate attempt to put the Americans
off al-Kuwaiti's scent; his act of defiance is often quoted by
those opposed to the extreme methods as proof that such
means do not always work.

However, another al-Qaeda courier, Hassan Ghul, said otherwise. Al-Kuwaiti was a trusted part of bin Laden's inner circle, and was working with Abu Faraj al-Libi, KSM's successor. When al-Libi was captured in May 2005, he also tried to divert attention away from al-Kuwaiti, making up the name of a courier whom he said was the key player. Attention was focused on the courier network, but leads were in short supply.

When he took power in January 2009, President Obama made the capture of bin Laden one of the CIA's priorities, and on 2 June 2009 he ordered his new D/CIA Leon Panetta to 'provide me within 30 days a detailed operation plan for locating and bringing [bin Laden] to justice'. Hopes were pinned on an apparent defector from al-Qaeda, Jordanian doctor Humam al-Balawi, but hope turned to tragedy when al-Balawi blew himself and seven CIA operatives up on 30 December 2009. Al-Qaeda continued operations, even as the CIA turned up the heat against them further – an attempt to down a commercial jet was foiled, and Faisal Shahzad, an American of Pakistani descent trained by the Taliban, tried to blow up his SUV in Times Square on 1 May 2010.

Surveillance on al-Qaeda operatives around the world paid dividends in the summer of 2010 when one of them contacted al-Kuwaiti, who revealed that he was 'back with the people I was with before'. This was taken to mean that he was back in bin Laden's inner circle. Human intelligence came to the fore now, as a Pakistani agent, working for the CIA, tracked al-Kuwaiti to Peshawar in Pakistan, then followed him back to the town of Abbottabad, two hours to the east. Al-Kuwaiti was living in a compound that struck the CIA as odd, since it had neither phone nor internet services.

When Panetta heard of this 'fortress' he ordered the Agency to investigate every avenue for getting inside the compound. It was clear that there was a chance that this was bin Laden's location, but after the Curveball fiasco over WMDs seven years earlier, they were determined to ensure that any intelligence used to launch a mission was absolutely certain. The number of families in the compound seemed odd, as did the Pakistani intelligence service's complete lack of knowledge about it. As deputy director Michael Morell pointed out at one stage, 'The circumstantial case of Iraq having WMD was actually stronger than the circumstantial case that bin Laden is living in the Abbottabad compound.'

The CIA set up a safe house in Abbottabad, and deduced from the various movements to and from the compound, as well as observation of the amount of laundry left to dry, that there were three families within the compound rather than the two which there would appear to be at first glance. The composition of the third seemed to match bin Laden's immediate family. It did seem as if the hunt might be over.

The relationship between the Americans and the Pakistanis took a knock early in 2011 when a CIA contractor, Raymond Davis, killed two Pakistani citizens in Lahore. There was already little trust between the two countries and their respective intelligence agencies: the Times Square bomber wasn't the only anti-American terrorist who had come from Pakistan, and there was a feeling that the Pakistan intelligence agency might not be playing it straight with the CIA. Consequently, the Pakistanis were not informed of the CIA suspicions over the Abbottabad compound.

As plans were drawn up, the information the CIA had painstakingly gained was subjected to a 'Red Team' inquiry once more, this time by experts outside the Agency. This meant that every piece of evidence was checked to see if there was an alternate explanation that provided as likely an explanation as the one ascribed by the CIA. The week before the raid went ahead, the Red Team concluded that none of the alternate hypotheses was as likely as the theory that bin Laden was there.

Obama's DNI, James Clapper, was one of those who felt

that it was 'the most compelling case we've had in ten years' of hunting for bin Laden. Leon Panetta felt that they were 'probably at the point where we have got the best intelligence we can get'. Both Vice-President Joe Biden and Secretary of Defence (and former CIA DCI) Robert Gates were against a raid; Foreign Secretary Hillary Clinton was in favour. So, after considering everything, was the president.

The raid went ahead on 1 May and at 11.35 p.m. President Obama informed the American people that 'the United States has conducted an operation that killed Osama bin Laden, the leader of al-Qaeda, and a terrorist who's responsible for the murder of thousands of innocent men, women and children.'

Leon Panetta remembered one of the most unusual events of that night. As he drove from the White House, he heard chants from Lafayette Park. 'CIA! CIA! CIA!' Maybe some of the failures of the past were now forgiven.

15

A NEW COLD WAR?

The conflict in Syria during 2012 brought the idea of a 'new Cold War' back into focus. With the CIA assisting the rebels and the Russians helping to maintain the existing regime, at the time of writing it seemed as if 'proxy wars' like those waged in the fifties and sixties are being fought once more, as the ideologies of East and West clashed. But beneath all the rhetoric about a change in Russian attitudes following the collapse of the Soviet Union, did anything really change? Wouldn't it, perhaps, be more accurate to say that the fall of the Berlin Wall and the end of Communism marked a new phase in the Cold War, which has been fought constantly since then?

It is open to debate as to how much difference there is between the KGB and the agencies that were formed from its members and apparatus. The KGB's First Directorate – responsible for overseas operations – became the Foreign Intelligence Service, initially headed by Yevgeni Primakov. As its spokesman Yuri Kobaladze pointed out in 1994, their main purpose was information-gathering from overt and covert

sources: 'That does not mean we will stop gathering information on you, and you on us, right? There are friendly states
but no friendly intelligence services.' The Second Directorate
eventually became the FSB after Boris Yeltsin disbanded the
Ministry of Security following questions about its loyalties
during his struggles with the Russian parliament in 1993.
Disingenuously, it claimed that it too could close down if the
CIA activities in Russia were discontinued.

There was little chance of that. The discovery of Russian
spies Aldrich Ames in 1994, and Edwin Pitts and Harold
Nicholson two years later – all of whom were willing to work
for the KGB's successors – seemed to justify the pessimistic
outlook of some in America who felt that the overt friendli-
ness that was being displayed by the Clinton administration
to the former Soviet Union was unwarranted.

FSB Director Nikolai Kovalev commented in 1996 that
'There has never been such a number of spies arrested by us
since the time when German agents were sent in during the
years of World War II.' Around four hundred foreign
intelligence staff were either arrested or placed under surveillance in Russia over the previous two years, and the FSB were
quick to publicise their successes: Platon Obukhov, a former
Russian Foreign Ministry staffer, was arrested in April 1996,
for allegedly communicating by radio with a member of the
British Embassy staff and passing on political and strategic
defence information to MI6. The FSB claimed this was the
biggest failure by the British since the time of Penkovsky.
Obukhov was sentenced to eight years in prison, but was
re-tried in 2002 and sent to a psychiatric hospital for
treatment. Vladimir Sentsov was also tried for spying for
Britain, and received ten years in jail: the worker at a defence
institute was charged with selling technological secrets to MI6.

Strategic Missile Forces Major Dudinka was caught while
trying to get $500,000 from 'a foreign intelligence service',
according to the FSB. He had classified information ready on

a diskette, including the command and control system for a missile army. Lieutenant Colonel Andrei Dudin of the FAPSI (the Russian equivalent of the NSA) was sentenced to twelve years' imprisonment after making contact with the German BND. Major Dudnik from the Russian Centre for Space Reconnaissance was caught handing top-secret satellite photos over to Israeli intelligence; they were also running an agent inside the GRU, who was arrested too.

The CIA lost an asset only referred to as Finkel in the FSB reports after he was convicted of passing on secret defence research to the Agency for 'monetary reward'. A former adviser in the Ministry of Foreign Affairs was also caught by the FSB. Known only as Makarov, he had worked for the CIA since his time at the Soviet Embassy in Bolivia back in 1976, but according to the FSB records, he had only received $21,000 for his efforts.

The FSB weren't overly keen on the new culture of openness that was supposed to characterize the new Russia. A survey of the Russian press in the mid-nineties shows a number of cases where the FSB arrested people on charges of spying although what they were doing was revealing information publicly, rather than selling it to foreign governments.

Boris Yeltsin made a key appointment to the FSB in July 1998, when he placed Vladimir Putin in charge as director, a position he held until becoming Acting Prime Minister in August 1999. Putin had served in the KGB between 1975 and 1991, resigning on the second day of the attempted coup that August. His more hardline approach would be cited as the cause of Russia's sometimes more intransigent attitude during his presidency of the country in the first decade of the twenty-first century.

Echoes of the old Cold War tensions flared up more openly from time to time. When retired KGB officer Vladimir Galkin landed at JFK airport in New York in October 1996, he found himself an involuntary guest of the FBI, based on charges that a few years earlier he had tried to gain information on Reagan's 'Star Wars' programme from Data General Corporation. The FBI had caught the men he had been running, but without his testimony they didn't have a case, so in violation of the unwritten agreement between the CIA and the Russians that former intelligence officers would be left alone, they arrested Galkin. Although the Bureau offered him a choice between thirty years in prison or assistance as a defector, he created a third option, demanding a phone and calling his wife in Moscow. She alerted Russian intelligence, immediately escalating the situation. In response, DCI John Deutch put pressure on the FBI and the Justice Department to drop the charges; Russian Prime Minister Viktor S. Chernomyrdin personally complained to US Vice President Al Gore. The FBI caved in, which probably saved countless former CIA operatives then working in Russia from problems.

A clear distinction was made between intelligence operatives for foreign countries who had previously been enemies but were now (however loosely) allies, such as Galkin, and those who they ran, whose treacherous activities had not previously come to light. Some of these were uncovered as a result of the incredible and painstaking work carried out by Colonel Vasili Mitrokhin, who defected to the West in 1992 bringing with him the fruits of his labours in the KGB archives. Over a period of ten years, he made copious notes on classified files, which he concealed in milk churns near his dacha upon his retirement. These gave details on past and present KGB agents, and as they were analysed, provided the basis for numerous arrests around the Western world.

These included former NSA clerk Robert Lipka, who first started working for the KGB in the mid-sixties. According to the head of the Washington residency at the time, who was responsible for assessing the information, Lipka was passing over whatever he got his hands on, some of which was ultra-sensitive, but was mostly of little value. He was motivated by money – payments of $1,000 being standard – which he used to put himself through college. He worked for the KGB until 1974, and then was willing to be reactivated when approached by 'Russians' in 1996. MI6, who had access to Mitrokhin's papers after the CIA turned them down, had passed on a warning to the FBI, who set up a sting operation to catch Lipka.

The Mitrokhin papers also assisted with the eventual arrest of George Trofimov. They gave enough information to identify Trofimov and his KGB handler in 1994, but under Germany's Statute of Limitations, they could not be charged. It seemed as if he would walk clear but the FBI were determined to get sufficient evidence to arrest him. When Trofimov returned to Florida after his retirement, he was approached by an FBI agent posing as a member of the SVR. Trofimov would later claim that he made up a story of passing information to the KGB to try to gain cash: 'I can't explain the logic behind it anymore,' he told CBS in 2009. 'My major logic was, I need money, they need a reason to help me. They need a justification, so I'm going to try to provide them with that. And that's what I did.' In an unusual twist, one of the star witnesses against Trofimov at his eventual trial in 2001 was the KGB's Oleg Kalugin, who had described meetings with the American in his memoirs. Still maintaining his innocence, Trofimov was sentenced to life imprisonment.

If the upper echelons of the American agencies had hoped that information from the Mitrokhin archive, coupled with their own trawling of the various Eastern bloc countries' intelligence agencies' papers in the aftermath of the collapse of Communism, would mean there were no more nasty surprises coming similar to Aldrich Ames, they were in for a nasty shock in 2001. Robert Hanssen was finally caught red-handed; according to some accounts, his immediate reaction was: 'What took you so long?'

It was a fair question, and one that was asked at many levels during the inevitable post-mortem. Hanssen had curtailed his own work for the Soviets two weeks before the dissolution of the Soviet Union in 1991, shortly after visiting another priest and confessing his sins, as he had a decade earlier. He had warned the KGB that he was about to receive a promotion which would move him 'temporarily out of direct responsibility' although he quoted General Patton's remark before the Normandy invasion: 'Let's get this over with so we can go kick the shit out of the purple-pissing Japanese.' It wasn't the only time that he would cite the general – and this particular coarse phrase would prove to be Hanssen's undoing.

Hanssen briefly reactivated contact with the GRU in 1993, interested to see if the information he had previously passed to the KGB had been shared with Soviet military intelligence. However, although he introduced himself as 'Ramon Garcia', expecting to be recognized, the GRU man he approached thought it was an FBI entrapment, and nothing further happened. Hanssen kept an eye on the FBI computers for any hint he was under suspicion, occasionally causing questions to be asked about his behaviour when he claimed to be testing the system security or was found with a password hacker on his hard drive. Surprisingly, no one thought more of it, even when Earl Pitts mentioned Hanssen's name during his interrogation. FBI Special Agent Thomas K. Kimmel Jr. was convinced that there was a second mole within the Bureau, but couldn't find enough evidence to prove his theory.

Believing that he was in the clear, Hanssen contacted the Russians again in October 1999. The SVR couldn't believe their luck: 'We express our sincere joy on the occasion of resumption of contact with you,' they wrote back. Delays in communication started to worry Hanssen: 'I have come about as close as I ever want to come to sacrificing myself to help you, and I get silence,' he wrote in March 2000. They replied in July asking him for 'information on the work of a special group which serches [*sic*] [for a] "mole" in [the] CIA and [the] FBI' to help ensure his security, but warning him not to send them messages through the mail. Hanssen asked for the funds the Russians had put aside for him to be transferred to a Swiss bank, but they refused 'because now it is impossible to hide its origin'. A dead drop was set up in Foxtone Park for 18 February 2001.

Hanssen's luck continued to hold. The molehunt focused its attention on CIA agent Brian Kelley, since he matched the profile they had prepared. Kelley was completely innocent, but three years were wasted investigating him; the cloud over him only began to lift after Hanssen's arrest.

Hanssen was unaware of the molehunters' plan to find a Russian source that might be persuaded to reveal the mole's identity, at this stage still expected to be Brian Kelley. A retired former KGB officer, living in Moscow, was targeted: he wanted to expand his business overseas so was invited to a meeting in New York in April 2000. To the surprise of the FBI, he claimed that he had access to the KGB file on the mole, which he had removed from KGB headquarters before his retirement. It didn't contain the name of the agent, but had all the details that he had given the KGB over the years. He even had access to a tape of the mole speaking. After considerable negotiations, he sold the file to the Americans for $7 million.

When the file was extracted from Russia by the CIA and passed to the FBI, it was treasure far beyond what the molehunters could reasonably have hoped for at any stage of their investigations: descriptions of the documents the mole had provided; computer disks with copies of the letters exchanged between the Russians and their asset. When they listened to the tape, they realized that it wasn't Kelley speaking, but it was someone who sounded familiar – and the phrase 'purple-pissing Japanese' had also been heard at the FBI. To their horror, the team realized that the person they were seeking was Robert Hanssen.

At this closing stage of his career, Hanssen was assigned to the Office of Foreign Missions at the State Department, but in order to watch him properly the Bureau wanted him back at FBI headquarters. He was therefore offered a new posting, which apparently recognized his computer expertise, and brought him back in-house. There he was watched constantly, and his home phone tapped. When he went to meetings, his office was searched, where messages from the SVR were found on a memory card.

Hanssen began to get suspicious, both of the 'make-work' element of his new job and 'repeated bursting radio signal emanations' from his car. He wrote to the SVR noting that his 'greatest utility to you has come to an end, and it is time to seclude myself from active service . . . Something has aroused the sleeping tiger.'

However, he still made his appointment on 18 February 2001, which the FBI knew about from the memory card. Maybe by that stage he had a death wish anyway. He had once told a friend, Ron Mlotek, 'A person would have to be a total stupid f***ing idiot to spy for the KGB because you would be caught. Because we're going to get you.'

And they did. Robert Hanssen was arrested as he slipped a package of documents in the dead drop location under a bridge in Foxstone Park. As Attorney General John Ashcroft said at the press conference announcing the capture: 'This is a difficult day for the FBI.' Hanssen pleaded guilty and promised to cooperate; it saved him from the death penalty. He was sentenced to life in prison with no possibility of parole.

Some observers, notably including former CIA chief Milt Bearden, believe that another mole has yet to be found who was operational simultaneously with Ames and Hanssen. Neither of them had access to some of the information that found its way into the KGB's hands, and led to the arrests of, among others, Oleg Gordievsky. With the current level of tension between East and West, the spy's identity is unlikely to be learned, at least while he or she remains alive.

Although much of their concentration was, of necessity, on countering potential and actual terrorist threats from radical extremists in the months following 9/11, MI5 were still actively involved with counter-espionage. Two sting operations successfully led to the arrest of British Aerospace employees who were trying to sell highly classified documents to the SVR. Both Rafael Bravo and Ian Parr were caught after they'd contacted the Russian Embassy offering their services, although, intriguingly, the official MI5 history doesn't explain how the Security Service discovered their approaches! Bravo was sentenced to eleven years, Parr to eight. And MI5 received a formal protest from the SVR that their operative had impersonated a Russian intelligence officer to trap Bravo.

There was an element of humour to the first exchange between the Russian Federation and the UK in 2006. In a programme on Russian television, the FSB accused four British diplomats of spying, in concert with a Russian citizen. A fake rock on a Moscow street contained electronic equipment that was used to transmit and receive information. The FSB filmed its use and linked it to allegations that the British were making covert payments to human rights groups. Asked about the allegations at the time, Prime Minister Tony Blair commented, 'I'm afraid you're going to get the old stock-in-trade, of never commenting on security matters. Except when we want to, obviously.' In 2012, his chief of staff Jonathan Powell admitted to a BBC documentary that the rock affair was 'embarrassing', but 'they had us bang to rights'.

The discussions later in the year were anything but comical, and soured relations between the two countries, particularly as it seemed as if Cold War tactics were back in use. Former KGB spy Alexander Litvinenko apparently died of poisoning after drinking a cup of tea that had been laced with radioactive

Polonium-210 on 1 November 2006. He had been an outspoken critic both of Vladimir Putin's regime, and the Russian leader personally, claiming that the FSB under Putin had ordered him to assassinate Russian oligarch Boris Berezovsky; that it had been responsible for a series of explosions blamed on Chechen separatists, which had been instrumental in bringing Putin to power; and even that Putin was a paedophile. He was granted asylum in the UK in 2000, where he advised both MI5 and MI6 and wrote increasingly vitriolic attacks on the FSB and Putin, accusing them of supporting terrorists, including al-Qaeda, and being responsible for the London bombings of 7/7. Two weeks before his fatal drink, he said that Putin had ordered the assassination of Russian journalist Anna Politkovskaya.

Litvinenko met with former KGB agents Dmitry Kovtun and Andrei Lugovoi on 1 November and fell ill shortly afterwards. He died in hospital on 23 November. The police investigation led to the preparation of an extradition request for Lugovoi from Russia, which was not processed. Lugovoi claimed the request was politically motivated, and was even willing to undergo a polygraph test. The test was carried out by a French media company who supply tests for daytime television programmes such as *The Jeremy Kyle Show*. Lugovoi said he had not been involved directly or indirectly with the murder, or had anything to do with polonium. 'After careful analysis of all the diagrams obtained from the test, we have determined that the answers to these questions were not false. Thus, in our professional opinion, Andrey Lugovoi was telling the truth when answering the above questions,' came the result. This seemed to fly in the face of evidence of polonium traces in his hotel rooms, and on the planes that he had used between London and Moscow. Lugovoi now has parliamentary immunity from extradition as a sitting Russian member of parliament; an inquest ordered in October 2011 had still not convened in July 2012, when Litvinenko's widow lobbied the British parliament to assist with helping her find final answers.

The relationship between Russia and Britain has not fully recovered from the incident. Diplomats were expelled by both countries. Long-range bomber aircraft sorties were recommenced by the Russians in 2007, requiring RAF planes to scramble from time to time when they came too near to British airspace. The following January, the Russians claimed that the British Council in Moscow was riddled with spies. That July, a 'senior security source' told the *Daily Telegraph*: 'Russia is a country which is under suspicion of committing murder on British streets and it must be assumed that having done it once they will do it again.' Six months later it was revealed that the number of Russian intelligence agents in the UK was at the same level as during the height of the Cold War, a piece of information that MI5 considered serious enough that it placed it on its website. 'If a country, such as Russia or Iran, can steal a piece of software which will save it seven years in research and development then it will do so without any hesitation,' a 'Whitehall source' said. 'Russian agents will target anybody that they believe could be useful to them. Spying is hard-wired into the country's DNA. They have been at it for centuries and they are simply not going to stop because the Cold War has ended.' And it was clear that Britain wasn't the only target.

The spy ring that was broken in America in 2010 was a gift to journalists, thanks to the involvement of future model and cover star Anna Chapman. It had all the ingredients of a classic spy thriller: sleeper agents planted a decade earlier in the heart of suburbia, a beautiful honey trap who got so close to a key member of President Obama's cabinet that the FBI were forced to act, and a dramatic swap of agents at Vienna International Airport.

Ten Russian agents, including Chapman, were arrested on

27 June, 2010; an eleventh was detained two days later in Cyprus on his way to Budapest; two further members of the ring escaped back to Russia. In the indictment laid against the agents, the FBI included the instructions that the SVR had given the sleepers: 'You were sent to [the] USA for [a] long-term service trip. Your education, bank accounts, car, house etc. – all these serve one goal: fulfill [*sic*] your main mission, i.e. to search and develop ties in policymaking circles in [the] US and send intels [intelligence reports] to C[enter].' They weren't particularly competent though – evidence against Chapman was provided in part by the laptop that she herself gave to an FBI agent posing as her SVR contact, and she bought a cellphone giving the address '99 Fake Street'.

The FBI had been running the operation to catch them – Operation Ghost Stories – for many years. Documents that have been released on the FBI's website, although heavily redacted, indicate that the ring was under surveillance as far back as 2002 and provided copious amounts of video evidence against them showing them using dead drops, 'brush past' exchanges of information with Russian officials and other elements of tradecraft. The Russians had in some cases taken the identities of American citizens and built a complete cover for themselves, including enrolling and graduating from universities and joining professional organizations. They started families as part of their cover and even, according to one of the children, intended to recruit them to work for the FSB when the time was right.

Chapman was a recent addition to the spy ring, and was targeted by the FBI. However, she felt uncomfortable when, on 26 June, the fake SVR agent asked her to pass a counterfeit passport to another spy. She contacted her father, a former KGB officer, for advice; he told her not to carry out the instructions and hand the passport in at a police station. This she did the next day, and was arrested. This attempted entrapment by the FBI may have been a ploy to get stronger evidence against her. According to Bureau counter-intelligence chief Frank Figliuzzi: 'We were becoming very concerned,' he told a British Channel 4 documentary in 2012. 'They were getting close enough to a sitting US cabinet member that we thought we could no longer allow this to continue.' This was the first confirmation that Chapman was more competent than the original reports had indicated.

Even before the spy ring was arrested, preparations were in hand for a spy swap with the Russians. When the approach was made by the CIA, and the requisite faux protestations and denials had been made by the FSB, the details were quickly arranged. Chapman and the other Russians were exchanged for: Igor Sutyagin, convicted of passing details on submarines systems to the CIA; Sergei Skripal, a GRU colonel who had been working for MI6; SVR Colonel Alexander Zaporozhsky, sentenced to eighteen years for spying for the Americans in 2003; and Gennady Vasilenko, a former KGB officer who was, incorrectly, believed to be a double agent for the Americans, thanks to information supplied by Robert Hanssen. No evidence had been found against him, but he had been imprisoned on other charges. He was the only one who hadn't committed treason against the Soviet Union or the Russian Federation. According to some reports, he was included in the swap after a personal request from his former counterpart, CIA officer Jack Platt.

The returning spies were eventually hailed as heroes (once they'd been debriefed, and the SVR could be sure that they hadn't been turned as double agents). Chapman now hosts a TV show and has made appearances in the Russian version of *Maxim* magazine, as well as on the catwalk. This might make it seem as if what she did isn't to be taken seriously, but, as former MI5 Director General Sir Stephen Lander pointed out, 'The fact that they're nondescript or don't look serious is part of the charm of the business. That's why the Russians are so successful at some of this stuff. They're able to put people in those positions over time to build up their cover to be useful. They are part of a machine ... And the machine is a very professional and serious one.'

The Chapman affair had a knock-on effect in Britain when MI5 believed that they had found another honey trap agent shortly after Chapman and her colleagues had been repatriated. Twenty-six-year-old Russian student Ekaterina Zatuliveter was arrested and told she would be deported as a risk to national security. This followed an investigation into her relationship with Portsmouth MP Mike Hancock, during which she had potential access to secret documents.

The evidence against her seemed strong. Either Zatuliveter had a penchant for men in positions of power, or there was something sinister in her choice of partners. Before her affair with Hancock, she had been involved with a Dutch diplomat. Then when she and Hancock went their separate ways, she dated both a NATO official (asking him about a meeting he'd attended with US Secretary of State Madeleine Albright), and a senior UN official.

Zatuliveter met Hancock when he visited St Petersburg University in 2006 and she eventually travelled to Britain to become his unpaid researcher at the House of Commons. MI5 suspected that she had been instructed by the SVR to seduce Hancock – who had a reputation for extra-marital affairs – to gain a pass to the building and knowledge of his work on various defence committees.

During a series of interviews with both MI5 and MI6, standard for any foreign national working in such a restricted area, Zatuliveter vehemently denied that she was in any way involved with the Russian secret service. When she was served with the deportation order, she determined to fight it, and appealed to the Special Immigration Appeals Commission.

The case was heard in October 2011. It didn't help that she had actually met with a known Russian agent during her affair with Hancock, although she claimed that she had no idea he really was a spy. She had also joked in an email that her affair with the NATO official had meant that half of NATO was disabled, and that the Kremlin were calling her with congratulations. However, although the Commission agreed that the Security Service had 'ample grounds for suspicion', they did not believe that they had proved their case, and in November 2011 Zatuliveter was allowed to stay in the UK. Nonetheless, she returned to Russia the following month.

It may not officially be called the Cold War any more, but it's clear that the 'Great Game' between East and West is still very much alive. Sub-Lieutenant Jeffrey Paul Delisle was arrested in Canada for passing documents to the Russians from the Canadian navy intelligence centre in Halifax, Nova Scotia in January 2012. A sixty-year-old German was arrested in Holland in May 2012, accused of passing 450 secret files to one of Anna Chapman's former contacts. Former FSB colonel Valery Mikhailov was sentenced to eighteen years in prison on 6 June 2012 after passing papers to CIA officers in Moscow.

According to MI5's website: 'The threat of espionage (spying) did not end with the collapse of Soviet communism in the early 1990s. Espionage against UK interests continues and is widespread, insidious and potentially very damaging . . . The ultimate aim of our work is to make it as difficult as possible for foreign spies to operate against the UK.'

In February 2012, outgoing Russian President Dimitri Medvedev told the FSB that Russian counterintelligence exposed 199 foreign spies in 2011, proving that 'activity of [foreign] intelligence services is not decreasing'.

The FBI agree:

Spies haven't gone the way of the Cold War. Far from it. They're more prolific than ever – and targeting our nation's most valuable secrets. As the lead agency for exposing, preventing, and investigating intelligence activities on US soil, the FBI works to keep weapons of mass destruction and other embargoed technologies from falling into wrong hands, to protect critical national secrets and assets, and to strengthen the global threat picture by proactively gathering information and intelligence.

Will we ever reach a stage where spies aren't needed? As MI5 Director-General Jonathan Evans said in a speech in the City of London on 25 June 2012:

> Those of us who are paid to think about the future from a security perspective tend to conclude that future threats are getting more complex, unpredictable and alarming. After a long career in the Security Service, I have concluded that this is rarely in fact the case. The truth is that the future always looks unpredictable and complex because it hasn't happened yet. We don't feel the force of the uncertainties felt by our predecessors. And the process of natural selection has left us, as a species, with a highly developed capacity to identify threats but a less developed one to see opportunity. This helps explain the old saying that when intelligence folk smell roses they look for the funeral.

Spies have been around for as long as there have been opposing groups of mankind. Sun Tzu was counselling, 'Be subtle! be subtle! and use your spies for every kind of business,' in *The Art of War* 2,500 years ago. The threats may change but the need for information about them will never go away. And while that remains the situation, spies will continue to thrive.

ACKNOWLEDGEMENTS

My thanks to everyone who has assisted with the preparation of this book, including a couple of sources who need to remain anonymous, and especially to:

Brian J. Robb for many things, especially the introductions and the wise words on the text. It's my turn to buy the DVDs!

Duncan Proudfoot and Clive Hebard, my editors at Constable & Robinson, for their help in shaping this manuscript and for their patience when real life intervened; and my copy-editor Gabriella Nemeth, for helping me avoid some pitfalls of my own making.

Robert J. Sawyer for the recommendation of the Writers Blocks software which was a great help in plotting out the best way to frame the narrative.

Michael, our Cold War tour guide in Berlin at Easter 2012, for some very interesting insights and tales of the CIA in its early days.

Lee Harris, Amanda Rutter, Lizzie Bennett, Scott Pearson, Jenny Miller, Caitlin Fultz, Patricia Hyde and Adina Mihaela Roman for coming to the rescue when things were looking difficult.

As always, the staff at the Hassocks branch of the West Sussex public library, who provide a ready reminder why the library service needs to be maintained.

My partner Barbara and my daughter Sophie for their love and support; and our terriers, Rani and Rodo, who have finally realized that when I'm sitting at my desk, it doesn't mean that I'm doing nothing and therefore it's time to start playing with them!

SELECTED BIBLIOGRAPHY

Aid, Matthew M.: *Intel Wars: The Secret History of the Fight Against Terror* (Bloomsbury Press, 2012)

Aid, Matthew M.: *The Secret Sentry: The Untold History of the National Security Agency* (Paperback edition Bloomsbury Press, 2011)

Andrew, Christopher and Oleg Gordievsky: *KGB: The Inside Story* (HarperCollins, 1990)

Andrew, Christopher and Vasili Mitrokhin: *The Sword and the Shield* (Paperback edition: Perseus Books, 2001)

Andrew, Christopher: *The Defence of the Realm: The Authorized History of MI5* (Updated edition, Penguin, 2011)

Bearden, Milt and Risen, James: *The Main Enemy: The Inside Story of the CIA's Final Showdown with the KGB* (Random House, 2003)

Bergen, Peter: *Manhunt: The Ten-Year Search for Osama bin Laden* (The Bodley Head, 2012)

Bischof, Günter; Stefan Karner and Peter Ruggenthaler: *The Prague Spring and the Warsaw Pact Invasion of Czechoslovakia in 1968* (Lexington, 2011)

Boer, Peter: *Canadian Security Intelligence Service* (Folklore Publishing, 2010)

Butler, Rupert: *Stalin's Instruments of Terror* (Spellmount, 2006)

Cherkashin, Victor with Gregory Fiefer: *Spy Handler: Memoir of a KGB Officer* (Perseus Books, 2005)

Drogin, Bob: *Curveball: Spies, Lies, and the Con Man Who Caused a War* (Ebury Press, 2008)

Gehlen, Reinhard: *The Service: The Memoirs of General Reinhard Gehlen* (Popular Library, 1973)

Gordievsky, Oleg: *Next Stop Execution* (Macmillan, 1995)

Hathaway, Robert M. and Smith, Russell Jack: *Richard Helms as Director of Central Intelligence* (CIA internal, declassified version available via the CIA website, 1993)

Howe, Sir Geoffrey: *Conflict of Loyalty* (Pan Books, 2005)

Ingram, Martin & Greg Harkin: *Stakeknife: Britain's Secret Agents in Ireland* (The O'Brien Press, 2004)

Jeffrey, Keith: *MI6: The History of the Secret Intelligence Service* (Paperback edition: Bloomsbury Press, 2011)

Kalugin, Oleg with Fen Montaign: *SpyMaster: My 32 Years in Intelligence and Espionage Against the West* (St Martin's Press, 1994)

MacRakis, Kirstie: *Seduced by Secrets: Inside the Stasi's Spy-Tech World* (Cambridge, 2008)

North, Oliver with William Novak: *Under Fire: An American Story* (HarperCollins, 1991)

Philby, Kim: *My Silent War* (Modern Library edition: 2002)

Rimington, Stella: *Open Secret* (Arrow Books, 2002)

Soufan, Ali H. with Daniel Freedman: *The Black Banners: Inside the Hunt for Al-Qaeda* (W.W. Norton & Co., 2011)

Tenet, George with Harlow, Bill: *At the Center of the Storm: My Years at the CIA* (HarperPress, 2007)

Thomas, Gordon: *Gideon's Spies: The Secret History of the Mossad* 5th Edition (St Martin's Press, 2009)

Trahair, Richard C.S. and Robert L. Miller: *Encyclopedia of Cold War Espionage, Spies and Secret Operations* (third edition), Enigma Books, 2012)

Wallace, Robert and H. Keith Melton with Henry Robert Schlesinger: *Spycraft* (Dutton, 2008)

Wise, David: *Nightmover* (HarperCollins, 1996)

Wise, David: *Spy: The Inside Story of How the FBI's Robert Hanssen Betrayed America* (Paperback edition, Random House, 2003)
Wright, Peter with Greengrass, Paul: *Spycatcher* (Heinemann, 1987)

The CIA website at www.cia.gov is an invaluable source of declassified documents and articles, giving the American perspective on events after the Second World War. Similarly, the FBI's site at www.fbi.gov provides much inside information on the counter-espionage activities of the Bureau.

The British Security Service can be found at www.mi5.gov.uk with MI6 represented online at www.sis.gov.uk These are considerably less open than their American counterparts but do reveal some choice nuggets.

The *New York Times* and *Time* magazine online archives are the primary sources for contemporary reports of trials and investigations.

Although we have attempted to trace and contact copyright holders before publication, this may not have been possible in all cases. If notified, the publisher will be pleased to correct any errors or omissions at the earliest opportunity.

GLOSSARY OF TERMS AND ACRONYMS

Agency, The: see CIA.

ASIO: Australian Security Intelligence Organisation. Counter-espionage.

ASIS: Australian Secret Intelligence Service.

AVH: The State Protection Authority. The Hungarian secret police under the Communists.

BfV: Bundesamt für Verfassungsschutz. (West) German counter-intelligence.

BND: Bundesnachrichtendienst. The German secret service; prior to unification, it served that function for West Germany.

Bureau, The: common nickname for the FBI.

Cheka: see KGB history.

CIA: Central Intelligence Agency. America's intelligence agency, based in Langley, Virginia.

cover: the identity assumed by a spy.

cryptology: the study (and breaking) of codes.

CSIS: Canadian Security Intelligence Service. The Canadian intelligence and counter-intelligence agency. Prior to its creation, such work was carried out by the Royal Canadian Mounted Police.

CSS: see DS.

CTC: the CIA's Counterterrorism Center.

DCI: Director of Central Intelligence. The head of the CIA, and, until 2005, the head of the American intelligence community. Replaced by the D/CIA.

D/CIA: Director, Central Intelligence Agency. The head of the CIA since 2005, who reports to the DNI.

dead drop: a procedure for passing documents between an agent and his handler. The agent will leave the items at a pre-arranged location (e.g. under a rock, beneath a bridge), and at a suitable time the handler will collect it.

DGSE: General Directorate for External Security. The French intelligence agency since 1982.

DNI: Director of National Intelligence. The head of the American intelligence community following reforms brought in after 9/11. Much of the work of the DNI was formerly carried out by the DCI of the CIA.

DPRK: Democratic People's Republic of Korea. North Korea, under a Communist regime.

DS: Duzhavna Sigurnost (State Security). The popular name for the Bulgarian Committee for State Security under the Communist regime.

ELINT: Electronic INTelligence. Data received from electronic sources, such as listening devices or satellites.

FAPSI: Federal Agency of Government Communications and Information. The Russian equivalent of America's NSA, concentrating on SIGINT.

FBI: Federal Bureau of Investigation. The American counter-intelligence agency which also has responsibility as a criminal investigative body.

FSB: The Federal Security Service of the Russian Federation. Russia's counter-espionage agency since the fall of Communism.

G-2: the intelligence gathering section of the US Army. It is also the title of the Irish intelligence agency.

GCHQ: Government Communication Headquarters. The SIGINT wing of British intelligence. Its main base is at Cheltenham, Gloucestershire.

GPU: see KGB history.

GRU: Main Intelligence Directorate of the General Staff of the Armed Forces. Soviet, now Russian, Army intelligence.

GUGB: see KGB history.

HUMINT: HUMan INTelligence. Information derived from human sources (i.e. spies on the ground)

HVA: Hauptverwaltung Aufklärung. The foreign intelligence arm of the East German Stasi.

IJS: Irish Joint Section. A group of MI5 and MI6 officers working together regarding problems in Northern Ireland between 1972 and 1984. MI5 took over responsibility towards the end, leading to its phasing out.

IRA: The Irish Republican Army. Group opposed to the presence of the British in Northern Ireland, which waged a campaign during the twentieth century. Offshoots include The Continuity IRA and the Real IRA. Its political wing is Sinn Fein.

JIC: Joint Intelligence Committee: A group reporting to the British Cabinet, which oversees the work of the various British intelligence agencies.

KGB: The Committee for State Security. Although only officially existing between 1954 and 1991, the title is often used for Russian foreign intelligence throughout the twentieth century.

KGB history: The Soviet State Security organization would go through many name changes in the period leading up to the Cold War. The Cheka (The All-Russian Extraordinary Commission for Combating Counter-Revolution and Sabotage) operated from December 1917 to February 1922, when it was incorporated into the NKVD (the People's Commissariat of State Security) as the GPU (the State Political Directorate). From July 1923 to July 1934 it was known as the OGPU (the Unified State Political Directorate) before reincorporating into the NKVD, this time as the GUGB (Main Administration of Soviet Security). For five months in 1941 it was referred to as the NKGB (the People's Commissariat of State Security) before returning to the NKVD. It became the MGB (Ministry for State Security) in 1946, before Beria merged that with the MVD (the Ministry of the Interior) in 1953 following Stalin's death. After Beria's fall, State Security was separated from the Ministry, and became the KGB. The KGB was disbanded in 1991 to be replaced by the SVR.

Langley: term often used to describe CIA Headquarters, or the senior officials of the CIA.

MGB: See KGB history.

MI5: The British Security Service. Officially, this was only its title between September 1916 and 1929 but the abbreviation is used even within the service.

MI6: term commonly used for the British Secret Intelligence Service (SIS). Properly, it only refers to a period during the Second World War when it was used as a counterpart to MI5, but the phrase has entered common usage. Officially the title SIS was given in 1920, and enshrined in law in 1994. The service itself uses SIS rather than MI6 as an abbreviation.

Moscow Centre: term used for those giving instructions to Russian/Soviet intelligence agents.

Mossad: the Israeli foreign intelligence agency.

MSS: Ministry for State Security. The foreign intelligence agency of the People's Republic of China.

MVD: see KGB history.

NCS: National Clandestine Service. Since 2005, the operational arm of the CIA.

NIA: National Intelligence Authority. A body overseeing American intelligence work between the end of the Second World War and the creation of the CIA in 1947.

NKGB: see KGB history.

NKVD: see KGB history.

NSA: National Security Agency. The SIGINT arm of US intelligence.

NSC: National Security Council. Chaired by the American president, this was designed to oversee American intelligence after 1947. It came to prominence during the Iran-Contra affair. Its functions were merged with the Homeland Security Council in 2009 to form the National Security Staff.

OGPU: see KGB history.

ODNI: Office of the Director of National Intelligence.

one-time pad: a method of sending messages which is nearly impossible to decode unless you have a copy of the pad. Agents are supplied with a set of tear-off sheets which are used to encode the message and then destroyed; their handlers have the only duplicate set, which they use to decode the information.

ONI: Office of Naval Intelligence. The American Navy's intelligence arm.

OSS: Office of Strategic Services. The American intelligence agency during the Second World War. It was effectively a forerunner of the CIA.

PFLP: Popular Front for the Liberation of Palestine. Terrorist organization fighting for a separate Palestinian state.

PFLP-GC: Popular Front for the Liberation of Palestine – General Command. Splinter group from the PFLP.

PLO: Palestine Liberation Organisation. Political and paramilitary organization aiming to set up a separate Palestinian state.

Politburo: the leading members of the Communist party. Usually referring to the USSR, but each country had its own politburo.

SDECE: External Documentation and Counter-Espionage Service. The French intelligence agency between 1944 and 1982. Replaced by the DGSE.

SIG: Special Investigation Group. A team set up by James Jesus Angleton to investigate potential spies within the CIA.

SIGINT: SIGnals INTelligence: information received from messages passed between opposing forces.

SIS: See MI6.

SMERSH: derived from the Russian term SMERt' SHpionam (Death to Spies). This was a part of the NKVD during the Second World War. Its notoriety derives from its use by Ian Fleming in the James Bond novels written in the 1950s, although the real SMERSH was disbanded in 1946.

SOE: Special Operations Executive. The sabotage wing of British intelligence during the Second World War. It derived from MI6's Section D, and was folded back into MI6 after the end of hostilities.

SPG: Special Procedures Group. Part of the CIA tasked with aiding anti-Communist parties to win the Italian elections after the Second World War.

SSA: South African State Security Agency. The South African intelligence service since 2009.

Stasi: Staatssicherheit. The Ministry for State Security in East Germany. The intelligence agency for the East German Communist regime.

StB: Státní Bezpeènost (State Security). The Czech secret service between 1945 and 1990.

Sûreté: the French police.

SVR: Foreign Intelligence Service of the Russian Federation. The successor to the KGB.

tradecraft: the ways in which a spy operates in order to maintain their cover.

TSD: Technical Services Division. The real-life Q Branch of the CIA, creating all the gadgets and technology required by agents. And the occasional Acoustic Kitty.

watchers: counter-intelligence agents monitoring a target.

wet work/wet affairs: a euphemism for murder and assassinations, deriving from the spilling of blood.

INDEX